"To produce this excellent manual, Nathan Ory has combined his decades of careful, methodical analysis of the motivations and ways of resistant behavior with a deep compassion and respect for each individual as a competent person. Catering not to pathologies and disabilities, but building on the person's strengths, he offers a brilliantly strategic and creative method for effectively and skillfully managing the most difficult of behaviors. He uses rich, graphic metaphors that teach directly to the unconscious; insightful concepts that stimulate the intellect; and clear, practical, step-by-step interventions. His positive attitude instills self-confidence in both the person receiving support and the practitioner."

–Donald T. Saposnek, Ph.D.
Clinical Child Psychologist, Dept. of Psychology, University of California–Santa Cruz
Author, *Mediating Child Custody Disputes*
Editor, special issue, *Family Court Review*, "Special Needs Children in Family Court"

"Nathan Ory's book, *Working With People With Challenging Behaviors*, has become a powerful tool in the delivery of both the theoretical and the practical components of the curriculum in the CEA (Education Assistant Certificate) program at Okanagan College. His book addresses all levels of behavior identification; both the obvious and the underlying causes and factors. It is easy to read and to understand. The breakdown into ten categories of behavior provides an easy-to-follow path toward understanding and working effectively with the individuals affected."

–Lorrie Forde
Continuing Studies Program Administrator
Okanagan College, Penticton, British Columbia

2nd Edition

Working
with People
with Challenging
Behaviors

A Guide for Maintaining Positive Relationships

by Nathan Ory

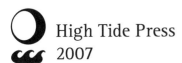

High Tide Press
2007

Working with People with Challenging Behaviors
A Guide for Maintaining Positive Relationships, 2nd Edition

By Nathan Ory

Published by High Tide Press
2081 Calistoga Dr., Suite 2N, New Lenox, IL 60451

Ory, Nathan, Working with people with challenging behaviors: a guide for maintaining positive relationships /
by Nathan Ory – 2nd Ed. Foreword by Thane Dykstra, Ph.D.

ISBN 978-1-892696-38-0

Printed in the United States of America

Second Edition

High Tide Press

This book is dedicated to persons living with challenging behaviors, their parents, educators and caregivers. May we continue to learn together how to offer support to those in need.

This book is also dedicated to my wife Bonnie and our children, Meghan and Jesse.

Table of Contents

Chapter 1 | Introduction to Values and Methods   3

Chapter 2 | Agitation, Stress and Panic Behaviors in People with Severe and Profound Developmental Disabilities   29

Chapter 3 | Resistive Behavior   **49**

Chapter 4 | Dependent and Functionally Dependent Behavior: Understanding and Overcoming Some Special Learning Problems   **67**

Chapter 5 | Persistent, Repetitive Behavior: Perseverative Responding **97**

Chapter 10 | Challenging Sexual Behavior   **235**

Foreword

By Thane Dykstra, Ph.D.

I have had the pleasure of attending workshops facilitated by Nathan Ory that help professional staff effectively work with individuals who present with challenging behaviors. I have also had the opportunity to observe Nathan firsthand as he provided behavioral consultation to individuals receiving services and supports at our agency, Trinity Services, Inc. During these experiences, I was struck by Nathan's ability to help staff members gain a hopeful perspective on the possibilities for people with complex and multiple challenging behaviors. In part, Nathan accomplished this by helping staff understand the phenomenology of the problem behavior from the perspective of the person receiving services. In addition, Nathan was able to empower staff by formulating individualized, systematic interventions. This was not the case for just a single consultation, but for all that occurred over the course of two days.

For professionals not fortunate enough to have direct experience with Nathan, this publication is probably the next best thing. Nathan draws upon his wealth of clinical experience—over 30 years—in creating this useful guide. Those problems range from agitation, stress, and panic behaviors among persons with severe and profound intellectual disabilities to challenging sexual behaviors. In his writing, Nathan draws upon numerous metaphors and real clinical examples that help professionals understand the experience of individuals who exhibit challenging behaviors. A significant hurdle confronting professionals working with individuals with challenging behaviors is the tendency to personalize these behaviors, and consequently engage the person in an ineffective manner.

In contrast to other texts that address this important topic, Nathan's writing avoids relying heavily on technical jargon. Although his framework is based upon a behavioral analytic perspective, it is not necessary for the reader to have significant prior exposure to learning theory. Nathan provides a very practical guide to overcoming challenging behaviors. He provides very specific recommendations that can be employed in the home, classroom, workplace, and community settings. To facilitate learning, Nathan provides frequent reviews of key concepts and includes memorable visual cues, which come back to the learner during times of crisis or during day-to-day experiences with challenging behavior. Although the book should be read cover to cover (at least once), its organization readily lends itself to use as a reference tool for particular content areas.

The two keys to overcoming challenging behaviors are establishing a positive relationship, and modifying the environment to accommodate individuals' unique goals and needs. Nathan Ory's writing provides a blueprint for accomplishing both tasks.

Nathan has had a profound impact on the lives of persons with disabilities and this text is a "toolbox" for professionals seeking to become ramp builders, behavior artists, and behavior choreographers.

Thane Dykstra, Ph.D.
Director of Behavioral Health Services, Trinity Services, Inc.
February 2007

Second Edition Features

This second edition updates some terminology to reflect people first. It also includes gender-specific language, alternating male and female pronouns for the purpose of balance. None of the behaviors described herein are specific to one gender.

In addition, readers will find several features to help them navigate these pages and make the best use of the author's ideas. Following are some examples of visual elements and what they represent.

Icons

 An example from real people in real situations

 An idea or reminder concerning positive relationships

 A warning or reminder that is particularly important

Text Boxes

Quotes taken from the text (example at right) offer the reader visual cues and reinforce key ideas.

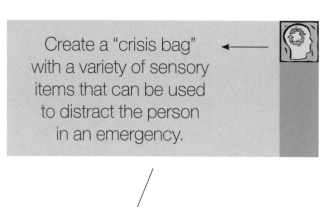

Create a "crisis bag" with a variety of sensory items that can be used to distract the person in an emergency.

Highlights in every chapter that make learning easy

The author wishes to acknowledge Dave Hingsburger for his substantial contribution to the chapter on challenging sexual behavior.

Working with People with Challenging Behaviors

A Guide for Maintaining Positive Relationships

In This Chapter

1 ■ Introduction to Values and Methods

- How We View Challenging Behavior
- Motivating Self-Control While Maintaining Positive Expectations
- Causes of Disruptive and Challenging Behavior
- Positive Assumption about the Causes of Behavior
- General Approaches to Challenging Behavior
- Sources of Emotional Distress
- Emotional and Behavioral Responses to Distress
- Metaphors for Building Positive Relationships
- The Nature of Learning

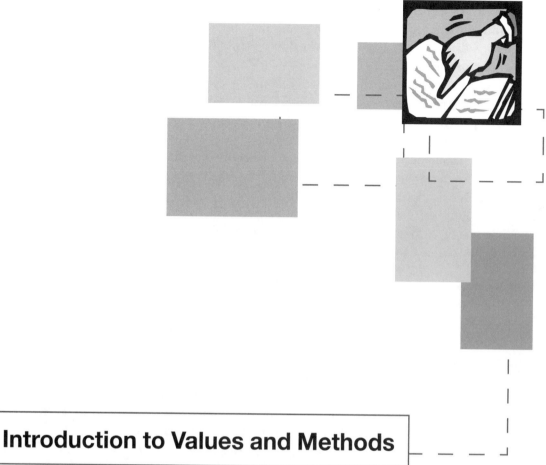

Introduction to Values and Methods

How We View Challenging Behavior

Who can use this information?

This material introduces general practices and specific solutions to behavior problems that will work with people who display difficult and challenging behaviors regardless of who they are. It is especially suitable for working with individuals who have developmental or intellectual disabilities coupled with a behavior disorder. The methods also apply to the person with emotional or psychiatric disturbances, or another serious mental health problem. Finally, they are helpful in providing support to elderly individuals who display challenging behavior.

What is challenging behavior?

Challenging behavior involves disruptive actions by someone who does not respond as expected regardless of another person's attempts to redirect or calm him. We may employ the usual procedures of extra prompting, guidance, motivation, training, or explicit direction or correction—all to no avail. This person simply becomes more passive, more resistive, more emotionally agitated, or more violent in response.

Why are common approaches not working?

Usually, the competent use of environmental prevention and positive guidance adequately accommodate the needs of a person who displays disruptive behavior. But, sometimes people with very persistent, challenging behavior do not respond to either common sense approaches or professional efforts to teach alternative coping skills.

For these people, the answer is not found in more sophisticated techniques. Instead, the support person will discover the answer by approaching each person as a unique individual and realistically accommodating his needs.

Though infrequent, some individuals do not respond regardless of the variety of methods used, or the level of skill or professional training the support person has. In these cases, we conclude that the problem lies elsewhere.

What are typical goals for the person's behavior?

Typically, when we provide services or support to a person displaying challenging behavior, we are pursuing three goals:

- We want the person to stop the challenging behavior.
- We want the person to respond to us in a positive manner.
- We want the person to participate voluntarily, cooperate socially and comply with directions we give.

In these instances, our goal is to stop disruptive and challenging behavior when it occurs. So, we spend our time and energy tailoring our approaches to just that goal. Unfortunately, the intense focus on methods to control disruptive behavior means a focus on ineffective interactions, making it difficult or impossible for the person served to cope.

What should our goals be?

We must realize that it is not just our classroom, workplace or home. It is also the challenging person's classroom, workplace or home. Often, a display of challenging behavior is what makes us most aware of this fact. What we really want from a person displaying challenging behavior is responsible self-restraint.

In the long term, our goal is not to become expert at behavior control, or for the person to become expert at complying with our direction after demonstrating the problem behavior. We want him to understand our expectations, develop appropriate coping skills, and feel motivated to use those skills. We want to understand the person's needs well enough to accommodate them, and we want to prevent circumstances that lead to challenging behavior.

First, our role is to form a positive relationship with the person and understand who he is trying to be. Then we lead, model and reward the person's existing coping skills, building on his spontaneous interests and personal attachments so as to improve his interactions. This requires strategies for leading, guiding and training individuals to cope. In addition, it requires a coping strategy for the support person to fall back on when a person does display challenging behavior.

Positive Goals for the Person Displaying Challenging Behavior

- We do not want to control behavior.

- We do not want to just teach the person to accept our control of his world.

- We want to teach the person to control his own behavior. If he cannot independently control his own behavior, we want him to accept our positive guidance about how to control his world successfully.

- We want to teach the person to control his behavior as an acceptable means of gaining control of his world.

- We do not want to put the person "into a box" where we control his behavior. We want him to walk into the "box of positive expectations" where he will feel safe and certain of a successful interaction and an attached relationship.

These goals are accomplished only in an environment where the person is able and willing to accept positive guidance. We establish such environments to protect those who cannot protect themselves. And, we start by looking in a slightly different manner at the situations in which people display challenging behavior. That is the reason for this book.

The wheelchair ramp and the ambulance

One useful metaphor for responding to challenging behavior begins with a person who has a physical disability and must use a wheelchair, but has many other capabilities. She wheels down the street, orders a meal, buys clothing and accomplishes many other things independently. She is doing as she pleases. In the course of her travels, she gets to a high curb where she expects a ramp. But there is no ramp, and she falls to the ground, suffering injury. Someone calls an ambulance. The sirens wail, an ambulance comes, and a crowd gathers.

Trained experts attend to the woman on the ground, then pick her up and transport her to the hospital. Health care professionals treat her bruises and cuts, and send her back home in fairly good shape. Unfortunately, she never got her half-gallon of milk at the corner store!

A support person will often respond to a display of challenging behavior, whether disruptive or resistive, as though the person with a disability had fallen off a curb. But, we do not wish to become expert ambulance drivers. Nor do we wish to become highly skilled at crisis response. We want to spend our time paying attention to the person while she is wheeling down the sidewalk or buying milk. We want to use preventive strategies so that no crises occur—so no one falls off the sidewalk. To achieve this with a person whose behavior is persistently challenging, and who does not respond to traditional teaching approaches, we must adopt two crucial attitudes.

Become expert at prevention and guidance.

Becoming expert at guiding people to avoid curbs where they might fall off and get hurt starts with showing them how to recognize their areas of difficulty. When do they feel confused? When are there too many demands at once? When are the surroundings becoming too crowded and confusing? How do they calm themselves? How do they ask for help?

Next, we must become expert at teaching people how to ask for assistance when they face a difficult situation. We want to become expert at building ramps, and helping people seek those ramps no matter what the situation. We want to protect them by keeping demands manageable and distractions minimal.

Finally, we want to teach the person to recognize dangerous or threatening situations, and be able to say to himself, "I have been here before, and I don't like what I see. What did I do last time? What is going to happen next? Who can rescue me before this situation becomes too much for me to handle?"

Adjust expectations to the person's realities.

If someone falls out of his wheelchair, we do not expect him to learn from the experience that he must avoid the street entirely! (When Rick Hansen, a man with a spinal cord injury, can successfully wheel around the world, we do not expect him to spend a lot of time learning to walk ten feet with crutches.) We change our expectations to work with the person's areas of strength and success, accepting his physical limitations.

It also means that we acknowledge, accept and reach for what is achievable for the person and tailor our approach to allow him to be as normal as possible, while expressing who he is trying to be in the world (e.g. a person who likes to be helpful to others; one who has meaningful work and relationships with others). We have to work with him using the methods to which he best responds.

This approach may result in the use of methods that are essentially unique to each individual and his knowledgeable support person. We must work until his positive coping responses become thoroughly established parts of his repertoire. But, we must be careful not to expect him to cope by using skills that he has learned only partially.

Motivating Self-Control
While Maintaining Positive Expectations

It is helpful to look at one behavior where people almost always demonstrate voluntary self-control, or at least active cooperation. Regardless of the disabling condition, almost everyone is willing to wear a seatbelt. Why is there so little challenging behavior in this area?

The reason is that no support person allows out-of-seat behavior while the car is moving. When a passenger refuses to buckle up, the driver does not start the vehicle until the person complies. If someone unfastens the seatbelt, the driver typically stops the car immediately. Regardless of the method, background or training of the drivers, they all stop, direct, train, motivate, correct, or control the unbuckled behavior before it has a chance to be carried on in transit. The person with a disability is never given the opportunity to rehearse and learn incorrect safety practices. As a result, the positive expectation quickly becomes an automatic habit.

And, why is the driver so consistent in teaching this behavior? Because she knows she can be fined if she is stopped when any passenger is not wearing a seatbelt. She also has specific expectations for cooperation and compliance. Therefore, she is crystal clear when she communicates her expectations to the passengers.

As you learn the many strategies available for attaining cooperation, keep in mind the differences among these: *voluntary self-control*, *encouraging compliance*, and *external control*. To maintain positive relationships, we begin by modeling, coaching and expecting voluntary self-control. We only move toward more intrusive means of establishing behavioral habits when it is necessary for the safety of the person and others.

Establishing Expectations for Desired Behavior: Four Keys

We can use the wearing of seatbelts as a model for "error free" teaching of any other behavior where safety requires cooperation.

Be precise about the expectations.

Make sure all persons providing services or support agree on what the expectations are. Everyone knows the seatbelt law. If we knew that every time a person presented a challenging behavior, it was going to cost us seventy-five dollars, we would be precise about what we expected him to do for his own safety. We would institute all the support and structure required to ensure that he knew how to perform—and was well motivated to demonstrate—the alternative behavior.

Likewise, if we knew we would receive five dollars for every minute a person was cooperating and participating voluntarily, we would communicate that expectation in a variety of creative ways. We would structure situations by prompting, motivating and teaching the necessary skills to make the person absolutely certain about our expectations and how we wanted him to help.

> Make sure all persons providing services or support agree on what the expectations are.

We want the people we support to perform effective, adequate coping skills consistently. In pursuing this goal, individual differences in methods and approaches do not matter as much as consistency among support staff and their expectations for behavior.

Act as if you expect self-control.

We expect cooperation and participation at the person's level of ability and a consistent display of adequate coping behaviors. Everyone must wear a seatbelt, and he will receive the support he requires. Anyone who cannot fasten it will get help doing so, and no one will be asked to remain fastened in longer than he can tolerate.

- Model the appropriate behavior. For instance, all the other passengers put on their seatbelts.
- Use natural rewards for modeling the behavior of others. The car starts as soon as everyone puts on his seatbelt.

Encourage cooperation.

- Give direct prompts or reminders for the appropriate behavior. "Remember the rule about seatbelts."

- Use an implied contract for mutual cooperation. "We will leave when everyone is buckled in," or "We can't leave until everyone is buckled in."
- Use rewards to gain attention and motivate voluntary participation. "If everyone is buckled in quickly, we will have time to stop for ice cream (or coffee)."

Establish compliance.

- Use direct instruction. "Do it up like this."
- Use diversion and indirect methods. For example, say, "Count the number of red cars we pass." By giving the student something to keep him occupied, you leave him too busy or too distracted to touch his seatbelt.

Establishing Expectations about Undesired Behavior: "Left Arm" Methods

An education professor, Dr. Charles Galloway, used the "right arm/left arm" technique for behavior management in the classroom. He found that, to enable children to sit and work at their desks, we must give them lots of "squeezy hugs" with our right arm when they are working at their desks. But, they must be actually sitting at their desks to get the hugs. ("You have to be there to learn there.") At the same time, we must be ready to use our left arm to keep a child in the seat long enough for us to give him praise and positive contact.

Certain of his expectations, Dr. Galloway knew how much control he would use to help his students successfully meet his expectations. He wanted to use just as much control as necessary, as soon as necessary, to ensure that he would employ as little control as necessary. Following are three left-arm methods.

Use negative reinforcement.

When we introduce an unpleasant situation (or stimulus), then offer to take it away if the person complies, we are using negative reinforcement.

- Stop the car, and inform the passenger that the car will not move until he stops touching the seatbelt. You may also need to state that everyone will have to walk if the undesired behavior does not stop. Be prepared to follow through.

Use negative consequences.

Applying punishment might include raising our voice; removing the person from the situation or location; or imposing the loss of a planned privilege for being uncooperative.

- If he handles the seatbelt, remove the person from the car and have him walk to the destination.

Establish control.

Two methods are available: provide continuous verbal prompting and direct physical control. For instance, a verbal prompt in the car might be: "Touching your belt is against the rules. Hands down." Direct physical control might involve calmly holding the person's hands to prevent him from touching the seatbelt.

These strategies use external control and evoke involuntary compliance through threat and emotion. They pressure people into practicing the desired behavior in addition to giving attention to persons showing uncooperative behavior.

Roles and Relationships with the People We Serve

Your role: police officer or mayor

Think about how a police officer catches a person violating a traffic rule. He informs the driver that she broke the rule, then applies a negative consequence (gives her a ticket), and tells her not to do it again. His job is to maintain order by catching the persons who violate established rules of conduct, exerting external control and applying consequences. The goal is to suppress undesired behavior.

Look at the effect on our behavior. Even if I am not breaking any rules, I tend to slow down, becoming inhibited when I see a police car. My spontaneity vanishes as I anxiously observe every aspect of my driving. Knowing I will be given a ticket if I break any rules, I am self-controlled. I feel the touch of the "left arm" around my shoulders.

In contrast, the mayor notices citizens who help the community. She praises them and uses instructional and motivational procedures to encourage repetition of the desired behavior. For example, she sets up a driver education and model citizen program. When she gives out safe driving certificates to residents who have driven without any accidents, she recognizes, acknowledges and rewards model behavior.

How did I learn such effective driving behavior! In driver education, I practiced and started out slowly under direct instruction. I established a habit pattern that I know will transport me safely from point A to point B. Every day, I use self-control without thinking because my driving pattern is so well rehearsed.

The mayor praises the citizens and uses instructional and motivational procedures to encourage the desired behavior.

We, as support staff, should think of ourselves as driving instructors and mayors rather than police officers. Yes, we must have the resources to intervene and calm out-of-control behavior, just as the mayor must have access to a police force to bring control when rules have been violated. But, the purpose of the city is not to have a police force. It is to facilitate a group of people working cooperatively toward common and individual goals (including safe transportation) with procedures and structures (including a political process for creating traffic laws and driver education) to accommodate needs and sort out differences.

We can also motivate voluntary cooperation with the right arm while encouraging positive self-control in other ways. These methods ensure attention to desired behavior with the left arm without causing inhibition and loss of spontaneity.

Reward all or punish all (Promoting accident-free days)

The Worker's Compensation Board puts up a sign at the front of a sawmill that employs five hundred people, showing that the plant has gone seventy-two days without an accident. The next day, a person with a thirty-year safety record drops something on his foot and goes to the hospital. On the following day, the board posts a sign showing zero days without an accident. In effect, the mistake of one person punishes everybody and erases the warm glow of a ten-week winning streak. This mirrors the approach to giving feedback to people about how they perform. We focus on the positive, but if one negative occurs, we debit all previous positives.

As an alternative, consider the effect of putting up a series of posters at the front of the plant, showing how many workers had gone twenty years, fifteen years, ten years, five years, one year and six months without an accident. If the person on the twenty-year record dropped something on his toe, his name would come off, but the good citizenship of everyone else would remain. Even the person whose name was withdrawn after twenty years would reappear on a poster after another six months of good safety practice. This provides a daily reminder of what is preferred and expected, and constant positive recognition for the person whose behavior followed good safety practices.

Motivating self-control through positive contracting

Think about the shopping cart at the grocery store. It is hard to find one when customers leave them all over the parking lot. Some major retailers install a coin slot on the back of each cart and keep them chained to each other in a central location. Shoppers insert a quarter to get a cart (make a commitment and enter into a contract), and get their money back when they return the cart to a designated spot. The retailer is contracting cooperative behavior. The shopper cannot participate without paying up front and agreeing to play by the rules (or pay for breaking them). The retailer is leading with the right hand while making it clear that the left hand will be used if necessary. The shopper has a choice; therefore, cooperation is strictly a matter of self-control.

Many stores are paying customers for reusing plastic bags. The practice illustrates the same idea, but the motivation may be too small. For many people, paying three cents for a bag does not provide sufficient motivation to cause them to choose environmental sensitivity. Contracting with a child to clean up his room before going out to a movie, or clear the table before eating dessert is another application of the same strategy.

Maintaining positive expectations for active cooperation

In a classroom situation, it is helpful to use visual cues when, for example, children have a list of classroom expectations on the wall. Those who follow the expectations earn points for rewards (daily for younger, weekly for older children) such as a chocolate milk break at recess and receive much praise from the teacher. The ones who ignore the expectations have their names put on the board.

If a child's name appears on the board only once, she has missed points for that moment but is still able to earn points for the daily or weekly rewards. The teacher makes no comment and imposes no other consequence. (The message is that anyone can make one mistake. The name on the board is just a reminder of the expectation.) The teacher interprets a minor episode of disruptive behavior as the action of a person who has made a mistake, rather than an act of deliberate malice.

The second time the teacher writes the child's name on the board, points are subtracted, and the child is given an opportunity to "work off" the points lost or receives a detention. The third time, the teacher calls a parent, and institutes increased direct instructional contact and control. The purpose is to communicate powerfully the expectation for, and desirability of, exercising self-control by following classroom guidelines. The rules are established as a fair way for people to interact in equal-rights relationships.

If a child is not mature or mentally competent enough to operate in such an environment of mutual respect, the structure should increase to create a more structured setting with more frequent, direct feedback for self-control, and more direct guidance to maintain positive participation.

Prompting self-control with a timer

The instructor can initially set the amount of time expected for a specific task, and prompt the student back to task whenever she loses focus. As she works with visual cues, he can move farther and farther away. However, when she goes off-task, he should come closer and become more directive. Initially, he gives her no chance to be off-task or misbehave. And, he sets the timer for her. But, as she needs less and less direction, she can eventually set the timer for herself, determining how long she will sit and work without interruption.

Prompting self-control arising from personal pride

When a student does well, the instructor can send a letter of praise to a person significant to her. If she fails once to maintain self-control, the instructor does not say anything to others. He simply reminds her that he will not send a note to significant persons about how the day went. The message to her is that she is in control and can avoid the next step. If the student fails to maintain self-control a second time, the instructor informs her that he will send a note to the significant person explaining what happened.

Rather than attending to the disruptive behavior, he prompts the individual to use self-control.

This method works well for people who have a lot of pride and are able to exercise self-control when the cues are strong enough. However, if employed more than once, it loses its corrective impact. It is useful for individuals who exercise self-control in response to the first prompt, and gives them another chance to feel pride and avoid losing "face."

The instructor can also say, "I would love to be able to tell (a significant person) about how well you did." Rather than attending to the disruptive behavior, he prompts the person to use self-control. This approach appeals to her pride and desire for positive recognition. It reminds her that reinforcement is close at hand. But, it is never productive to say something like, "If you don't smarten up, I'll tell so-and-so, and you will be in big trouble."

Causes of Disruptive and Challenging Behavior

One behavior can stem from a number of causes. For example, what we typically call shy behavior—someone holding back when first entering a room containing a group of people—may have several explanations. In general, behavior is caused by one or more physical, developmental, neurological, psychological or environmental factors.

Physical

A physical cause for shy behavior, for instance, could be a hearing impairment. The person may prefer to avoid groups when it is difficult to understand the words others speak.

Developmental (part of the growth process)

A developmental cause for shy behavior may be lack of experience or familiarity with group settings. The person may simply not know what to do or how to act.

Neurological (part of the brain process)

A neurological cause for shy behavior may be a language processing dysfunction. For example, a central auditory processing dysfunction could cause an inability to discriminate language from background noise. In addition, a short attention span could cause a person to understand only the last few words of a spoken sentence. In either case, the person might hold back and avoid being in a group situation where she might not understand what others say.

Psychological (part of the adjustment process)

Psychological causes fall into two categories, behavioral and emotional.

- *Behavioral learning.* A youngster may have been regularly coddled when she acted shy early in life. As a result, she could have learned to attract special attention–a strong positive reinforcer for behavior–by holding back and acting like she did not know what she was supposed to do.
- *Emotional learning.* When a person has previously been embarrassed in a group setting, he may have learned to fear this happening again–a strong negative reinforcer for avoidance behavior. He would then hold back in anticipation of being embarrassed again.

Environmental

The person might be shy because there is a "bad fit" between who he is, how he copes and what the environmental demands are. For example, the person might not be at all shy when in the company of only one or two persons. But, he may feel very uncomfortable with a larger group that does not allow the level of intimacy or feedback he enjoys, so he might hold back or leave the situation.

Not only can several different causes exist for the same behavior in different people, but several causes may exist in the same person for the same behavior. Because it is so difficult to tell precisely what is happening, we recognize that a person who displays any behavior deserves the benefit of the doubt. That is, we cannot assume that the observed behavior is purposeful or deliberate since we cannot be certain of the cause.

So, what do we do about behavior when we do not know the cause?

Positive Assumptions about the Causes of Behavior

Our assumptions about why a behavior occurs determine our responses to it. Not only should we be aware of our responses, we need to develop a set of positive assumptions about the individuals we serve. Furthermore, we should exercise caution when interacting with those who display challenging behavior since our responsibility involves keeping them safe, but also protecting ourselves from harm. On many occasions, we may not be sure what is happening with a person, or what approach to take, but we can follow a hierarchy of assumptions. Each one leads to a different practical response.

Though behaviors may seem to indicate malicious intent, we should not assume that distressed people are out to get us. We begin with the simplest assumption and move to the next more complex assumption only when our current practical responses have proved ineffective.

Do not assume deliberate malice.

When a person hits me in the face, it is very hard not to take it personally. His resistive and extremely challenging display of distressed behavior makes it very difficult to deal with him. Responding wisely requires taking a close look at the coping responses he has available. Typically, the person only knows how to act out or withdraw from situations he finds distressing.

Observe closely any persistent problem behavior that does not respond to common sense or traditional teaching/learning behavior modification approaches. The behavior may occur because of processes that are very hard to detect and seem to make no sense, such as a cognitive or emotional dysfunction.

Before assuming malice, first assume the person is doing the best he can to cope. For instance, he may be forgetful, unaware of what to do, confused or unmotivated.

If all of the following possibilities for the behavior are taken into account, and the person is still displaying the behavior, then you can reasonably consider the behavior to be deliberate. At that point, consider using some corrective procedures rather than suggestive, motivational or instructional procedures.

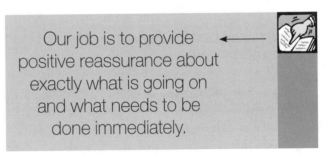

Our job is to provide positive reassurance about exactly what is going on and what needs to be done immediately.

Assume that the person is confused and unable to understand what is expected.

Uncooperative behavior might be caused by a language processing or hearing problem. The person may not be thinking clearly at the moment. Some aspect of the situation distresses him, and his coping skills are inadequate. He may, for example, have an attention deficit. Do not assume that he prefers not to participate or cooperate.

Many times, we find that once we overcome confusion, we instantly acquire voluntary participation and cooperation. The first step is to clarify expectations. We often use the word "firm" to make sure the person knows that we mean business. We say, "We have to be firm with this person." But, we do not become firm until the behavior angers us. Being firm works because we have become clear, certain and explicit. Fortunately, we do not have to wait until we are angry to be absolutely clear. In fact, confusion is often a signal that we have been unclear or not firm from the beginning. So, our job is to provide positive reassurance about exactly what is going on and what needs to be done immediately. We can focus on actions the students already have as part of their repertoire so that working with them is a success; for example, "We are doing this right now!"

Assume that the person is distracted or forgetful.

Our second assumption should always be that the person requires a repeated suggestion to provide him with verbal or visual reminders. This accommodates the person with intellectual disabilities who is distractible and/or has a short, immediate attention span. For instance, he may have seen and heard an instruction, but did not pay attention, or paid attention but rapidly forgot it. We must shorten the length of the instructions; use simple, concrete words; and present requests one at a time. People sometimes show distress behavior when we make multiple requests and exceed their capacity to process the information. This person may be able to work quite well if asked to do only one thing at a time.

Envision this scenario: You must send an expensive, five-word telegram to Australia. It costs twenty-five dollars for every five words you send to the person with a disability. You quickly recognize that you must be very careful about choosing your words. You are sure to send only one simple message at a time.

Fortunately, you may send the same message up to one hundred times at no additional charge. However, if you send a new message before getting a correct response to the first message, it will cost five thousand dollars. Under these circumstances, you are sure to wait for the person to be focused, attentive, and clear in his own mind that he understood the expectation you are communicating. You are also sure to wait until he has successfully responded before giving him positive feedback, and moving to the next step.

Assume that the person is able, but inadequately supported or motivated, to participate.

Next, we assume that the person is insufficiently supported–that is, not receiving enough prompts and/or rewards–before concluding that he is untrained or unable. Often, the person with disabilities knows how to participate, but requires additional cues or prompts. He may be able to respond to an immediate reminder of what comes next, such as, "Finish this, then you can play cards." The additional motivator is not offered as a bribe, but rather as an additional activity that he could expect anyway. It is the anticipation of pleasure that is being offered to increase motivation. Giving the person a cue that may register "puts the ball in his court" and allows him to perform.

We do not look at reluctance to participate as a behavior problem. Assume that the person's reluctance results from his need for extra cues or motivation. A person can frequently exercise excellent self-control if a support person offers him powerful reinforcement for positive participation.

Assume that he is able, but inadequately trained, to perform the behavior.

Our fourth approach assumes that structured training is what is lacking. We do not assume that the person cannot perform the expected behavior. Rather, we assume that he is untrained or experiencing some subtle learning dysfunction. Perhaps we need to teach the person in a different manner, or break down the expected social behaviors into specific skills. He may be cue-dependent and need to be shown exactly what he is expected to do.

- One woman learns only through step-by-step instruction, because she does not pick up on abstract instruction or cues from the social context. She learned over half a lifetime, like a marionette, to act the roles she was trained to perform. She cannot recognize what she is supposed to do in a given situation and only responds well in the ways she has been trained. She does not have a problem with forgetfulness; the problem is extreme difficulty making choices or judgments between options.

The woman lived adequately on her own until different workers came into her life and tried to incorporate new activities into her well-learned act. Different meals, different clothes, and a different time of day for bathing, among other changes, rendered her totally dependent and unable to do anything for herself.

- A boy who was unable to learn through step-by-step instruction could not be directly taught to tie his shoelaces. However, he learned to operate a chain-saw by watching his father teach his brother and sister. Even though he can "recognize" what he is supposed to do by watching others being taught, direct instruction sends him into a violent rage.

In this instance, the best option is to give him the answer before you ask him the question. The person is capable of learning self-control when calm, motivated and adequately trained. Make life a multiple-choice test where he has the answer key. Let him always be able to observe someone else being shown the right way to do something before he is presented with the task, because he is able to exercise good self-control when the learning environment is the "right fit" for him. This may solve the behavior issue.

Assume that the person is desperate and unable to learn.

A specific disability can prevent some individuals from learning what the support person is attempting to teach. They find it impossible, for instance, to exercise self-control when they are overwhelmed by fear or anxiety. We assume that the person is doing the best he can to cope under the circumstances, and our approach is to provide calm guidance. We reduce the circumstances that generate desperate behavior, and attempt to teach emotional coping skills.

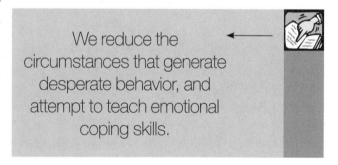

We reduce the circumstances that generate desperate behavior, and attempt to teach emotional coping skills.

It is possible that the person simply cannot respond to our assistance, no matter what approach we offer. If so, we may have to assume control to guide him back to a state where he can regain self-control. We then create opportunities for the person to practice relationship-sustaining behaviors. And, we continue to assume that the person is acting out of disability and desperation, not with deliberate malice.

Finally, consider that the challenging behavior may be deliberate.

The last assumption we should ever consider is that the person consciously resists and deliberately intends harm. Carefully constructed, restrictive guidance procedures may be necessary for the person who acts with intent to harm, especially when he is aware of and able to choose alternative forms of expression.

We set up rewards for relationship-sustaining behaviors. We assume that the person is capable of learning to value and voluntarily choose behavior that draws others into positive contact. So, we provide him with many good reasons for wanting to be cooperative and participative.

Be cautious with an individual who constantly attempts to seize control over his support person, and reacts against all efforts to provide assistance. Also, be cautious with a person who constantly argues for control, complains and demands. While this may be the only behavior he has for engaging in social interactions, his maladaptive responses may lead us to engage in relationship-breaking behaviors. It is essential to avoid becoming confused by, or overly engaged in, the content of the person's complaint.

It may be that the person reacts so strongly that he cannot respond to positive expectations. The difficult solution is to provide extreme structure, maintained by support staff with "compassionate detachment" from the behaviors of concern. They care for the individual but do not expect his behavior to change while maintaining a safe environment where there is opportunity for him to participate as he is able and ready.

Letting this type of person do things his way within the rigid structure provided by his support person is a very difficult solution. But, once a person has shown no concern about the consequences of his dangerous behavior, he must be protected from circumstances in which he cannot function safely without the constant presence of supportive and restrictive structure.

How to Think about Distressed and Challenging Behavior

1. Do not assume deliberate malice.

2. Assume confusion, uncertainty or inability to understand expectations.

3. Assume distraction or forgetfulness.

4. Assume ability but lack of sufficient guidance or external motivation.

5. Assume a subtle learning dysfunction, lack of training or inability to learn.

6. Assume inability to cope with overwhelming fear or anxiety.

7. Assume inability to exercise self-control and the need for external structure.

8. Only then, consider the behavior to be deliberate.

General Approaches to Challenging Behavior

Throughout this book, regardless of the kind of behavior, support staff should consider four strategies for behavioral intervention. Rather than responding only to the impact of the disruptive behavior through crisis management, support persons should include prevention, guidance and training techniques. Crisis management is a final option only after the first three have failed.

Prevention

Prevention techniques anticipate and avoid the problem behavior. They begin with acknowledging the person's disabling conditions, and they continue with an accepting attitude while accommodating the person's needs and deficiencies. For the shy person who holds back, we would provide:

Key to Prevention

Use intervention with the environment and people providing support. Remember the six A's: Acknowledge, Anticipate and Avoid problem behavior. Have an Accepting Attitude; Accommodate the person's needs and deficiencies.

- A hearing aid if she has a physical, hearing impairment
- A welcoming, encouraging attitude if she is a developmentally young or fearful person
- Quiet corners if she is neurologically impaired and unable to discriminate language from background noise, so she can communicate with success
- Reduced expectations for group interaction if she is more comfortable in a more intimate environment.

Guidance

These techniques divert the person in a non-confrontational manner, and redirect his behavior. We provide him with positive motivation to perform cooperatively. We show our expectation for a behavior we know he can employ.

Key to Guidance

Use positive intervention with the person. Use human relations techniques to engage him in other behavior without confronting him about problem behavior. Use suggestion, positive motivation and humor along with the three D's: Displace, Divert and re-Direct the person's behavior.

The developmentally young person (the shy one who holds back) could be guided with supports that motivate him to join in a well-known group activity that allows him to participate with the feeling that he knows what is expected. We do not pay a lot of attention to the shy behavior. This illustrates the use of good human relations. We are helping the person to displace an inadequate behavior with a more adequate one that he knows well.

Training

Training techniques help develop long-term, positive motivation and alternative coping skills. The shy person displaying emotional learning that inhibits his participation in a group would be exposed to desensitization training. At first, he would participate in a social setting with only one other person. Gradually, support staff would introduce other people until he developed confidence in his ability to interact. (See Appendix A: Fundamental Training Approaches for a Person with Severe Intellectual Disability.)

Key to Training

Use positive intervention with the person. Employ motivation and skill development programs, and teach alternative coping skills over time.

Crisis Management

These techniques use direct intervention that gives support staff effective control over the individual who is unable to exercise self-control. The best crisis management strategies are the same ones used in giving the person non-confrontational guidance. They accommodate his special needs and disabilities; address sources of distress; and allow support staff to bring the problem behavior to a stop.

The short-term goal of all crisis management is to control those environments in which the person cannot exercise self-control. We never lose sight of the long-term goal: to prompt, motivate and train him to use adequate coping strategies, and exercise adequate self-control over his environment and his behavior. The belief that underlies all crisis management strategies is that people involved in problem behavior are most often desperately doing the best they can under the circumstances.

Key to Crisis Management

Use direct intervention with the problem behavior. Remain calm and always use guidance techniques first. Accommodate the person's special needs and disabilities. Respond to chaotic behavior with a prearranged plan for surviving the crisis while bringing challenging behavior to a stop! Interact positively with the person as soon as he exercises a degree of self-control. Have a plan for how to re-enter normal life.

Sources of Emotional Distress

Think about the various circumstances that create distress. All of them involve learning– starting with the who, what, when, where and why of what is currently happening. Next comes learning how to respond to what is happening, or if we know how, learning how well we respond. Anyone will experience distress when faced with other people's unrealistic expectations.

- How did you learn to drive a car? Imagine if the instructor had taught you how to drive in snowy conditions by taking you out on an icy field and saying, "Floor it, then step on the brake and see what happens." Or, suppose that one rainy night the instructor took you on a busy street in a brand new car, and yelled at you the entire time, "Watch out! No, don't do that! Be careful!" Imagine instead the words, "Let's learn how to get control of this car before we begin. No problem. Take your time."

It makes an enormous, negative difference to your experience as a learner if a person–whether it is you or someone else–places an expectation on you that, though achievable, lies beyond your present level of competence. Being a new learner is a distress-creating circumstance no matter what. Remembering our own distressful situations can enable us to understand better the sources of emotional distress in the person with disruptive behavior.

Unrealistic social expectations

Unrealistic social expectations place a demand for action beyond the person's present competence. In these situations, the expectation is achievable, but you need time to gain more training or experience. Examples are learning to drive a car, master a sport, or work at a new job. Time constraints can create undue pressure, setting you up to feel inadequate and insecure.

Long-term exposure to a "new learning" situation can also create pressure, setting you up for burnout. This fact is important to both the support person and the person with disturbed and challenging behaviors. If either one is reaching a burnout stage, both of them are at risk.

- When learning tennis, there is no chasing or sense of distress if no one pressures you, and you have all the time in the world to hit balls against walls. But, if you are trying to learn in competition with a skilled player, you will feel inadequate. Similarly, if you can work with people without feeling pressured to perform perfectly right from the beginning, your sense of distress will diminish.

Unachievable social or task requirements

A demand for action that is impossible to meet is the second type of situation that creates distress. Situations with unachievable expectations have the following characteristics:

- No one could meet these expectations, no matter how much skill, training or experience he had.
- The quality or quantity of pressure is too intense. Tasks, clients or caseloads are assigned with inadequate resources (skills, space, people, money) to service needs.
- Time pressure, such as an external deadline, is too great.
- Values, roles or personal expectations conflict.
- The task involves too much risk. If the person fails, he loses his job or a relationship.
- Some combination of these factors is present, setting the person up to feel frustrated and incompetent.

Think about individuals with mental, emotional or psychiatric disabilities. Support staff may force them to perform activities such as eating with a fork, dressing themselves, or entering a demanding social situation that it is beyond their present capabilities. Then consider the corrective feedback they receive after they fail to perform. This is the wrong approach, one that unintentionally makes them feel incompetent and inadequate.

Unknown or unfamiliar social expectations

Think about a situation that involves an activity in an unfamiliar environment with unknown expectations such as a first date, a new school, the first day at work or a new boss. You know the expectations are achievable with enough experience, but you are sure someone will make you aware if you act inappropriately. These situations set you up for fear of criticism.

Now, think about the people you serve who display challenging behaviors. Are you sure they are familiar with your expectations? Are they certain of them? Do they know you? Every time a person comes into contact with a new support person, he faces unknown and unfamiliar expectations. He also faces his own fear of criticism as a potential source of personal distress.

Unrealistic personal expectations

Look at the kind of unrealistic and unachievable personal goals and expectations we put on ourselves. Some people will try to master a sport or musical instrument in three months even though it takes most people two years. We begin activities or projects wanting to do well, but meet with frustration because we underestimate the time it takes to acquire the relevant skills. A person with a disability is no different. Whether or not he can describe them, he has personal goals, both realistic and unrealistic.

Unachievable personal expectations

These expectations may involve lack of ability, a disability, or goals that must change due to loss, illness or other causes. Unrealistic and unachievable personal expectations are a set-up for constant self-criticism, personal disapproval and disappointment.

Emotionally disturbed individuals make urgent goals for themselves that are almost always unrealistic, unachievable or beyond their current capability. For example, they may want to live completely on their own, work in a "normal" job with no external support, or have major changes in their life take place immediately. This leads to feeling incompetent and inadequate, and constantly criticizing themselves and others. Unfortunately, support staff sometimes exacerbate these feelings with approaches that do not acknowledge the person's disabling condition.

Emotional and Behavioral Responses to Distress

We all need coping skills to adequately deal with distressing experiences. Otherwise, the experience leads to emotionally distressing behavior. But, what emotional responses does the person with a disability have at his disposal in a distress situation?

When unable to cope with unknown, unfamiliar, unrealistic or unachievable expectations, the person will often respond with one or more of the following feelings: frustration, anxiety, confusion or dependency. His perception of who is at fault for those feelings determines how he will respond. If the person thinks his inability is his fault, he may feel embarrassed, ashamed and inhibited. If he finds someone else at fault, he will probably be angry, disappointed or demoralized.

Three categories of behavior are displayed by every person, with or without a disability, when experiencing emotional distress.

Behavioral Responses to Distress

Coping

These behaviors involve seeking a solution or resolution to both the problem and the distress it brings. They require skills such as assertiveness and flexible thinking.

- If I think it is my opponent's fault that I am not able to return any of the tennis balls he hits, I might assert myself and say, "Look, don't hit them so hard." If I am being taught to drive in icy conditions with too many cars around and someone is yelling at me, I might say, "I can't do this. You will have to take me somewhere else." These reactions illustrate adequate coping responses.

Behavioral Responses to Distress		
Coping (adequate)	**Acting Out** (inadequate)	**Withdrawing** (inadequate)
Assert self	Reject others	Reject self
Ask for help	Make demands	Injure self
Try again another way	Try the same thing more forcefully	Do not try at all
Be focused	Be focused	Be helpless
Be determined	Be destructive	Be dependent
Change your mind, give it up and go on to something else	Fixate neurotically	Avoid reality
Accept reality	Deny reality	Leave reality

Acting Out

These behaviors involve a negative and often harmful reaction to the problem and the distress it brings.

- If I believe it is my fault that I am inadequate, I might say, "I can't play this game," or I might curse at myself. If I think it is someone else's fault for putting that kind of pressure on me, and I do not have good emotional coping skills, I might say, "I'm not going to play with you anymore!" or "You're no damn good as a teacher." I might even yell back at the person, "Don't you talk to me like that."

These are emotional, acting-out behaviors we use to defend ourselves. What we also may do is fixate, perseverate, and almost neurotically work on things when we feel distressed.

Withdrawing

These behaviors involve a decision not to face the problem or the feelings it causes.

- If I am feeling inadequate and distressed because I cannot get the car started, I may walk away and say, "I can't do this," without trying something different or asking for help. The opposite, of course, is to remain focused, determined and persistent, while accepting the situation. The person who is acting out would repeatedly grind the starter. The new driver with an adequate coping response would say, "Okay, stop. Let me go over this again. Let me try it a different way. Maybe I have to touch the gas first."

When we observe inadequate responses to distress, we must teach an appropriate, alternative coping response, such as how to be assertive, how to ask for help or how to refocus. But, we must recognize that coping behaviors are often difficult to practice, regardless of intellectual ability. They require knowing when something is a little bit beyond our abilities and when we need to ask for help. And finally, they require practice. That is why training is invaluable.

Essential Approaches to Emotionally Distressed Behavior

Initially, let the person just watch and tag along. Later, ask him if he wants to help. Offer him a chance to participate in just one meaningful part of your activity. Use few words. Let your nonverbal communication say, "I'm here, you're here. It's okay just to be here together." Share a basic experience with him. Do what you like to do: listen to music, cook, play cards, garden or walk. Do not think that you necessarily have to train a skill or be productive to be meaningful and helpful.

If you know about a specific weakness, be aware of it, but do not focus on it excessively. Just protect him from having his weakness become an issue.

- Some individuals will only be able to keep their minds on one thing at a time. In these cases, you should finish completely what you are doing at the moment before suggesting the next activity.

- Some individuals can understand language quite well but can only follow what is said if sentences are no more than five or six words long. In these cases, be aware of the length of your phrases, and speak slowly–"speaking down"–to the person.

Metaphors for Building Positive Relationships

Developing a positive relationship with a person who displays disruptive behavior can be a very difficult endeavor. But, the human imagination is a powerful tool. We can use it to constantly define our role in a positive, energizing way.

Be a dotted line on a highway in deep fog.

Imagine how you feel on a steep, mountain road when thick fog makes the highway difficult to see. You try to keep your eye on the yellow, dotted line as you also look out for traffic ahead of you. Then, imagine how you feel when the fog becomes too thick to see the dotted line. You panic! You freeze in space! You have no idea where the side of the cliff or the other traffic is. You needed that constant view of the familiar guideline to allow you to function.

Now, imagine the person with a short attention span. He can only work on what he sees at the moment. If immediate, familiar cues are missing, he tends to lose sight of where he is and panics.

In another scenario, remember what it is like to memorize a speech or a song. You generally start out pretty well, but then lose your place or forget what comes next. Sometimes, you return to the beginning and start all over again. This developmental behavior pattern is common in young children; they have to go back to a familiar place to reorient themselves and find their way.

Effective Human Relations Practices

1. Remove social/emotional expectations that provoke disruptive behavior.
2. Ensure that the individual is familiar with clear, concrete, realistic and achievable expectations to reduce emotional avoidance.
3. Do not demand performance beyond the person's present level of competence. Remove time pressure.
4. Remove any social/emotional pressure to work better. In addition, remove time pressure.
5. Never criticize performance. Use encouragement and positive direction.
6. Expect success, and modify your approach until the student is successful. Acknowledge and reward each success, moving from success to success, one small step at a time.
7. Familiarize the person with a situation to remove the fear of the unknown. Teach him how to cope!

The natural coping response for the people we serve is to freeze and resist, or to make some strong demand for a familiar face to lead them out of their situation. We must remember that new faces represent the unknown. A person who is unable to cope without familiar cues cannot be expected to trust an unfamiliar face until he is convinced that person knows what she is doing. So, we show ourselves as the dotted line so the resistive person always knows where he is. We show him that he can rely on us for guidance, so going over the cliff never enters his mind. Acknowledging his need to be shown what is going on and where he is on a constant basis, we talk in a reassuring manner and explain what we are doing. Since a new support person does not know the person's abilities or how well he can respond, we use activities he is familiar with to initiate his involvement. The familiar activities become the dotted line until the fog clears and the new support person becomes a familiar, reassuring part of the journey.

Be the ramp builder, not the ambulance driver.

Do not try to be a great ambulance driver or an expert manager of behavioral crises. Be a good builder of sidewalk ramps. Teach people how to stay on the sidewalk and ask for help when they think they are going to fall off.

Be a behavior choreographer.

The people you work with have many moves, many dances with which they respond. They provide the music and create the dance floor for themselves. Many of the behaviors they choose are appropriate activities of daily living and adequate social responses. Others are extremely distressed, inadequate coping responses.

When a person makes a move that exhibits an inadequate coping response, you would like to prompt him to move with a behavior that is a strong, positive part of his repertoire.

You want to say, "Look, that's not a very interesting dance. I have this wonderful piece of music and this lovely dance floor. I know you love to do this dance. Why not come over here and do your other dance to this music on my dance floor?"

Be a behavior navigator.

Imagine that you and that person are both powerboats navigating in your own directions. Imagine that a very slack rope is attached from your boat to his. He is going his way, but your positive direction leads him steadily like a water-skier, cruising along outside the wake of a boat.

In a storm of challenging behavior, you drop the sails and head for calm waters. In guiding individuals, we keep a hand on the tiller, steer steadily, and leave lots of slack in the towrope. You do not try to sail close to the rocks with the tide coming in, but rather aim for deeper, safer water.

Be the bank in a Monopoly game.

The banker in a monopoly game gives out two hundred dollars just for passing GO, surviving the round and continuing to play. Similarly, you do many nice things for those you support for no reason at all. This is especially important for those with many challenging behaviors, who do little to make people want to be nice to them.

Be a person delivering manna from heaven.

You are providing something to sustain the person in a wilderness of negative behavior. You always want to communicate, "It's okay just to relax and be here. We're looking after you." Some people only know how to initiate an interaction with a negative behavior, but you want to avoid that trap and remain in the business of wholesome, free deliveries.

Be a behavior artist.

Imagine that you are an artist trying to paint over an old oil painting with only a box of watercolors. How do you make your picture–the new image–stand out? You manage it with lots of repetition.

The pigment is the person's behavior. The brush stroke symbolizes your prompting of relationship-sustaining behavior. And, since the canvas represents what happens between you and the person you serve, every moment provides an opportunity to paint.

Do not expect to get rid of the old painting totally, or feel like a failure when something comes up and reveals the old picture every now and then. Just pick up a clean brush and keep painting.

We also prevent the person from picking up the old oil brush and repainting the original image. Do not present him with an opportunity to practice habitual, maladaptive behavior.

The Nature of Learning

We must always keep in mind the nature of learning. What we can do well some of the time, we do not necessarily do well all of the time. Golfers, for example, know that they can only hit some of the golf balls very well, perhaps twenty out of one hundred. No one can hit every one of those hundred balls because human behavior is variable. We are not able to control all aspects of an activity even when we are highly skilled. In working with the behavior of individuals with developmental disabilities, intellectual disabilities, mental illness or emotional distress, we must acknowledge that variability.

This becomes easier when we accept the fact that people sometimes cannot even perform as well as they did just fifteen minutes ago. With our patient help and encouragement, those we serve will make further attempts and eventually be able to accomplish their tasks. (See Appendix B: The 6-Step Training Ladder: How to Support a Setback in Training.)

The goal is not to prevent the person from trying to control his environment. Rather, we should allow him to act in any area where he is competent, and encourage whatever he does well. We constantly seek opportunities for him to experience success, confidence, competency, self-control and a sense of belonging to the human community.

> We should allow the person to act in any area where he is competent, and encourage whatever he does well.

In this book, we examine a number of behaviors: agitated, impulsive, resistive, dependent, emotionally distressed, and special learning problems, among others. We regard challenging and disruptive behavior as the person's attempted coping response, and study a range of prevention, guidance, training and crisis management interventions. In each case, we investigate the ways we can enhance that person's dignity, self-control and personal responsibility. Our goal is to teach the person to choose meaningful social interactions under his own self-control, rather than avoid disruptive social interactions solely because someone constantly controls him.

In This Chapter

2 ■ Agitation, Stress and Panic Behaviors
in People with Severe and Profound Developmental Disabilities

- ■ Definition
- ■ Generative Factors
- ■ Reflexes
    - *The Innate Pain Reflex*
    - *The Innate Startle Reflex*
    - *Innate Defensive Reflexes*
    - *Learned Fear Response*
- ■ Intent to Communicate Distress
    - *Non-Directional Communication*
    - *Active Approach Communication*
- ■ General Approaches to Agitation, Distress and Panic
- ■ Friendship Box Training Program
  for People with Severe and Profound Developmental Disabilities

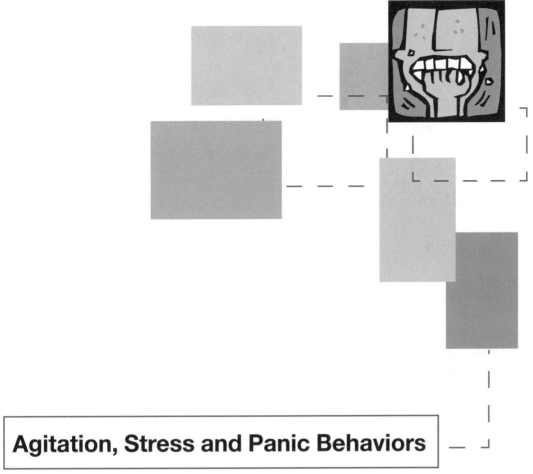

Agitation, Stress and Panic Behaviors

in People with Severe and Profound Developmental Disabilities

This chapter provides guidance to support persons who work with individuals who are entirely dependent on others for their physical care and survival. All examples involve individuals with extremely limited behavioral repertoires, who communicate exclusively through full body physical reactions. Chapter 3: Resistive Behavior covers active avoidance behaviors among individuals who have a wider behavioral repertoire.

Definition: This category includes any behavior that indicates that the person is stirred up, excited, extremely worried, anxious or alarmed. All of the behaviors are:

- Emotionally intense; all involve a fear or panic reaction
- A response to the perceived presence or anticipation of danger or suffering.

Generative Factors

At least two factors can generate agitation, distress and panic behaviors in a person who has severe to profound disabilities and requires extensive supports. They are a reflex and an intent to communicate distress. Each of these generative factors is summarized below with suggestions for intervention.

Factors That Generate Agitation, Distress and Panic Behaviors

Reflexes	**Intent to Communicate Distress**
• Pain reflex (innate)	• Non-directional
• Startle reflex (innate)	• Active approach to support staff
• Defensive reflexes (innate)	• Active avoidance of supports.
• Learned fear (conditioned reflex).	

Reflexes

A reflex response occurs when a neural impulse is transmitted inward to the brain from a receptor or sense organ, then transmitted outward to muscles. This type of response may be innate (that is, built into the organism through heredity), or acquired through conditioned learning.

An agitated reflex response is reactive and involuntary. The reflexive agitation is not intentionally, deliberately or purposefully directed at the support person.

We will consider four types of reflex responses: pain reflex, startle reflex, defensive reflexes and learned fear response (a conditioned reflex).

The Innate Pain Reflex

Pain reflexes include screaming, hand flapping, self-injurious behavior, destruction of nearby objects and striking out aimlessly.[1]

BEHAVIOR CHARACTERISTICS
- The reflex may take the form of a total-organism reaction to a sharp, intense, or lasting sensory or visceral pain, such as a burn, prick, cramp or stretching bowel.
- The behavior may originate from a reflexive spasm within the spinal cord.
- The behavior may include pain that is triggering a defensive "fight or flight" reaction.
- The behavior may be cued by the immediate onset of a specific, environmental event or circumstance.

INDIVIDUAL CHARACTERISTICS
- The person often functions below twenty-four months developmentally.
- The person does not have to be able to think about the pain or the source of the pain to be able to feel and be affected by it. In other words, cognition is not part of the response.
- The person has no effective method of coping with or escaping from discomfort.
- The person does not understand that she can get help, or how to get someone to help her. She has no other, more acceptable means of communicating.

Interventions ————————————————————————————————
Pain Reflex

PREVENTION AND GUIDANCE

■ Avoid stimulating circumstances.

■ Carefully note what happened just before the person became agitated.

■ Nurse and treat the hurt. Calm the person with gentle touch and loving communication techniques. (These are described on pages 41-44, General Approaches to Agitation, Distress and Panic Behavior.)

■ Recognize that restraining the person may trigger a fight-or-flight reaction.

■ Get "wise" to the person's idiosyncrasies.

■ Watch your own emotional and physical response. You may be unintentionally adding to the person's agitation.

Key to Prevention

Use intervention with the environment and people providing support. Remember the six A's: Acknowledge, Anticipate and Avoid problem behavior. Have an Accepting Attitude; Accommodate the person's needs and deficiencies.

TRAINING

■ Teach the person how to relax to control spasm reflexes.

■ Use desensitization training procedures (described on pages 42-43).

■ Train the person to control the situation, if possible.

CRISIS MANAGEMENT

■ Back off. Then, use calming touch and loving communication techniques.

The Innate Startle Reflex

The startle reflex, also called the Moro reflex, is a reaction to a sudden, unknown, unexpected or unfamiliar movement or sound. The arms go out and the back, elbows and fingers extend. The back also arches. Then, the arms go in and flex toward the midline. This generally occurs in a person up to about the nine-month developmental level.[2]

- Startle reflex reactions include screaming, hand flapping, self-injurious behavior, destruction of nearby objects and striking out aimlessly.

BEHAVIOR CHARACTERISTICS

■ The behavior is cued by the immediate onset of a specific, environmental circumstance.

■ The behavior is a defensive/protective reaction.

■ The behavior is not deliberately directed at the support person.

INDIVIDUAL CHARACTERISTICS

■ The person often functions below twenty-four months developmentally.

■ The person has no effective method of coping with or escaping from distress or discomfort.
  - Thresholds differ regarding the intensity of stimulus and suddenness of reaction.

Some individuals startle to any unfamiliar stimulus while others only to specific stimuli. One person may take three seconds to assimilate a new stimulus, while another person takes ten. Also, some individuals react only to loud sounds while others respond to anything that is not anticipated.

Interventions
Startle Reflex

PREVENTION

- Avoid stimulating circumstances.

- Get "wise" to the person's idiosyncrasies. Train unfamiliar support staff to recognize idiosyncrasies so they can avoid stimulating the startle response.

- Let the person see and hear you coming. Before beginning any interaction, use a gentle, calming touch. Go slowly.

GUIDANCE

- The support person must "read the individual's mind" by reading her behavior.
    - Carefully note what happened just before she became startled and agitated.
    - Attempt to work within the person's frame of reference. If she seems focused on one object, activity or thought, go with the flow. Talk about or interact with her wherever she is at the moment.
    - Next, gently refocus her onto sensory aspects of her environment other than the ones that startled her.
    - Then, orient her toward your voice and movement. Lead her to the activity you want her to pursue.

- Use loving communication techniques, heaping praise on the person.

 Watch your own emotional and physical response. You may be unintentionally adding to the person's agitation.

TRAINING

- Use desensitization training procedures. (See pages 42-44.) The goal is to train the person to control the situation, if possible.

CRISIS MANAGEMENT

- Back off. Then, use calming touch and loving communication techniques..

Innate Defensive Reflexes

Defensive reflexes are self-protective reactions in individuals who are tactile sensitive.[3]
    - Defensive reflexes include screaming, hand flapping, self-injurious behavior, destruction of nearby objects, and striking out aimlessly, especially during feeding.

Reflexes of the Head

Gagging-choking reflex: stimulated in the mouth on several touch centers—any part of the soft palate, and between the root of the tongue and last molar. This reflex never disappears.

Sucking and rooting reflex: turning toward touch on mouth or face, indicating a seven- to twelve-month developmental stage. Also, tongue thrusting–a primitive feeding response.

Reflexes of Other Parts of the Body

Galant reflex: withdrawal reaction to touch on side or back. Trunk curves and arches away from the stimulus, up to a six-month developmental level.

Flexor withdrawal: leg withdraws from stimulus on the sole of the foot, indicating up to a three-month developmental level.

Grasp reflex: hand closes down on any item in the palm, indicating up to a seven-month developmental level.

Asymmetrical neck reflex: turning the head to right side and right side limbs extending on same side and contracting on the opposite side, indicating up to a seven-month developmental level. It is especially important when feeding to keep the body symmetrical.

Key to Guidance

Use positive intervention with the person. Use human relations techniques to engage her in other behavior without confronting her about problem behavior. Use suggestion, positive motivation and humor along with the three D's: Displace, Divert and re-Direct the person's behavior.

BEHAVIOR CHARACTERISTICS
- These are involuntary reactions. The person has no control over them until they are developmentally integrated into voluntary responses.
- The behavior is a defensive/protective reaction.
- The behavior is cued by the immediate onset of some specific stimulus.

INDIVIDUAL CHARACTERISTICS
- The person often functions below one year developmentally.
- The person has no effective method of coping with or escaping from distress or discomfort.
- The person does not understand that she can get help, nor how to get someone to help her. In other words, she has no other more adequate means of communicating.

Interventions
Defensive Reflexes

PREVENTION
- Avoid the stimulating circumstance.
- Carefully note what happened just before the person became agitated.
- Watch your own response. You could be accidentally reinforcing agitation.
- Get "wise" to the person's idiosyncrasies.

GUIDANCE

- Recognize these defensive reflexes by their behavioral characteristics. Read the person's mind by reading behavior.

- Accept reflexes for what they are, and do not treat them as purposefully resistive behavior.

- Use loving communication techniques.

TRAINING

- Use desensitization training procedures.

- Train the person how to control the situation, if possible.

CRISIS MANAGEMENT

- Remain calm.

- Back off. Then, use calming touch and loving communication techniques.

Learned Fear Response

This reaction cannot occur until the brain is developmentally mature enough to recognize stimuli that trigger pain, startle and defensive reflexes. This recognition leads to a conditioned anticipatory fight-or-flight reaction (that is, the stimulus leads immediately to a response).

Individuals with multiple disabilities have many opportunities to learn a fear response. The following examples demonstrate only a few.

- A person with a poor swallowing reflex may learn by experience that being fed may lead to choking. She comes to associate the sight of someone approaching with a spoon with her own panic reaction that follows a choking episode. Thus, she learns to be afraid and will react with panic, distress and defensive resistance.

- An individual with contractures may learn that changing clothes can lead to painful limb extensions. She associates the sight of a support person approaching with clothing with pain. In her distress or panic, she strikes out aimlessly and attempts to bite anyone who touches her.

- A man who requires medical care learned that he will experience discomfort, and sometimes pain, when he receives a certain treatment. The sight of a support person approaching with treatment materials triggers his distress and panic. He may grab at the support person's arm. Or, he may scratch at his own ear until it becomes raw.

These anticipation-of-fear reactions make any situation more difficult for the person. The increased tension and resistance:

- Make it harder for the person to relax enough to swallow
- May lead to even greater spasms
- May lead to more painful treatments since the person is less likely to be passive.

The goal is to ensure as much comfort and relaxation as possible before a potentially painful interaction so that any discomfort remains as brief and pain-free as possible.

BEHAVIOR CHARACTERISTICS

- The fear/panic behavior is a conditioned reflex. It is learned in order to avoid a stimulus that triggered a fear reaction in the past. (It is cued by the immediate onset of a specific, environmental circumstance. It is not deliberately directed at support staff.)

Key to Training

Use positive intervention with the person. Employ motivation and skill development programs, and teach alternative coping skills over time.

- The reaction has survival value as a defensive/protective response.

- The reaction has functional value as a primitive communication response that signals that the individual is experiencing panic. (Her response may indicate: "I don't want this to begin!" "I'm scared!" "Go away! Get away from me!" "Help me!")

INDIVIDUAL CHARACTERISTICS

- A learned fear response is possible in any individual whose brain is developed enough to interpret her environment and recognize stimuli that trigger pain, startle and defensive reflexes. (A learned fear response is not possible without this characteristic.) These responses can be "accidentally" learned by stimulus response association throughout our lifespans.

- Typically, the person functions below twenty-four months developmentally.

- The person has no effective method of coping with or escaping from distress or discomfort.

- The person does not understand that she can get help, or how to get someone to help her. She has no other, more adequate means of communicating.

- The person often wants to be somewhere quiet or wants you to remove the stimulus that she finds aversive.

Interventions
Learned Fear Response

PREVENTION

- Carefully note what happened just before the person last became agitated. Recognize what provokes the panic reaction, and avoid the situation that stimulates it. Find another way to achieve your goal.

- Reduce demanding interactions to a minimum. Greatly increase non-demanding interactions.

- Watch your own emotional and physical response. You may be unintentionally aggravating the person's agitation.

- Get "wise" to the person's idiosyncrasies.

GUIDANCE
- Read the person's mind by reading her actions.

- Initiate any interaction by first using a gentle, calming approach.

- Use loving communication techniques; comfort and reassure her.

TRAINING
- Use desensitization training procedures.

- Teach or condition incompatible responses. Teach the person how to relax within the context of the panic situation.

- Teach her how to control the situation positively.

- Teach her alternative communication for expressing fear.

CRISIS MANAGEMENT
- First, control the escalating behavioral cycle.

- Then, back off and allow the situation to cool off.

- Next, re-approach the person with a gentle, calming interaction.

- Finally, reintroduce an appropriate training approach.

Intent to Communicate Distress

This group of behaviors is distinguished by its message value. Agitated behaviors begin as spontaneous responses to distress that allow the person to release emotional tension. However, if the agitated behavior results in the removal of the distressing stimulus by the support person, the individual may learn that the behavior can be intentionally used to elicit a desired response. Thus, the agitation/distress/panic behavior becomes one element of a primitive communication system.

In each case, the message behind the behavior is directed at the support person, even if the behavior itself is not always directed at him. We can divide communication-based behaviors into three categories relating to the direction of the behavior.
- Non-directional
- Active approach toward support staff
- Active avoidance of support staff. (See also Chapter 3: Resistive Behavior.)

Non-Directional Communication
This category encompasses a wide range of behaviors including screaming, shrieking, yelping, self-injurious actions and wandering aimlessly.

- One young lady produces a high-pitched scream in the bathtub when her soother, a pink sock, is taken away so it will not get wet.

- A man bangs his head whenever he is in an overly noisy environment.

- A woman scratches her arms when her toy is not working properly.

BEHAVIOR CHARACTERISTICS

■ The behavior is cued by the onset of a particular circumstance.

■ The behavior is a reactive, agitated response. Initially, it is not deliberately directed at the support staff.

■ The behavior may eventually become a functional means of avoiding or correcting the distressing situation.

■ The behavior is a primitive form of expressive communication. It communicates: "I don't like what's happening!"

INDIVIDUAL CHARACTERISTICS

■ The person often functions at a one- to five-year developmental level.

■ The person is most often nonverbal, with no formal means of alternative communication.

Interventions ———————————————————————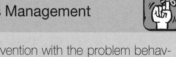
Non-Directional Communication

PREVENTION

■ Avoid actions or circumstances that set off distress behavior.

■ Constantly try to provide the person with items that are important to her.

GUIDANCE

■ Divert and distract the person. Interrupt her agitation by offering a new activation opportunity to distract her from focusing on whatever is distressing her.

TRAINING

■ Teach her how to cope with distress.

■ Train her to use an alternative form of communicating needs such as "No," "Don't want," or "Don't like."

■ Train the person to control the situation, if possible. Wait for the first moment when she is not agitated. Then, attempt a communication approach. Using words or gestures, say, "Show me" or "Take my hand." Show her how to ask for help, and reinforce her for any attempt to ask appropriately.

Key to Crisis Management

Use direct intervention with the problem behavior. Remain calm and always use guidance techniques first. Accommodate the person's special needs and disabilities. Respond to chaotic behavior with a prearranged plan for surviving the crisis while bringing challenging behavior to a stop! Interact positively with the person as soon as she exercises a degree of self-control. Have a plan for how to re-enter normal life.

CRISIS MANAGEMENT

■ Back off.

■ Try again later when the person has settled down.

■ Prevent the situation from escalating.

■ Remove her from all stimuli until she has become calm.

Active Approach Communication

- One man lunges and strikes out at the support person if his shoes and braces are taken away from him.

- One girl becomes agitated and aggressive when she cannot find a possession.

BEHAVIOR CHARACTERISTICS

- The person becomes distressed if she does not have something. Her response says, "I'm upset if I don't have it!" or "Don't take that away from me," or "Give it back to me!"

- The individual has no better way of asking for what she wants.

- The behavior may occur at the moment something is taken away from her. For instance, she grabs at or lunges toward the support person as something is being removed.

- She may escalate to greater distress–screaming, agitation, destructive handling of clothes or objects if a substitute item is not available.

These behaviors are not the same as impulsive behaviors. The extreme distress quality is not present in impulsive responses.

INDIVIDUAL CHARACTERISTICS

- The person initiates the behavior as an expression of some state of need.

- The person actively engages her environment with a seeking or approach behavior.

Interventions
Active Approach Communication

PREVENTION

- Avoid stimulating circumstances. Do not suddenly take away an object whose removal will trigger this response.

- Ensure that the person always has an activation item to fill the identified need.

- Beware of the person using active distress behavior as a form of non-verbal "request" to be removed from noise or another aversive stimulus. If this occurs, arrange for private or quiet time in the following manners:
  - Using a prearranged schedule (such as a nap every three hours)
  - Following a request by the person for quiet time
  - Checking periodically to make sure the person still wants to remain in a quiet environment.

GUIDANCE

- Provide the person with alternative activities. If the item has to be taken away, do so gradually, with an explanation and a replacement.

TRAINING

- Teach the person how to request what she needs properly, if possible.

CRISIS MANAGEMENT

- Control the escalating behavioral cycle.

- Then, provide an alternative activity.

- Next, attempt to teach her how to request what she needs. (See also Chapter 5: Persistent, Repetitive Behavior: Perseverative Responding.)

General Approaches to Agitation, Distress and Panic

Two methods provide the basis for a successful approach: the support person's communication skills and desensitization training to reduce the individual's fear. These methods communicate nurturing and affection, contributing to a trusting relationship between the support person and the person served.

Communication Skills

The support person's communication should convey calm, relaxation, affirmation, healing, loving and caring acceptance. To achieve this, employ these simple skills:

- **Tone of voice**: mellow, melodious, even rhythm, flowing tone, humming.
- **Eye contact**: smiling eyes and a smiling mouth.
- **Touch**: firm, secure, constantly holding. Contact should be flowing, not abrupt, and the individual's body should always be supported. Rub hand lotion on the individual's hands to help yourself become comfortable and secure giving touch. Make this a regular part of each day's activities.

All human beings hunger for loving, caring touch that affirms, relaxes and heals, especially touch that makes no demands. We also all need acknowledgement, recognition and acceptance. The support person can greatly reduce fear by recognizing and meeting some of these needs during regular routines as well as non-routine interactions. (See also Chapter 7: Socially Disruptive, Attention-Seeking Behavior.)

> The support person's communication should convey calm, relaxation, affirmation, healing, loving and caring acceptance.

Desensitization Training to Reduce Fear

Many people have learned to fear some specific stimulus–a person, object, event, situation or procedure. (These learned fears are discussed in more detail later.) Fortunately, any fear that has been learned can also be unlearned. The support person can facilitate the process of fear reduction through an emotional retraining procedure called desensitization.

 Any time a person displays fear during a procedure such as feeding, washing or hygiene, the priority for the moment is not to complete the procedure but to teach the person to become calm, trusting and less fearful.

Desensitization Principle (Fear Reduction)

To help a person overcome fear of a particular stimulus:
- Begin by providing minimal exposure to the fear stimulus, ensuring that she is comfortable, relaxed and secure.
- Gradually increase exposure to the fear stimulus in very small steps.
- Make sure that at each step the person becomes comfortable, relaxed, secure or rewarded before moving on to the next one.

A desensitization program should include the following six steps, based on the desensitization principle.

1. Stop and observe. When you observe a person's fear, ask yourself, "What is she afraid of?" Help the person back off from her encounter with the feared event. Never force her through an activity while she is in a defensive spasm or other state of fear.

2. Reassure. Calm the person down using comforting touch and voice. Wait until she is relaxed, accepting and trusting before proceeding.

3. Reintroduce the situation. Bring the person into the situation in a non-demanding manner. Teach her that she can be in the feared situation without experiencing any negative event. This teaches her to have an emotionally neutral reaction to the situation. It tells her, "See, nothing bad happened here."
- Teach the person to accept physical contact in a play environment where no demands will be made of her. In this manner, she learns that some contacts are pleasurable.
- Bring the person into the feared situation with something pleasurable to do. The message is: "See, some good things happen here, too."

4. Reintroduce the activity. Go slowly, being very gentle and comforting. Do only a little bit at a time. Progress at a speed that allows you to maintain the person in a relaxed and accepting condition. If pain or panic reactions arise, stop the procedure until the pain reflex or panic subsides. Carry on when the person is completely settled once again. This teaches the person to learn to trust and remain relaxed–to be less sensitive about being touched, washed, moved or fed.

4. Distract. Provide the person with an object of interest, such as a book. While the procedure is being carried out, talk soothingly or have someone else calm her.

5. Enhance communication. For some individuals, every physical encounter with support staff (bathing, feeding, positioning, medical treatment, and so on) is associated with a painful demand on their bodies. If possible, teach some method of communicating, "Stop," "Slow down" or "It hurts." Even if the person still experiences discomfort or pain from a procedure, the experience will be milder and last a shorter time if she is relaxed and comfortable.

Un-Teaching the Learned Fear Response

Any time we observe signs of learned fear, our priorities with the individual must change. The goal of the moment must no longer be feeding, dressing or giving a treatment. It must be teaching the person to be unafraid and to relax. The following desensitization training is designed for the person who displays a learned fear response to certain grooming routines.

The person does not like feeding or tooth brushing.
- Take your time.
- Start with the lips. Gently touch them, then rub them softly with a warm cloth, then a cool cloth.
- Rub the cheeks softly. Tap the person under the chin with your finger.
- When she accepts your touch, be sure to reward her with a sensation, smell or sound that she likes.
- Do not attempt to feed her while she is tense. Relax her with the Ways to Move techniques described on page 44.

The person does not like a facecloth.
- Take your time.
- Stroke the person's face with a very soft tissue while letting her smell, feel or hear things that she likes.
- Gradually build up her acceptance to gauze, a soft cloth, and finally a washcloth.
- First, use very gentle stroking with a soft cloth. Once she tolerates this, introduce more and more pressure until a normal pressure level is reached. Then, switch to a washcloth.

The person does not like a towel rub.
- Take your time.
- Lay a soft, flannelette cloth on the person's body.
- Rub with this soft cloth, starting very gently and gradually building up pressure.
- Switch to a washcloth, then a towel.

The person does not like water.
- Take your time.
- Play with her fingers in lukewarm water in a cup, then a bowl, and finally a basin. Vary the temperatures. As she shows that she tolerates the sensation, move up her arms to her neck. Do this same procedure on each body part, coming to the genitals and face last.
- Be sure to stroke and verbally reinforce her for complying. Also, be sure to let her feel, smell or hear what she likes when she relaxes and accepts contact.

The person does not like movement, touch or dressing.
- Take your time.
- If the person resists movement or touch, initially touch or handle her gently while she is busy with a pleasurable activity like eating or bathing. Then, gently stroke her with various textures—smooth, soft, fluffy or furry—during non-routine periods.
- Use the Friendship Box activities with the person. (See section below.)
- Touch the person from feet to face. Start with her hands and rub up to her neck, head and face.

Ways to Move

These methods work especially well with a person who is blind. Before initiating any movement, play and talk while you approach the person. Then, make first contact with her feet, soothing and rubbing her feet then her legs. Do the same beginning with her hands and moving up the arms, shoulders and neck to the head.
- Gently rock the person back and forth with your hands, rubbing her head gently.
- Rub her head and squeeze her shoulders gently. Turn her head in your hands from side to side.
- Clap the person's hands together in pat-a-cake. Move her arms over her head to clap, then down to the front and clap again. Wiggle her limbs and body parts while giving the person firm overall support. Pump her legs up and down to simulate kicking.
- Push and turn her in the wheelchair or on the stretcher. Note what seems to make her feel good.
- Pull her in a padded wagon, or gently bounce her on a trampoline.

Friendship Box Training Program

for People with Severe and Profound Intellectual Disabilities

Many individuals who are easily agitated have few interactive skills. For the support person, it is difficult to develop interactions with them because they react and scream each time someone approaches them for basic care and feeding. The Friendship Box Training Program addresses this issue.

Friendship boxes are containers the support person can create and fill with play-stimulation materials for use in desensitization training. The boxes offer activities and interactions for working with a person who functions in the infantile to four-year mental age range.

They are arranged from the most passive ways of interacting without creating a startle reflex to increasingly complex interactions. People with limited or no sight should particularly enjoy these activities.
- It is important to be enthusiastic and positive when approaching the person with an activity. Your confidence rubs off.
- Feel free to make up your own activities to add.

- Attempt the activity suggested for each box with every item in the box. Demonstrate each activity at least three times to attract her attention.
- Give manual guidance to get her to participate. When she accepts this or tries even a little, let her feel, see, hear or smell what she likes as a reward. If she shows any interest or active response, continue to explore the activity. Try to get her to repeat the response several times.
- Note your successes. If there is no response or interest, go on to the next activity, then the next box.

 This program is designed especially for volunteers who have no training in working with and establishing relationships with people with severe and profound intellectual disabilities.

Box 1. Things to Smell (Smelling Activities)
Several types of food flavors and spices: peanut butter, pineapple, onion, nutmeg, chili powder, vanilla, raspberry, celery salt, banana, perfume samples and aftershave.

Place the substance on a cotton ball inside a small prescription vial. Then, place that container into a larger prescription vial. This will preserve the smell for long periods of time and prevent the person from accidentally ingesting items. The box requires direct supervision.

Set up several open containers on a table or on the floor beside you. Pass each briefly (for no more than two seconds) under the person's nose. Look for and note any special signs of preferences. She will move her lips, smile, quiet down, interrupt self-stimulatory behavior or make a noise.

> Progress at a speed that allows you to maintain the person in a relaxed and accepting condition.

When you notice what seems to make her feel good, repeat it several times with a variety of smells. Pause seven to ten seconds between smells. Good smell may act as a reward for reducing agitation. Be sensitive and pace your interaction to avoid over-stimulating her.

Box 2. Things to Listen To (Listening Activities)
Whistles, noisemakers, horn, your voice, bells, the radio, an audio player (CD, DVD, MP3, et al.) with a variety of recordings—music, conversation, stories, sounds from nature, funny sounds, and so on.

From behind and from the sides of the person's head, place or hold a radio or music maker. If she turns toward the sound, smiles, wakes up, makes noise or responds in another fashion, move the object into and across her field of vision. Try different tunes to see if you get different responses. Use the music, horns or bells in different places in a quiet room. Note whether she orients to the sound.

Sing or hum to the person while gently stroking her. Repeat her name in different tones of voice. Vary your tone of voice while speaking to her: excited, purring, rhythmic or soft. Use music for ten- to twenty-second periods. Then, vary the tune or sound source so it does not lose its value.

Begin with sounds within a few inches and move away as the person pays attention. Help her turn her head toward the sound. Note what seems to make her feel good. (Clean horns and whistles with tissues and antiseptic before using.)

Box 3. Things to Feel and Touch (Tactile Activities)
Sponges, cloth samples, textures glued on blocks, carpet samples, bean bags, rings from a ring stacking game, clay in a bag, your hands touching her, tissue paper and hand lotion.

Teach the person to hold. If she can see, hold the small objects so she can see them. Touch the inside of her hand with the object and let her fingers close around it. Take your hand away. When she drops it, repeat. Gently wrap her fingers around the object if she does not grasp it.

Do not force her to hold the object. Gradually lessen the pressure on her fingers. Stroke her arms, hands and face with each thing to feel. Make soothing sounds or play music she likes while stroking. Note what seems to make her feel good. Then, rub hand lotion on her hands.

Box 4. Things to Look At (Visual Activities)
Hand puppet, hand mirror, mobile, your face, bubble solution and flashlight.

Hold the puppet near the person's face. Make voices and play games to get any response. Move any bright object across her field of view–above her head and around both sides to try to catch her eye. Put your face twenty-four inches from her face while talking to her. Hold any bright object near your face and call her name.

Turn the person's face to look at you and let her smell or hear what she likes while looking at you. Stroke her face during the period of eye contact. Blow bubbles with your face near hers. Let her see bubbles blowing past and away from her. Place a mirror over her head, by her side. Flash lights in the mirror to get a response. Note what seems to make her feel good.

Box 5. Things to Make Sound With (Audio-Kinesthetic Activities)
Squeaky toys, clog sticks, wrist bells, cowbells, roly-poly ball, cloth cubes with bell and rattles.

Teach the person to imitate simple movements. Squeeze, shake, ring or rattle the object within a few inches of her face. With your hand over her hand, help her reach out and touch or grab the object. If she can do this, hide the object out of sight, and reward her for looking around to find it. Help the person hold the object by placing your hand over hers. Help her shake or squeeze it. Release the pressure.

Stimulate her several times with each object, and reward her by letting her smell or hear what she likes for any slight, participating response, or any attempt to participate. If she seems to like this, try taping a bell or rattle to her hand so the object makes sound as she moves her hands.

Box 6. Things that Help the Person Imitate Coordinated Movements

Xylophone: Help the person pull the instrument by a string or hit it with a wooden player. Put your hands over hers, and show her how to do the motion several times. Encourage her to imitate your action.

Tambourine: Help her hold and shake it with one of two hands.

Slinky toy: Hold one end, and put the other end in the person's hand. Lift and drop your end while she holds onto hers.

Pop beads: Hold one end, and show the person how to hold on while you pull the beads apart. Then push them back together while she pushes against your bead.

Play peek-a-boo: Clap hands with her and encourage her to imitate your movements.

Box 7. Things that Help the Person Learn to Work on Simple Tasks

Stacking rings: Help the person stack the rings by placing your hands over hers. Encourage her to imitate your movements.

Clothespins and cans: Help her take each clothespin off one can and drop it into another can. Then empty the can, help her put the pins back on and repeat the process. Encourage her to imitate your movements.

Nuts and bolts: Help her put on and take off the nuts by twisting with one hand while holding them in the opposite hand. Encourage her to imitate your movements.

Cymbals: Show the person how to hold the cymbals and clap them together. Encourage her to clap with you, both with and without cymbals.

Pop beads: Help her hold both beads, then put them together and pull them apart.

Slinky toy: Hold one end of the toy. Help the person hold the other end. Raise and lower your end as long as she is holding her end.

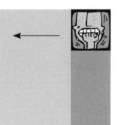

When you notice what seems to make her feel good, repeat it several times.

Tambourine: Help her hold the instrument in one hand and hit it with the other.

Blow bubbles: Show the person how to blow bubbles. Encourage her to imitate your movements. Show her how to dip the wand in the bottle and wave it.

Crayons: Encourage scribbling with crayons.

Box 8. Problems and Puzzles

Lego blocks: Show the person how to stack blocks and build simple structures.

String and beads: Show her how to hold large beads and push a stiff cord through them to make a bracelet.

Stacking cups: Start with the largest cup and the next two sizes. Show her how to stack the cups in the correct order. Then, slowly add more cups as she learns to do the activity correctly on her own.

Divided container and selection of small objects: Show her that one type of object goes in each division. Encourage her to sort all the objects.

Tupperware shape ball: Hold the ball and pick up a circle shape. Show the person where it goes. Let her practice putting a single shape in and out of the appropriate space. Repeat the activity. When she is continuously successful, add another shape.

Bubbles: Show her how to blow bubbles, and encourage her to imitate you.

Drawing: Encourage the person to copy lines and circles.

In This Chapter

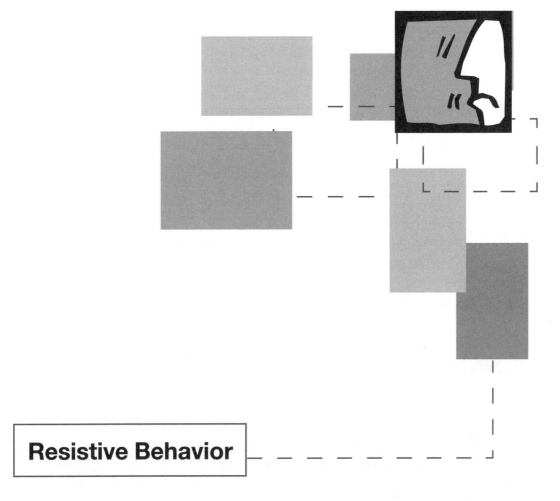

Resistive Behavior

Definition: For the purpose of this chapter, resistive behavior is an oppositional reaction to a support person's approach, direction or control.

Generative Factors

Resistive behavior arises from four main factors and may involve more than one. Each behavior—feeling overwhelmed, a communication problem, accidental learning, and power struggle—is summarized below with suggestions for intervention.

Feeling Overwhelmed

Every person will feel overwhelmed at some point, and will experience the negative feelings that come with fear, confusion, avoidance or even panic.

- A woman screams, "No! No! Go away!" She bites, lunges, spits and curses in response to direction.

- A reclusive man throws food in the dining room. The behavior increases when the number of people in the dining room rises and with greater distance between him and the door.

- • A woman tries to bite anyone who comes near her. This makes hygiene care very hazardous.

- • A normally affectionate child cries, squirms and thrashes about when the support person tries to put him on the toilet, brush his teeth or give him a drink out of a glass.

BEHAVIOR CHARACTERISTICS

■ This behavior stems from confusion, fear or panic.
  - – An initial fear response may become functional in the short term. It may either relieve the need to respond to demands or simply make people back off for a moment. It may also result in the avoidance of pain or escape from discomfort.
  - – The behavior may become functional in the long term. The support person's responses may reinforce the learned fear response.

■ The behavior may be a response to a support person's abrupt approach or request for an immediate response. For instance, the person only tries to hit when the support person comes within arm's reach without warning.

■ The behavior may be a reaction to what the person cannot quickly accommodate or incorporate, such as circumstantial distress.

 A Reaction to Circumstance?

Resistive behavior is reaction to circumstantial distress if:

- • The person never displays the behavior if an identifiable circumstance does not occur.

- • The person stops reacting shortly after the offending stimulus or circumstance is removed.

- • Temporarily removing the person from a feared situation increases the frequency of the behavior. If so, the person was trying to get away from something or wanted to be left alone.

- • Escalation of the behavior often follows a predictable pattern. The person first becomes agitated, then becomes agitated about being agitated. This may cycle and build on itself. (See Chapter 5: Persistent, Repetitive Behavior: Perseverative Responding.)

- • As the behavior is escalating into ever more disruptive activity, the person accepts the offer of activity or quiet time, and soon settles.

Individual Characteristics

- Often, the person has an exaggerated startle response that can produce panic reactions. For instance, when he sees other people approaching, he may react with panic. He may be disinhibited by his startle response and unable to control his reactions.

- The person has had a long history of distressing experiences in similar circumstances.

- The person has difficulty responding and adapting to changes in the environment and/or difficulty with transitions. He becomes disoriented easily in interactions without extra help and structure.

- The person often displays perseverative, compulsive and ritualistic behavior.

Interventions

Individuals Who Are Overwhelmed

Prevention and Guidance

- General approach: Prevent the person from becoming frightened; avoid the stimulating circumstances.

- Get the person's attention. Help him look at and interact with you before you make your request; that is, orient him to you.

- Always orient the person to what is about to happen before requiring an action. Gently introduce him to the situation. For instance, give him time to get ready. Prompt with gestures, visually and verbally. Avoid physical prompts (touch).

- Attempt to work within the person's frame of reference. If he seems focused on one object, activity or thought, go with the flow. Do not be in a hurry. Draw attention to what you like about him. Talk about his smile or how nice he looks.

- Use a low-key, gentle tone of voice.

- Do not react immediately. Before you respond, wait for a brief moment of non-agitated behavior.

- Be gentle and non-demanding. Help the person feel good in the situation.

- Where possible, give him a choice. Put control in his hands.

- Be sensitive to idiosyncrasies.

- Be positive. Encourage, expect and recognize success.

- Give the person the benefit of the doubt. Consider that his resistive behavior may be motivated by fear before concluding that it is intentional.

Key to Prevention

Use intervention with the environment and people providing support. Remember the six A's: Acknowledge, Anticipate and Avoid problem behavior. Have an Accepting Attitude; Accommodate the person's needs and deficiencies.

- Use "kid gloves." Back off when the person is irritated, and do not provoke or pressure him. Give him time to calm down. Do not try to "teach him a lesson" or "teach him who's in charge." Do not confront him about the behavior or reprimand him; instead, try to calm him down, refocus and redirect him. Then, repeat the request or resume the activity. This prevents the problem behavior from becoming functionally effective.

■ Do not take resistant behavior personally or hold a grudge. We must look at the situation from the resistive person's point of view. He is stuck in his emotional reactivity and needs assistance. (See Chapter 8: Emotionally Fragile and Reactive Behavior and Chapter 9: Violent, Aggressive and Destructive Behavior.)

TRAINING

■ Train the person by finding powerful reinforcers (rewards). Use them to motivate his self-control and cooperative participation. Tell him, and consistently show him, that he will get the reward.

■ Use a desensitization program to remove the person's anticipation of a distressful experience. (See Chapter 2: Agitation, Distress and Panic Behavior.)

CRISIS MANAGEMENT

■ Stay calm.

■ Interrupt early in the build-up of agitation. Do not let the person get carried away!

Communication Problems (A way of saying, "No!")

• A person with cerebral palsy and a speech deficit is aggressive and resistant any time a support person attempts to place him on the commode when he does not need to use it.

• A woman fights as a way of refusing the clothes that a support person offers her.

• One man beats his head when he wants to be alone.

• An adolescent woman huddles in a corner with her shirt pulled over her head. She cries and strikes out when a support person tries to get her to stand up.

• Halfway through a meal, a man will throw his plate on floor because he is no longer hungry.

BEHAVIOR CHARACTERISTICS

■ The behavior begins as a spontaneous, unlearned response to distress or dislike of a situation.

■ The person learns that resistive behaviors can be used to achieve goals of avoidance or release from pressure to perform an undesired activity. Therefore, the spontaneous behavior becomes reinforced behavior.

■ The behavior has message value once the person has learned that it is an alternative to saying "No." The support person's response reinforces the functional aspect; that is, she drops the demand.

INDIVIDUAL CHARACTERISTICS

- The person exhibits a deficit or developmental delay in expressive communication. He may have no other way of letting you know he does not want to cooperate.

- The person has a deficit in his ability to inhibit emotional responses and limited ability to tolerate frustration.

- The person often sends initial, small signals that he is becoming frustrated with a situation or demand.

Interventions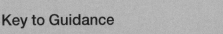
Communication Problems

PREVENTION

- Organize your schedule and the person's schedule so you can manage predictable confrontations at the optimal time.

- Try to anticipate where the person's lack of communication skill will cause problems. Be ready to interpret initial, small signals and respond to them before the person becomes disruptive. (If we listen to the whispers of behavior, we do not have to hear the screams.)

- Always try to build choice into the request situation. Give the person an option that he can refuse if he wishes.

- Try to prevent the person from becoming frustrated; avoid stimulating circumstances.

GUIDANCE AND TRAINING

 Our temptation to leave the person alone when he is resistive teaches him that acting out is the method he must use to communicate, "No, leave me alone," or "No, I don't want to do that right now."

- Use effective rewards for positive interactions. First, show the person the payoff for cooperating. Then, once you have learned how to read his behavioral signals, begin to give him direction.

- Teach him an alternate form of communicating "No," "Don't want," and "Don't like." Rehearse a more desirable communication form, such as a gesture, sign, picture, pointing and/or vocalization. Use multiple forms of communication simultaneously.

Key to Guidance

Use positive intervention with the person. Use human relations techniques to engage him in other behavior without confronting him about problem behavior. Use suggestion, positive motivation and humor along with the three D's: Displace, Divert and re-Direct the person's behavior.

- Encourage successive approximations. Accept and reward any attempt to use any appropriate means of refusal.

- Demonstrate that using alternate communication is the successful way of saying "no" and achieving his goals.

Once an alternative method of communicating "no" has been well learned, eliminate any payoff for the person's use of disruptively resistive behavior to say "no." Coach the positive alternative and then back off. This reinforces the alternative and reduces the likelihood of the disruptive action.

- Assess whether or not the person's resistance is due to the difficulty of the request. To address the issue of difficulty:
  - Remove his anticipation of a distressful experience using the desensitization program in Chapter 2: Agitation, Stress and Panic Behaviors.
  - Break the task down into smaller and easier steps.
  - Create interest to increase the person's motivation.
  - Remove any distracting features from the training environment.

CRISIS MANAGEMENT
- Remove the time pressure.

- Do not force the situation. Back off!

Accidental Learning

Accidental learning can take place at any age, but examples in this section describe individuals who function at a very young age developmentally (three years or less).

- When the support person tries to dress the child and says, "Come here," he giggles and runs away laughing.

- When the support person attempts to bring the child to the dining room for a meal, he runs away, dodges and slaps out when anyone tries to catch him.

- During feeding attempts, the child brings a cup to his mouth, but also twirls it around, tries to feed it to the support person and spills the liquid, causing an excited reaction. Then he does it again at his next feeding.

- The person mistakenly practices and learns many errors in the process of being trained to eat, dress, cooperate socially, and so on. When he makes an error, the support person corrects it. He rehearses this so many times that he believes the error/correction process to be what is expected. While the support person becomes frustrated with the person's constant failure to improve, he is only doing what he has practiced repeatedly in the situation.

BEHAVIOR CHARACTERISTICS
- These behavior characteristics may begin as a confusion response but become conditioned through support staff's unintentional reinforcement.

- The person's cooperative and responsive behavior surfaces when the support person first, indirectly, gains his attention. But, resistive behavior results when the support person makes a direct, unexpected suggestion.

- The person seems to be "playing a game."

INDIVIDUAL CHARACTERISTICS

- The person has receptive communication deficits (a language processing problem), which prevents him from understanding the link between his own actions and another person's response to his actions. He does not "get" cause and effect connections and simply reacts to "the thrill of the chase."

- The person is easily confused. He may misunderstand the intent of a request and interpret it, for example, as an invitation to play a game.

- The person may be inadvertently receiving an intrinsic reward, such as excitement and attention, built into the resistive behavior itself.

- Check out your interpretation of this behavior! The person may seem to be making a game out of resisting direction. His behavior appears to say, "You can't get me!" "Ha, ha! Try to catch me!" "Ha, ha! You can't stop me!" If the support person interprets his behavior as taunting, testing and manipulative, she may react and chase him, reinforcing the accidentally learned resistance.

Interventions
Accidentally Learned Behavior

PREVENTION

- Prevent this behavior by working up to clear, consistent expectations.

- In situations like dressing, start early so you can give the person enough time to do it his own peculiar way. Also if resistance arises, you will have time to walk away until he is ready to try again.

Key to Training

Use positive intervention with the person. Employ motivation and skill development programs, and teach alternative coping skills over time.

- Avoid giving undue attention to resistance.

- If one support person does not succeed with the individual, try having a different staff member make the request.

- Let the person perseverate a bit.

GUIDANCE

- Get the person's attention before you give instruction or direction. Instead of saying, "Go get your coat," try saying, "Look, the sun is shining. Let's go for a walk."

- Use certain, explicit and positive directions. "Be gentle," instead of "Stop hitting!"

- Revise your directions. If the person resists the explicit direction, make it indirect, so it appears less like an attempt to control him. "Where is your spoon?" instead of "Eat your food!"

- Use reverse psychology. You may get him to cooperate by acting as if you do not care whether he cooperates or not. "We're leaving at two o'clock. Since you're not getting dressed, I guess you're not going" instead of "Come here and get dressed."

- Be matter-of-fact in your interactions. Do not display your frustration.

- Everyone should prompt the person using the same cues, whether they are physical, visual, verbal or gestural.

- If safety issues permit, do not pursue him if he runs away.

TRAINING

- Do not give the person a chance to rehearse the accidentally learned, resistive response. Set up tasks so that he is only expected to complete very small steps, following an explicit demonstration. Structure the teaching so that practice is free of errors.

- Do not "chase mistakes." Lower expectations for the amount of participation, but raise expectations for the quality of participation.

CRISIS MANAGEMENT

- Remain emotionally detached and self-controlled.

- Remove time pressure. Back off!

- Do not be overly concerned about consequences. Try again, using different prompts, when the person calms down.

Power Struggle

Definition: Intentional resistance against the support staff's control.

While working with a person with intellectual disabilities, you may encounter different types of intentional resistance.

Desire for self-control: The person wants power to exert control over his own behavior. He wants to maintain self-control, sending the message, "Mother, please. I'd rather do it myself." These are not really challenging behaviors because it only requires an understanding of the person's intent.

- If rushed during his self-care routine in the bathroom, one man will refuse to hurry, sit down and, if pushed, strike out. When given enough time to finish grooming at his own pace, there are no problems.

- One young woman refuses to drink liquids required for a blood condition. When the support person puts down the cup and says, "You don't have to drink it," she picks it up and drinks the contents enthusiastically.

Desire to control others: The person wants to elicit some behavior from the support person. He wants not only to get others to do his bidding, but also to constantly establish how much control he has over their behavior. (See Chapter 9: Violent, Aggressive and Destructive Behavior.)

One large man will demand to be taken out to eat at a restaurant and will threaten to harm support staff if they refuse to take him.

Desire to avoid the control of others: The person wants to prevent or avoid the experience of having a support person exert power over his behavior.

- When someone offers one man his coat or tells him it is time for a walk, he says, "No!" If someone hands him the wrong coat and tells him it is time to walk, he laughs, teases the support person for being "dumb," and says, "That's not my coat." Then, he gets his own coat and willingly goes for a walk.

- When asked to dress, one woman says, "No!" If support staff try to assist her, she pulls away and screams. If they persist, she becomes violent.

Resistance and Developmental Processes

"It has to be my own idea."
Some individuals will always say "no" unless they are certain that doing an action is their own idea. For instance, one young man with autism cannot respond to coaching or direction to take a shower at home. It makes no sense to him to stop what he is interested in doing. But, he is cooperative and capable of showering when he is in the shower room following a swim at the public pool.

"I'm afraid if I try I will fail."
Some people are afraid that if they try something unfamiliar they may fail. Their defense against the unknown and potential failure is to avoid and resist. For this person, it is necessary to build on prior success and confidence. Reduce expectations for "rising to the challenge" and increase expectations for successful interactions at any level of positive participation.

BEHAVIOR CHARACTERISTICS
Certain behaviors indicate that the person's resistance is a power struggle reaction against external control.

- The behavior occurs only in response to support staff control. It does not occur for days, then "flares up" or cycles, especially with the change of support personnel, inconsistent approaches by a support person, or transitions from place to place.

- The behavior escalates or becomes more resistive when a support person reprimands or persists.

INDIVIDUAL CHARACTERISTICS
- The person appears to be testing you. Testing limits is normal for all people; we have a natural curiosity about "how far I can go." This is especially true if limits are not clear and consistent. The person with disabilities who "tests" may have an excessive psychological need to establish the degree of control he has over his own behavior.

- The person follows rules when they are well established, but becomes resistant if there is any indication that the support person is not adhering to the rules and limits.

■ The person seems to be reacting against your direction due to personality factors. However, he typically has a history of frustrating personal interactions, negative expectations and little success. He seems to barely cope.

 Watch your own interpretation and emotions. This person's behavior tends to make support staff feel angry or resentful since every direction, suggestion or instruction is met with intense resistance. In addition, other people often perceive the individual as stubborn, uncooperative or spoiled. His response seems to say:

- "You can't make me do it."
- "Ask me and watch me say no!"
- "Let me do this MY way!"
- "Don't you tell me what to do!"

- If this type of power struggle makes up a large part of the individual's behavior repertoire, the support person may become frustrated. And, she tends to feel relieved as soon as the person stops being resistive. As a result, she may leave him alone when no direction is necessary. But, if the person is not getting the attention he naturally needs, he may inadvertently learn to seek attention by initiating power struggle behavior. The power struggle then becomes compounded by the issue of inappropriate attention seeking.

Interventions
Power Struggles

It is important to accept that changing people with long histories of displaying such behavior–and perhaps organic reasons for the behavior–can be extremely difficult. Accommodating their personalities and individual needs, and successfully managing their tendency to be resistive, is often the path of least resistance and most success for all concerned.

PREVENTION

■ Try to prevent resistive behaviors through accommodation and management.

■ Do not "buy in" to the power struggle. Do not try to win! In other words, avoid forcing the person to follow a directive unless it is absolutely necessary.
- Do not counter his power with yours or engage his negative reactions. Take your wind out of his sails.
- Then, take your sails out of his wind. Back off when he pushes or tests because if you engage him at all, you may reinforce the power struggle as his effective mode of seeking attention.

■ Arrange the environment to prevent power struggles from occurring, or so that it does not matter if they do occur.

■ Let the person perseverate a bit.

■ When prompting a person to respond to positive direction, you should not expect an immediate response. Use the ten–second request method described below.

GUIDANCE

- Use human relations skills to motivate the person to cooperate with support staff.

- Let him have as much self-control as is reasonably possible.

- Be clear and consistent about expectations, standards and limits. Ensure consistency between support persons working at different times or on different days by keeping written rules and guidelines for working with the person.

- Do not ask the person to participate, and avoid direct demands. Use diplomacy! Give him directions in a way that appears as if you do not want control.
    - Wherever possible, present directions in the form of choices between alternatives that you provide.
    - Go with the flow of his spontaneous activity. Ask him to do what he is already showing interest in doing.
    - Be indirect: "Whose turn is it to set the tables?" rather than, "Gail, come set the tables."

- Give him time to respond before repeating your prompt. Do not "nag" or remind too often. Go on with other things or with other people.

- When compliance is necessary, try to use the ten-second request method. When prompting the person to respond to positive direction, do not expect an immediate response. Use the request method described below, which allows time for a response. This affirms the person's right to "test" support staff. It also establishes that the support person knows the limits, is able to communicate the expectations, and is willing to persist and "pass the test."

 The Ten-Second Request Method

- Your clear, explicit and positive direction is given to draw the individual's attention to the support person and establish a clear expectation for a compliant response.
- Give your request and remove your direct attention, but remain in close proximity.
- The first few seconds allows the person to slow the momentum of whatever he was doing before you made your request.
- The next few seconds allows the direction to "sink in."
- The last few seconds allows the person to feel that he is in charge; no one is pressuring him or pushing him around. He saves face and gets ready to respond.
- If the person still does not comply, separate him from the situation. Explain the alternatives that he would prefer to avoid in private.

- Remove time pressure. Do not push. Arrange the situation so there is time for him to do the task his own way and at his own pace.

- Do not intrude physically more than necessary.

- Always try humor and a light touch.

- Model the desired behavior yourself, and get others involved. If positive direction fails, try reverse psychology.

TRAINING

- Remember to attend to the person when there are no requests to make.

- Give praise and approval whenever his behavior is cooperative or responsive.

- Focus on his successes—how much better he is now than before.

- Let logical consequences follow. For example, the person cannot go on an outing if he does not get dressed.

 When designing consequences for a person with severe disabilities, be aware of his cognitive levels. For some individuals, the nature of the disability prevents them from learning the relationship between their behavior and its effects. If a person cannot learn from natural consequences, support staff must rely on prevention and guidance techniques.

As a complete model for positive training to overcome resistive behavior, consider the relative ease with which individuals learn to wear seatbelts. (See the section titled Motivating Self-Control While Maintaining Positive Expectations in Chapter 1: Introduction to Values and Methods.)

CRISIS MANAGEMENT

If you must intrude and force your direction on the person who engages in power struggles, be prepared.

- Give yourself plenty of time, and have staff backup ready.

- Prompt the person, making it clear what is going to happen before it happens.

- Pursue your action with calm confidence.

- Avoid taking resistance personally. Do not hold a grudge.

- Follow through with what you start. Do not give up.

- Adopt "a success is in the effort" attitude. In other words, do not be hard on yourself or other support persons for "never getting anywhere" with the person. To accomplish this, follow the guidelines in the next section.

> **Key to Crisis Management**
>
> Use direct intervention with the problem behavior. Remain calm and always use guidance techniques first. Accommodate the person's special needs and disabilities. Respond to chaotic behavior with a prearranged plan for surviving the crisis while bringing challenging behavior to a stop! Interact positively with the person as soon as he exercises a degree of self-control. Have a plan for how to re-enter normal life.

Extremely Disruptive Behavior in Children

Some children with long histories of disruptive behavior are like an elemental force every time they perceive a challenge or experience frustration. Often, the child's acting out with such force leads others to give in. He rapidly learns that it is functional for him to explode, disrupt, attack and confront as a quick method of "getting his way" or "getting what he wants."

Naturally, the parent will attempt to put a stop to this behavior. In the process, both parent and child can become caught up in a "negative spiral" of continuing power struggles. The child's behavior frustrates the parent so continually that it becomes very difficult to maintain or re-establish a positive footing with him. This leaves both of them–and other family members–feeling trapped.

The Power Struggle Trap

- The parent and child engage in daily power struggles.

- As the power struggles increase, this way of interacting becomes the family members' primary means of interacting with each other.

- Everyone forgets that there are other ways to interact.

- Negative feelings begin to dominate family life.

Interventions
Extremely Disruptive Behavior in Children

The initial goal for managing any of the disruptive behaviors is not to change them. It is to work out an adequate means for coping with them emotionally. Metaphorically speaking, if you are out sailing (trying to accomplish a task) and a sudden windstorm (power struggle) arises, you do not attempt to fight against the elemental forces of nature. You drop your sails (drop the task) and attempt to steer for calmer waters (switch to some pleasant, cooperative activity).

Increasing the Positive

To achieve this goal, both parent and child need to increase their focus on any pleasant and cooperative activities that remain a part of their relationship. Following are some guidelines.

Make smiles and happy times a common occurrence. This requires the parent to:
- Avoid trying to change multiple difficult behaviors at one time.
- Prevent as many predictable confrontations as possible.
- Identify any activity or circumstance the child is performing more adequately.
- Offer the child increased opportunities to engage in the more adequate activities and circumstances.

Offer him the activities he likes best. To use the sailing metaphor, this is not retreating but tacking. The captain takes another direction for a while that is less challenging for everyone. This allows the whole crew to continue making small, though steady, headway against the wind.

Train your eye towards the positive. In the short run, it is best for the parents or support persons to lower their expectations for direct control over the child's disruptive behavior. At the same time, they should raise their expectations for direct control over the child's appropriate and desirable behavior.

Give a little to get a little. For a parent who typically winds up giving in after a major tantrum and power struggle, a better approach is to give in before the power struggle has an opportunity to occur. At the same time, she must maintain some degree of control and ability to manage the situation. This requires giving the child what he is looking for, but modifying it somewhat to accommodate the needs of the situation.

 A girl begins to act out because she wants an extra snack. Her mother offers her a number of acceptable choices–yogurt, fresh fruit or carrot sticks. The girl chooses one, and no power struggle ensues. Though she really wanted a less healthy alternative like chips or cookies, the girl has gained some of what she wants. The child has agreed to cooperate and accept some degree of limitation, and a major power struggle is avoided.

Tip the scale towards the positive. However much the parent finds herself disciplining the child, she needs to make sure that she does something to evoke five to ten smiles on his face to balance out each episode of discipline. Otherwise, the whole world turns hard and nasty for the child, and that is not the purpose of discipline. The purpose is to show the child how he can exercise responsible control over his own behavior.

Maintain your own positive outlook. The parent or support person must continually create these positive opportunities, regardless of how much manipulation of circumstances it requires of them. When a parent becomes worn out, a second parent–or other responsible adult–can take over and allow the first adult a chance to wind down and regain his or her good humor.

Maintain the structure the child needs. Parents should also be aware that many children who display disruptive behavior are at their worst during unstructured times. Because they cannot organize their own behavior adequately, difficulties often erupt during transitions and times when they are not receiving explicit direction. Conversely, the child will often function best in highly structured, one-on-one situations, or in a group playing a game similar to Simon Says. In these situations, the child is provided with continuous, explicit prompting about what he should do with himself.

Ideally, life for the frequently disruptive child would be a continuous game of Simon Says. They would be shown or told what to do with themselves every few moments. Parents can use this game as a metaphor, understanding that the game depends on the leader's instruction. The child can occasionally go for a longer period of time without structure.

But more often, the child will quit if the structure ceases for even a minute. The parent ensures that the child will "stay in the game" by providing more guidance, support, structure and assistance the moment the child demonstrates lack of control.

Accommodate the child's specific disability. Frequently disruptive children often like to learn, but display wide variations between what they can understand and what they can actually do for themselves.

Do something to evoke five to ten smiles on his face to balance each episode of discipline. Otherwise, the whole world turns hard and nasty for the child.

The child's abundant energy for learning can quickly turn into intense and disruptive activity when no support person is giving him adequate assistance with a task he finds difficult. This can be the child's desperate attempt to experience some degree of control, regardless of the cost to himself.

 Parents and support staff must realize that for a child who desperately needs to experience structure, displaying violent behavior becomes quite functional. It brings him immediate attention, control and structure!

When assessing these children, we look for patterns in each child's disruptive behavior and try to identify causes. Factors to consider include behaviors reflecting:

- The person's cognitive dysfunction that will respond to alteration in approach and teaching strategies.

- Non-remediable brain dysfunction that must be accommodated.

- Reactions to social and environmental factors that will respond to extra supports or extra training for those who are supporting the child.

- Functional behavior that will respond to increased structure and development of alternative coping skills.

- Emotional and personality dysfunction, from which the child and others may need to be protected

- Mental illness or severe emotional distress that may respond to psychiatric medication, cognitive-behavioral therapy, or other psycho-therapeutic interventions.

Seek professional help. Creating and organizing the positive activities and procedures for these children always requires dedicated effort both at home and school. The parent or support person usually needs skilled assistance.

In addition, to prevent burnout, the support person or parent almost always requires predictable, frequent respite.

When seeking professional help, it is important to remember that children who depend on others to organize and structure their activities are usually quite dependent on their well-established, familiar cues. A new support person will often need several training sessions with the former support person in order to become familiar with the child and his established procedures and activities. Therefore, respite is often best delivered in the child's own home environment with minimal disruption to his familiar activities.

In This Chapter

4 ■ Dependent and Functionally Dependent Behavior
Understanding and Overcoming Some Special Learning Problems

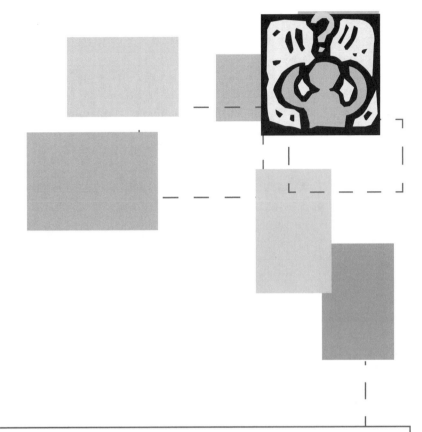

Dependent and Functionally Dependent Behavior

Understanding and Overcoming Some Special Learning Problems

Some people with multiple physical and developmental disabilities are truly dependent. They require total care and must have all aspects of tasks done for them by a support person, regardless of the amount of task structuring, extra incentive, or extra prompting given. This unit does not address the behavior of such physically dependent individuals.

Definition: For the purposes of this chapter, dependent and functionally dependent behavior refers to activities the person cannot perform unless given special assistance, such as increased task structuring, more explicit expectations, extra motivation and extra prompting.

Many individuals with developmental disabilities, who are competent and independent in some areas, show dependent or functionally dependent behavior in other areas. This can be particularly confusing when the person talks about plans that she is unable to carry out herself. The people described here are ready and willing but unable to carry out certain tasks unless a support person uses special approaches to address their areas of dependence.

Dependent behavior may become challenging when a person becomes frustrated and distressed by her inability to perform at the level of her own or a support person's expectations. As a result, she may develop low self-esteem, become emotionally fragile and engage in self-blame.

Those who are functionally dependent require a protected, limited and rigorously guided environment in order to function in a relatively independent manner. They may be described as "dependently independent." This functionally dependent characteristic exists to varying degrees. Some people are functionally dependent in only a few areas while others are in many areas.

Without rigorous support, a person who consistently demonstrates functional dependence may also display severely challenging behaviors. These behaviors can lead to the breakdown of community, educational and vocational placements, hospitalization and/or problems with the law. "Putting her back together" and rebuilding a support system is often extremely difficult.

Providing proactive support is essential. While the proper support requires intense expenditure of time and resources, it is a much better approach in the long run. It greatly reduces the chances of having to control a flood after the dam has already broken.

Generative Factors

One or more of at least four factors may generate dependent behavior. (See box below.) The support person's goal in each case is to give as little assistance as possible while always providing just as much assistance as necessary.

Generative Factors in Dependent Behavior

- Accidental learning (Changes in social interactions can make this irrelevant and overcome these environmental factors.)

- Hard-to-detect learning disability (Using strategies that work with the person's strengths can overcome many of her weaknesses and psychological factors.)

- Prompt dependence (Developmental brain dysfunctions require environmental adaptations to compensate for these biological factors.)

    - Inability to self-initiate action
    - Inability to self-sustain momentum.

Accidental Learning

The person has the potential to learn to perform a task adequately. She can perform the task, but has inadvertently learned to be dependent, non-initiating or withdrawn as a means of gaining assistance or having the task done for her. Her dependence or passivity is behavior that support staff have mistakenly reinforced, and/or rewarded.

- A man waits for the support person to wash his face for him during self-care procedures. He had done the task for several years, but was always slow at doing it for himself. He has been unintentionally taught to be passive and dependent.

- When finished in the bathroom, a woman remains seated on the toilet for long periods of time. Though staff lead her away every so often, they allow her to return immediately and remain there for extended periods. Support staff describe her as withdrawn, antisocial and wanting lots of time to herself. They even give her medications and drinks while she sits on the toilet. She has been unintentionally taught to be passive and socially isolated.

Individual Characteristics

■ The person is typically slow at processing directions and physical movements.

■ The person "used to do a whole lot more than she does now," according to long-term support staff.

■ The person will typically hand things to support staff as a way of requesting their assistance with tasks.

Check your interpretation and emotional reaction to this behavior! Support staff may interpret the person's behavior as deliberately lazy or manipulative. Actually, she has learned that passivity results in extra assistance.

■ Support staff may regard the person as good at disappearing when faced with a task or "fading into the woodwork."

■ She seems to be trying to get others to do tasks for her.

Interventions
Accidentally Learned Dependent Behavior

Prevention

■ Decide on consistent expectations and prompts for performance. Communicate these clearly to the person and all those who work with her.

■ Always leave plenty of time for the person to perform parts of tasks that she is capable of doing for herself or performing with assistance. Do not do her tasks when she has consistently shown that, given enough time, she can do them for herself.

■ Give the person a chance to err. Smothering her with prompts too quickly damages her performance, and inadvertently teaches her to wait for you to either tell her what to do, or do the task for her.

Guidance

■ Be kind but insistent about expecting the person to assist with or accomplish the task at the level of her ability.

- If she can do parts of a task some of the time, avoid doing the task for her entirely. At most, work with her, continually expecting her to do what she is able.
- Give her a chance to respond spontaneously before intruding with your assistance, but do not hesitate to intrude with graduated prompts when necessary.

TRAINING

■ Expect and obtain participation even if the person only participates through hand-over-hand interaction.

■ Reinforce any degree of spontaneous or prompted cooperation and participation, no matter how much assistance was required to initiate it. Praise any degree of effort, not just proficiency at the task.

■ Let the person see a reward. Otherwise, let her know she will receive a reward for her participation and cooperation.

Invisible Learning Disabilities

Definition: An invisible learning disability is an impairment in problem solving capabilities (cognitive processing) that is not easily detected.

The person with invisible disabilities has the potential to perform tasks adequately with the aid of special teaching procedures. This problem-solving impairment can be overcome through recognizing it, and employing special teaching accommodations and structured environmental approaches through it may still present a significant obstacle to learning.

The chart on the opposite page summarizes many of the common areas of functional dependence that reflect invisible learning disabilities that require both accommodation and structured approaches.

Understanding Functional Dependence

Some persons with developmental disabilities have a great deal of skill under certain circumstances, but are extremely functionally disabled by their inability to self-orient or organize their own behavior. This involves several psychological factors. The person may:

- Lack a sense of her own ability to affect others (does not understand that she can ask for help)
- Lack a sense of how cause and effect are related (When something goes wrong, she did not mean to be "bad." It just seemed like a good idea at the time.)
- Lack the ability to differentiate between the important and the irrelevant aspects of a problem situation (She has no idea where to start; everything goes over her head.)

Often, these factors result in a lack of any sense of continuity between her experiences. Without a sense of continuity or where one fits in the big picture, it is difficult to learn from experience or to generalize learning which takes place in one circumstance to other, similar situations. A person who is able to perceive situations only from her own, immediate-instantaneous point of view may repeat inadequate and maladaptive actions endlessly.

An inability to organize one's own behavior could be due to a number of cognitive-emotional factors such as extreme distractibility, severe attention deficit, severe deficit in

Themes of Functional Dependence	
Happy Themes	Sad Themes
"I can do things if I see someone else doing it first."	"I cannot do something until it becomes my own idea."
"I can do things if it's what I expected."	"Things have to be just the way I thought it was going to be or it blows my mind."
"If you focus me, I know what to do. When I know your expectations, I can follow them. I can do things when I am ready and sure."	"If you don't prepare me, I can't meet expectations. If I am uncertain, I can't figure out how to begin to begin."
"I can do things if it's part of my familiar routine."	"I can't do things if I don't know how they will turn out."
"When I am involved in what I do well, there are no problems."	"I don't know what to do whenever I don't know what to do. I act out when I'm not occupied."
"If you give me rules, I can use self-control and act like I have a conscience."	"Without your rules, I act like I have no conscience."
"If you set my beginning and end points, I can do the middle part all by myself."	"I can't be 'smart' without your telling me exactly what to do next."
"When someone is with me, I feel safe and secure."	"When I am alone, I am symptomatic."

immediate memory span, extreme anxiety and psychological dissociation. These functional features may be seen in individuals with a wide variety of diagnoses, such as autism, fetal alcohol syndrome/fetal alcohol effect, cerebral palsy, arrested hydrocephaly, severe depression, extreme mental health crisis, dementia, and others.

Features of functional dependence may be seen in any normal child who is developmentally very young. Older children and adults who are still functioning at a very young developmental level may remain dependent on others to keep them organized and focused, similar to the level of support that would be provided to a young child.

The difficulty arises with people who are obviously functioning at a much higher developmental level in some areas. They appear to be highly capable in certain areas, yet consistently encounter situations where they are obviously either incapable or dependent on others to be able to cope. They are able but cannot self-initiate or sequence their own actions. They seem to be "smarter than they can act." These individuals are functionally dependent on support staff.

The person may disclose the disabilities by making repeated errors at a task regardless of the support person's persistent effort to teach her. Typically, the support person will correct her mistakes constantly and inadvertently teach her that she is quite helpless in the task situation.

- The person can only clear one item at a time from a table and cannot coordinate his actions in response to a request to "clear the table." He can perform repetitive or spontaneous, well-learned actions such as floor hockey or ping pong but cannot carry out a sequence on demand.

- The person can pick out five visual items from memory but is unable to identify the order in which the items were shown to her. Or, she can do proficient manual work while working beside a coach but cannot follow a sequence of actions on her own.

- One man's assessed intelligence fell within the "normal" range. His psychologist dictated the following statement to him: "Sometimes people use too many words with me. I need to say, 'Talk shorter,' so I can understand." He could write the statement and read it aloud, but he could not answer the question, "What do you need to say to people?" His inability to describe his need persisted even with the statement directly in front of him.

- The person can read, write and connect a sequence of numbered circles randomly arranged on a page within "normal" time limits. She cannot, however, create a sequence of alternative numbers and letters (1-a-2-b-3-c-4-d, and so on.)

- When helping with the washing machine or dishwasher, the person always pours all of the soap from the box into the machine. He also uses the whole bottle of shampoo when washing his hair. He has the right idea but cannot stop himself when he reaches the right amount. However, if a support person tells him when to quit pouring, he will stop.

- A girl eats a whole tube of toothpaste every time she is alone in the bathroom, but not if someone is with her. She can also use it appropriately if someone reminds her just before she goes to brush her teeth.

- A woman becomes very frustrated by her inability to separate papers during a recycling task, and jumps out of her chair each time she does it incorrectly. If support staff guide her movements verbally, she can do the task well.

Some Diagnostic Categories of Individuals Showing Functional Dependence	
Developmental Brain Dysfunctions	**Genetic Syndromes**
• Anoxia at birth • Cerebral palsy • Seizures • Tuberous sclerosis • Microsephaly • Arrested hydrocephaly • Fetal alcohol spectrum disorder (FAS, FAE, ARND and ARBD)	• Fragile X Syndrome • Prader-Willi Syndrome • William's Syndrome
Pervasive Developmental Disorders (Autistic spectrum disorders)	**Neuropsychological Dysfunctions**
• Autism • Asperger's Syndrome • Pervasive Developmental Disability (NOS) • Rett's Disorder • Childhood Disintegrative Disorder	• Right Hemisphere Learning Disability • Sequential Processing Disorder
Attention and Memory Deficits	**Psychiatric Disorders**
• Severe Attention Deficit • Severe Short Term Memory Deficits • Working Memory Deficits • Dementia	• Extreme Anxiety Disorders • Psychotic Disorders • Attachment Disorders • Dissociative Disorders • Dementing Disorders

The chart above lists some diagnostic categories of individuals who may display functional dependence. Most individuals with these diagnoses *are not* functionally dependent. These categories simply demonstrate the many causal factors and emphasize their biological base.

Without a full assessment of the person's cognitive processing, including developmental level, language, learning functions, executive function, attention, memory functions and adaptive behavior (among others), it is not possible to know exactly what support she requires. However, it is not necessary to wait for a full assessment to be able to provide essential levels of support. (See General Tips for Teaching a Dependent Individual, page 89.) Many factors can lead to functional dependence; some common ones are listed below.

Causes of Functional Dependence

- Impaired receptive language
- Slower rate of processing language
- Impaired time concept
- Inability to hold more than one thought in mind at a time
- Inability to pick up cues from social context
- Inability to recognize the effect of her own behavior on others
- Inability to comprehend consequences of her own behavior on herself.

Functional dependence may be associated with:

- Extreme distractibility
- Inability to predict the behavior of others
- Inability to plan her own actions
- Inability to follow sequences
- Inability to do more than one thing at a time
- Inability to attend to the effect of her own behavior on herself or others
- Living the emotional moment.

Functional dependence can be the result of:

- Perseverative behavior
- Difficulty with transitions, initiation and sustaining her own momentum
- Inability to inhibit her behavior outside the presence of external reward/ prompt or structure
- The tendency to fill down time with disruptive behavior.

INDIVIDUAL CHARACTERISTICS

- The person may have very good long-term memory for familiar experiences though her immediate attention span may be extremely limited in specific areas.

- The person may not understand the effect of her behavior on others, or cause and effect. She may not be capable of learning from her mistakes or from correction.

- The person may have extreme deficiency in receptive language with no apparent deficit in spontaneous expressive language. Her ease with expressive language gives support staff a false impression of her ability to understand instruction. She needs extra time to figure out the meaning of what is being said to her. For example, she may be able to repeat a fifteen-word sentence exactly, but be unable to follow verbal directions such as "Pick up red or blue," "If there's a black, pick up red," or "After touching yellow, touch white."

- Her assessed cognitive skills may be significantly greater than her independent, functional skills. Therefore, a wide gap may exist between things she can do well and things she cannot do at all.

- The person may have extremely variable abilities, doing tasks at certain times but not others. She may be unable to perform unless the support person is present, prompting her to say or do the necessary action.

■ The person often experiences confusion and failure, while appearing unwilling to learn or passively resistant to efforts to teach her. She is frequently highly motivated but does not have the ability to tell support staff that a task is too difficult to perform.

■ The person often learns, after making repeated errors, that she cannot perform expected tasks independently and may become passive and unmotivated. One indicator of a growing sense of helplessness is her general work performance. Support staff may notice that, while she used to perform quite proficiently at some tasks, she no longer works as hard or she completes less than before.

Failure to recognize and accommodate invisible learning disabilities can lead to a psychological reaction referred to as "learned helplessness."

Learned Helplessness

Sometimes, a person learns through repeated negative experience that her efforts will not have any effect. This predictably impacts her learning process. Learned helplessness appears in the form of decreased attention span, and an inability to focus and learn from experience. Typically, it stems from one or more of the following experiences.

1. Anticipation of failure reduces the individual's desire to learn new things, so she does not try.

2. Expectation of failure increases her negative thoughts, so she no longer wants to try. To protect herself from failure, she may actively resist learning new things.

3. When the person does make an effort and it gets noticed, she discounts positive feedback. She refuses to build up hope that what she accomplishes has some impact.

4. Repeated failure decreases her potential to learn from experience. She actually becomes unable to perceive which efforts are successful and should be tried again the next time.

Interventions
Invisible Learning Disabilities

PREVENTION
■ Maintain high expectations for performance.

■ Discover and eliminate as many aversive aspects of a situation as possible, such as time pressure, unknown support staff, unfamiliar prompts, inconsistent procedure and/or unachievable steps. These aversive elements demotivate the person and reinforce passive avoidance and learned helplessness.

■ Provide the right task structure. Use task analysis to make a job less confusing, ensure success, and motivate the person to attempt tasks for which she has customarily received criticism or correction.

- Do movement-by-movement analysis of the task, observing closely where errors occur.
- Break the task down into smaller and smaller movements at points where errors occur.
- Make steps small enough for the person to experience success.

GUIDANCE

Give clear, consistent prompts. Observe where the person is making persistent errors (such as always using an entire tube of toothpaste). Give direct prompts at the precise point that will prevent the incorrect action (such as a reminder about the "rule" to use a small amount of paste immediately after she picks up the tube). Reinforce her good attention to the rule, "Good for you. You remembered how much to use."

Use simple language. Demanding verbal processing may create anxiety and expectation of failure. Some individuals stop processing language completely when they become emotionally distressed. Others will lose all previous coping skills and any ability to organize their actions. This can cause them to become anxious or depressed. A person may act as though she is only doing "sensory processing" in the moment. (See Chapter 8: Emotionally Fragile and Reactive Behavior.)

Make it visual. The support person can offer choices by presenting visible objects representing them—that is, pictures of options. Say, "What do you want to do?" Or, guide the person by showing a picture of the desired activity and saying, "I like to do…. Want to come with me?"

Avoid open-ended and two-part questions like "What do you want to do?" or "After we do X, do you want to do Z?" Also avoid using "if," "or," "maybe," "when," and "then." (See "Acknowledge responses to the presentation of choices" on page 94.)

Think of the reasons why being "firm" sometimes works! It tends to be visual and concrete direction, ensuring the person's visual or auditory attention. A firm request, usually delivered with a degree of emotional intensity, also tends to provide the best direct guidance when immediate action is necessary. Talk about only one thing at a time, using few words, and the directive will usually be clear, certain, definite and explicit! This allows a person with a disability to interpret expectations clearly.

- "Do this now!"
- "Help me with this right now!"
- "Come over here and sit down."

Sometimes, a support person does not provide explicit guidance until he is frustrated or angry about the person's inability to perform independently. But it is never necessary to be angry to give clear, certain and definite directions.

TRAINING

Many individuals with intellectual disabilities are able to perform adequately when given recognition tasks. But, often they suffer from an invisible learning disability that makes it difficult or impossible to perform when given recall tasks.

Key to Prevention

Use intervention with the environment and people providing support. Remember the six A's: Acknowledge, Anticipate and Avoid problem behavior. Have an Accepting Attitude; Accommodate the person's needs and deficiencies.

Recognition tasks use a form of "What's this?" or "Do what I am doing" as the support person works alongside her. This allows the person with disabilities to draw on long-term memory and familiarity, and select from an array of correct answers or an immediately present model. She is able to evaluate whether or not she knows what form of response is required. She can answer spontaneously, knowing she is correct and doing what is expected.

Recall tasks are much more intellectually (cognitively) demanding. The person must use her immediate, short-term memory. She has to recall when you first modeled a task and when you make a request like "Do what I just did!" or "Tell me what you just heard or just saw!" The model for performance is no longer present in her immediate awareness. This requires her to make a response on demand and leaves her unable to evaluate whether or not the response is correct. She cannot answer spontaneously and know that she is correct.

To work best with a person who has an attention-span disability, turn everything into a recognition task. This always gives a form of the answer before asking her the question, making it much less likely that she will misunderstand what is expected. The process builds her confidence in her own actions.

Using recognition tasks makes life into a multiple-choice test. So when a person is dependent, give her the answer key before asking the question.

- Use backward chaining, the technique of teaching the last step first, then the next-to-the-last step, etc.

- Help the person become proficient at each step before progressing to the next, more difficult step.

- Build in prompt redundancy by inserting as many physical prompts into the task materials as possible. For example, use color-coded matching, masking tape or another physical guide to limit excessive range of movement, and printed lists with numbered steps.

- Fade out prompts only after the person achieves proficient behavior.

- Record the person's progress. If small progress does not occur within a few weeks (maximum), work on an even smaller piece of expected behavior by altering the task or procedure. Always set her up to practice doing what she knows how to do. This builds motivation and trust.

Prompt Dependence

These forms of dependent behavior are an aspect of developmental brain dysfunction.

They are not learned behaviors, nor are they behaviors that "get better" through the use of special teaching approaches. These are functional disabilities that must be acknowledged and accommodated.

Definition: This behavior characterizes individuals who, when unsupported, may be withdrawn, passive, non-initiating or inconsistently initiating, and frequently appear helpless and unmotivated. However, when support staff provide appropriate prompts (cues), they are responsively interactive, self-motivated and able to sustain effort consistently with familiar activities. Their adequate performance is prompt dependent.

The inability to initiate, sustain, shift or stop an ongoing action is a characteristic of brain dysfunction that is often interpreted as a purposefully disruptive behavior. When movement sequences become "stuck" in any of these ways, they are referred to as "perseverative" actions. (The rest of this chapter discusses difficulties in initiating and sustaining momentum. The next chapter, "Persistent, Repetitive Behavior: Perseverative Responding" discusses difficulties in shifting and stopping behavior.)

Prompt Dependence: Inability to Self-Initiate Action

Definition: The person lacks the energy or arousal level needed to attend to or initiate a task. She requires external motivation to be able to initiate actions. She seems to have no "on" switch. The support person must prime the pump, though once turned on, the person with disabilities will continue the activity to completion.

- One woman will not take the next step in any motor sequence. She can tell the support person what the next step is, but cannot begin until told to do it now!

- Another woman stays in bed all day if she is not called. As soon as a support person calls her, she gets out of bed and dresses herself for breakfast.

- A boy will not initiate a request for food unless he sees a sibling with food. Then he says, "Where is mine?" For him, in sight is in mind.

- A girl sits and waits for the support person to do all her personal hygiene activities for her. She does not respond to hand-over-hand assistance. However, if her special "work song" is sung, she follows along to the words and actively participates in the hand-over-hand guidance.

- When given instructions for self-care, activation and feeding, one man will not respond to verbal, physical or gestural prompts alone. He does respond when all three are combined.

- One woman requires the prompt, "Find your spoon," before she can begin eating.

- One highly talented man frequently complains that he has nothing to do. If the support person suggests something like rug hooking, he will start and keep it up forever. He is happy to do anything suggested to him, but is often unable to initiate an activity without a suggestion.

- One woman lived independently at her parents' home for many years. When her parents died, she moved into a group home and lost all her old skills. Support staff had to tell her to put on every item of clothing from underwear to outerwear. However, when she roomed with another, more competent person, she dressed herself without being told by anyone. One day, a support person said in frustration, "Get dressed by yourself, and put all your clothes on at once." She did just that!

    The woman was clearly dependent on familiar prompts to accomplish tasks. Given a partial prompt, she did a task partially. Given a complete prompt, she could finish any familiar task completely.

INDIVIDUAL CHARACTERISTICS

- The person knows how, but not when to do things. She needs to be told or shown when to start. She cannot prompt (cue) herself.

- The person may only perform a desired behavior occasionally, or only for certain support persons. Or, she may only be able to perform when support staff provide optimal circumstances.

- The person may occasionally show a great deal of animation if a support person "really gets through to her." This type of person can learn, but only when she receives greatly enhanced, positive feedback in response to her efforts.

- The person may be very slow to orient to what is happening around her and becomes easily distracted from the task at hand. Support staff may find it difficult to lead her to focus her attention.

Check out your own interpretation and emotional reaction to this behavior! The person may be seen as unmotivated, over-dependent, withdrawn or lazy. This is a misperception! She simply lacks the ability to motivate herself internally, and her behavior is neither purposeful nor deliberate.

The initiative deficit is not behavioral. The person has a dysfunction that prevents her from being able to initiate her own behavior easily. Her inconsistency of response indicates a lack of adequate feedback or sufficient external motivation.

If the support person does things for her instead of giving adequate prompts to initiate action, it may reinforce her dependent behavior. Lack of self-initiation due to brain dysfunction can also become a learned dependent behavior.

- The person is often happy and willing to do a task, but cannot get started without an external prompt. It is as though she is missing an "on" switch. While she cannot initiate a behavior without being told, if prompted to begin an activity, she may do just fine and accomplish a great deal.

■ In addition to her inability to self-initiate, she may also lack the ability to sustain momentum during tasks. (See Inability to Self-Sustain Momentum on page 83.)

Some individuals are aware of their inability to initiate the actions that allow them to accomplish their goals. When "stuck in place," the person may sit passively and engage in no behavior until given an external direction.

Others will fill this "stuck" moment with an extreme focus on internal feedback, either sensory, kinesthetic, emotional or cognitive. For instance, they may display ritualistic behaviors such as regurgitation and rocking, or experience anxiety, panic attacks, depression, obsessive thoughts or even psychotic thoughts (such as hallucinations and paranoia). A person in any of these states may appear to be demanding attention for herself when she really needs direction for her unfocused or trapped energy.

Interventions
Inability to Self-Initiate Action

PREVENTION

■ Give the person something to work for.

■ Give the person time to orient to your prompts.

■ Remove distractions.

■ Organize the person's time for her. Structure her day on a moment-by-moment basis. Making a "Things to Do" list might help.

GUIDANCE

■ Provide the person with immediate feedback. Interrupt and redirect her inadequate response to being stuck.

■ Display extra enthusiasm and encouragement.

■ Increase the intensity of your prompts and directions.

■ Draw the person into the task or activity. Help her get started.

■ If the person reacts with an emotional crisis, lower your immediate expectations. Take a mental health approach, and focus on quiet, well-known, routine activities. Bring her into a familiar, predictable experience in which she knows what to do next.

TRAINING

■ Teach a ritualistic response for "what to do when you don't know what to do."

■ Create a "What to Do" book. Try to teach the person to recognize the feeling of "being stuck" and ask for help. Coach her to deal with her feelings of confusion. Teach this process to someone else, and let her watch. Then say, "Your turn." It can help to develop a sensory calming routine.

 It may help to develop some simple, routine interactions with the person and then purposely break them. This allows her to have an opportunity to practice "what to do when you don't know what to do."

Prompt Dependence: Inability to Self-Sustain Momentum

Definition: The person lacks the ability to sustain a sequence of actions independently. She does only one step at a time, requires refocusing on the task and needs frequent external prompting, or she will stop in the middle of an activity.

- One woman stands in front of a door for long time with a confused look on her face. When asked, "What are you trying to do?" she answers, "Get in." When asked, "What do you need to get in?" she answers, "A key." When asked, "Where do you get a key?" she answers, "From a staff person." Then the support person says, "Do it!" The person responds by asking for the key and unlocking the door.

- One man repeatedly lets down his pants to tuck in his shirt. The support person sends him into the bathroom to fix his shirt, but he stays there all day, repeating his "stuck" behavior over and over. When the support person tells him to go to the bathroom, fix his shirt and come right out when he is done, the man does exactly as he is told.

INDIVIDUAL CHARACTERISTICS

■ The person has a brain dysfunction that prevents her from sustaining a sequence of actions independently. Her lack of momentum is primarily a neurological rather than behavioral problem. However, if support person responses reinforce dependent behavior, the behavior becomes a learned dependency as well.

■ The person is often quite motivated.

■ The person depends on the exact prompts given to her. She requires frequently restated, external expectations. Without the prompts, her behavior lacks momentum.

■ The person may be quite competent and independent in all areas of familiar, previously well-learned activity, but never knows what to do next. She acts when prompted, but does not know what to do once she has finished doing exactly what was requested.

■ She is often quite confused, anxious or uncertain about what to do until she is given an explicit, direct prompt to carry on with a task.

■ She may ask frequent questions. Support staff can often misinterpret the questions as attention seeking when they are actually prompt seeking. Typically, the person can answer any questions she is asking, so the problem is not a lack of knowledge. Rather, it lies in her inability to sustain a sequence of unaided actions.

■ The person may have had few problems with memory or problem-solving ability. In fact, she may have very good memory for past events, but very poor memory for immediate instructions. She may also have co-existing language processing problems.

■ Often, the person finds it very difficult to learn by task analysis or step-by-step instruction. She may, however, learn quite quickly when she can observe others being taught the tasks.

- Sometimes, the person also lacks the ability to self-initiate action. (See Inability to Self-Sustain Momentum, page 83.)

 Check your interpretation and emotional reaction to this behavior! The person may be described as "inattentive" or "inconsistent." Or, she may appear to be an "expert actor," a master at standing and staring blankly. Support staff may believe she is "just playing a game with me."

- The person can carry out an instruction some of the time, but seems completely incapable of doing so at other times. Support staff may become very confused by this. The inconsistency often results from the manner in which the task or instruction is presented. The person may only work independently if working alongside, or as a helper to, another person. If sent to do a task alone, she may become "frozen" or anxious, and engage in distress behaviors, like nervous pacing or repetitive questioning.

- The person may become frustrated with support staff giving her inadequate direction or insufficient support to allow her to accomplish a task. This type of lack of momentum can sometimes be the underlying cause of aggressive behavior.

Interventions
Inability to Self-Sustain Momentum

PREVENTION

- Provide supervision so that prompts to "move on" can be given as soon as the person becomes stuck in a rut. The support person may only need a simple directive like "Keep going," "Do some more" or "Carry on."

- Provide clear, concrete expectations.

- Give additional verbal reminders frequently, and prompt appropriate behavior prior to each social situation.

- Give plenty of warning. Use visual prompts to direct the person to cease one activity and begin another.

GUIDANCE

- Aim the person at the target to help her organize her activities. For example: "Get dressed for breakfast" instead of just "Get dressed."

- If the person is capable, but tries to get you to make all the choices for her ("Should I use this bowl or that one?"), suggest that she choose for herself. Or, after a reasonable amount of time, say, "Make up your mind; we are leaving the room." In other words, direct the person to direct herself to avoid reinforcing dependent behavior.

- Give additional prompts and encouragement.

- Reassure and comfort the person when she is anxious about what she is supposed to do next.

- Provide any necessary bridges for the "gap" the person seems to be experiencing.
    - Use the "can't goof" method: ask the person to help you. Do the task with her,

or do the task for her, asking her to help with the last step.

- Suggest that the person do single-step, continuous actions such as rolling yarn, stacking wood and shucking peas. It is easier to sustain momentum at tasks when the next thing to do is more of the same activity.

> ### Key to Guidance
>
>
> Use positive intervention with the person. Use human relations techniques to engage her in other behavior without confronting her about problem behavior. Use suggestion, positive motivation and humor along with the three D's: Displace, Divert and re-Direct the person's behavior.

■ Do not reprimand or criticize! When giving correction, first try, "Can you fix it?" Then try, "Look, do it like this!" If the person is not following verbal cues, switch to visual and context cues. Rely on repetition, recognition and rehearsal of a role in the "play of life." Give the script to this person who is struggling to sustain momentum.

■ Bring behavior sequences under the control of specific external prompts. A number of devices can be used:

- Lists, timers and pictures
- Picture albums of "things to do when I don't know what to do"
- Picture sequences of steps to follow
- Video recordings of things to do next Tell the person, "Finish your task and turn on the recording with your next activity prompt." The last comment on the recording could be: "Turn off this recording now and go do your task."

■ Use a sliding scale of prompts to prevent individuals from becoming dependent on support staff for more prompts than they actually require. Be sure to give as little assistance as possible and just as much as necessary.

 Allow for variability. The amount of prompting necessary for a person to accomplish a task may vary from day to day.

■ Many individuals who are prompt dependent have fragile, reactive outbursts if not given sufficient guidance to be able to recognize that they are succeeding. They cannot tolerate the anxiety or panic of failing to meet expectations. Treat the person as if her life is a role in a well-scripted play, and provide her with the script. She may be at her best as a buddy or in the role of a shadow helper.

TRAINING

■ Some individuals are unable to learn through step-by-step training of sequences because they cannot make the connection between individual steps and the final outcome of the task. Many of these individuals can learn the tasks, but not by direct teaching. Try the following:

> ### Key to Training
>
> Use positive intervention with the person. Employ motivation and skill development programs, and teach alternative coping skills over time.

- Provide a model of someone else being taught the task.
- Work from a picture of what the completed task must look like.
- Model the whole task and use backward chaining.
- Give multiple repetitions of the task as a whole unit.
- Prompt each step of the task.

■ Form realistic expectations for persons with developmental brain dysfunction. Lack of momentum is not a behavioral or a learning problem; it is a brain condition.

■ Expect that the person will always need extra directives or your physical presence to prompt her to keep up her momentum.

■ Perhaps with many months in the same stable setting, doing things in the same sequence, she will eventually form new behavioral habits on the basis of repeated rehearsal. However, do not expect learned sequences of behavior to generalize to any new setting. Do not expect the person to be able to perform well-learned tasks when she is asked to do so outside of her well-learned routine.

CRISIS MANAGEMENT

 The following crisis management techniques will work for all forms of dependent behavior.

The person may have a disability that is not readily apparent (invisible) that prevents her from being able to accept assistance. She may be unable to initiate necessary action or sustain effort at necessary action. Furthermore, she may be momentarily overwhelmed because of her disability.

■ **The person may suddenly begin operating at her lowest functioning level.** If so, quickly accommodate her condition.
- Lower your expectations for the quantity and variety of interaction. Lower expectations for risk-taking behavior, participation in an unfamiliar activity and any response to a request.
- Increase expectations for the individual's spontaneous cooperation in whatever she can do routinely.
- List everything the individual ever does well, even some of the time. Offer her frequent opportunities to make these lists so they become her "curriculum in the moment."
- Avoid the use of "time out" with a person who is only able to function with structure and prompts. Increase the predictability of her day by offering one activity at a time. Use immediate, concrete feedback, and avoid abstract or confusing language and references to time.

■ **Individuals who are dependent on others to be able to function at their potential (functionally dependent) may have great problems coping with certain types of changes.** Unexpected new experiences may lead to a behavioral outburst. They may be overwhelmed by an unanticipated requirement to shift their momentum into a different direction.

For the person who is dependent on being prepared:
- Introduce changes gradually. Do not "spring" things on the individual.
- Give the person a positive mindset. ("You are going to love this.")
- Introduce something new in a non-demanding situation. Set it up so that the individual's first experience is a casual drop-by where all she needs to do is keep the support person company without interacting.
- Aim to create familiarity over a long period of time. Allow the new environment to become predictable.
- Focus the individual by asking her to "help" you do a familiar activity in the unfamiliar setting. Initial interactions must be very simple to guarantee success.

■ **The absence of an expected experience may lead to a behavioral outburst.** The individual might be unable to process verbal explanations, and be reliant on a familiar routine to be able to understand and predict what is going on. Finding out that an expected activity is not happening may "blow her mind."

For the person who is dependent on predictability:
- Prepare her for change by using visual description, such as photographs on a calendar.
- If there is to be a change in routine, use the picture calendar to show the individual when an expected experience will happen. Help her shift the photograph from the time or day she was expecting to the new time or day.

Key to Crisis Management

Use direct intervention with the problem behavior. Remain calm and always use guidance techniques first. Accommodate the person's special needs and disabilities. Respond to chaotic behavior with a prearranged plan for surviving the crisis while bringing challenging behavior to a stop! Interact positively with the person as soon as she exercises a degree of self-control. Have a plan for how to re-enter normal life.

- As much as possible, protect the individual from breaks in her routine.

■ **The individual may be actively avoiding participation.**
- Offer her an activity that she knows she can do well, providing her a way to engage herself. If this is wiping a counter, be happy with counter wiping. If it is copying words, be happy with copying words.

■ **The individual may not be trying to participate.** She may feel depressed, rejected, grief-stricken and/or completely overloaded. Any time it becomes apparent that the person is unable to do even those activities she can do well, investigate these possibilities: Did she just move from one residence to another? Did someone close to her become very ill or die? Has a support person to whom she was attached left the location?
- Give the individual a "temporary leave of absence." Back off and avoid confrontations that might provoke a meltdown. Instead, enjoy the sun and the flowers.

■ **Assist the individual in crisis by approaching her in a gentle, calm, almost reverential manner.** Your goal is to help her through the moment. Do not approach her as a behavioral adversary. Imagine how you would approach a respected acquaintance displaying the same crisis behavior as a result of a stroke.
- Momentarily drop all cognitive demands.

- Control your own emotional space, and self-meditate.
- Give the individual sensory-emotional feedback.
- Hum a happy tune. Lower your tone of voice. Slow the pace of your speech.
- Use more visual and fewer verbal cues.
- When speaking, say things that are familiar to the individual.
- Shift gears to shift the individual's momentary focus.
- Make the environment safe for the individual. Communicate acceptance. Offer calm, quiet, one-on-one interaction. Rely on a monotonous, familiar activity to decompress the situation, such as sweeping, eating, wiping a counter, sitting and watching a sport on TV, or looking at a picture album of a happy occasion.

■ **In crisis, the person may rely on her most regressed coping responses.** She may become dependent on the acceptance of others and the evident presence of external control. For example, she may run to a hospital emergency room or doctor's office. She may dial 9-1-1, or repeatedly call every person in her social network.
- Provide the individual with clear, explicit guidance about what to do in these situations. Give her a list of people, and identify whom she should call for each issue. Be sure to include medical, financial, social and work issues.
- Post the list with every person who provides critical support. Each support person should know how to direct the individual to the correct person. Build in one permanent back-up person who will take the last call before the individual dials 9-1-1. If necessary, this person can accompany the individual to the hospital. The goal is to accommodate the individual's dependent state of anxiety and still be able to give her the guidance and prompting she requires to function.

Generative Factors in Dependent Behavior

- Assume that the individual is able to perform but does not understand what is expected of her. She may be confused, unaware or uncertain about what to do.
- Assume that the individual is capable of performing but experiences memory or attention problems.
- Assume that the individual is able to perform but depends on some form of external motivation such as prompts or rewards, or lacks training in a specific coping skill.
- Assume that the individual is able to perform, but has a subtle, invisible learning disability that must be addressed, or has a brain dysfunction that impairs her ability to learn and cope. She may be overwhelmed by fear or anxiety.

General Tips for Teaching a Dependent Individual

Effective teaching requires that you adapt expectations and approaches to the basic requirements for learning. First, you must remove disabling learning conditions in order to provide the instructional environment that is essential for learning.

Learners have to pay attention. Get the best attention by eliminating distractions. Use task analysis to organize tasks, and train the individual to pay attention to what is important in making proper judgments about the task. Learning is disabled by:

- Any distraction that makes it hard for the learner to pay attention to what you are trying to teach, such as too much irrelevant information or too much emotional pressure.
- Disorganized information or material that is presented too quickly, making it hard to remember what has to be done first, second, and so on.
- Insufficient feedback to allow the learner to differentiate between what is important and what is not.

Learners have to practice in order to develop their memory and skill. Go slowly, focus on only one thing at a time and expect a much longer training time. Allow for many extra repetitions and practices. Expect forgetting between training sessions. Learning is disabled by:

- Insufficient opportunity for the learner to practice being competent at one step before moving on to the next step.

Learners must understand the instructions they are given. Be concrete and use pictures. Make the instructions meaningful and relevant to the learner's experience. Learning is disabled by:

- Giving demonstrations or verbal instructions that are ambiguous or open to interpretation.

Learners must be motivated. Make the training interesting, exciting or worth something special to the learner. Provide her with an ulterior motive to give the task meaning; encourage and reward effort and persistence as well as success. Learning is disabled by:

- Not understanding the purpose of an activity. Give learners a purpose.

Learners need to know if what they are doing is right or wrong. Encourage persons with disabilities to make judgments, but make important discriminations for them if they are not succeeding. Be concrete and specific with your directions and feedback, increasing their knowledge of results. Tell them how they are doing. Learning is disabled by the following:

- Insufficient feedback (Tell the learner if she is doing the right thing or not, so she does not repeat her errors indefinitely.)
- Too much feedback, robbing the learner of the opportunity to test and use her own judgment, and then learn from her mistakes. Without this opportunity, the person may never try to self-correct or do her tasks better.

The Realities of Invisible Learning Disabilities

Acknowledge language deficiencies.

The individual may only get a part of your message, such as the first phrase or the last few words. To be successful, keep messages short, visual and specific to the action required.

For support staff, language is like a horn of plenty. We can draw nourishment from anything the horn provides. But, the language-impaired individual can eat only one piece of fruit at a time, so imagine that the horn of plenty you offer students contains only one piece of fruit at a time.

You might also use the metaphor of a telegram. When you speak to the person, imagine you are sending her a telegram that costs you twenty-five dollars for a five-word message. If you know it is going to cost you twenty-five dollars for five words, you will be very careful about the words you pick. You will send only one clear message at a time. In addition, imagine that you are allowed to send the same telegram as many times as it takes to receive a reply, at no additional cost.

Now, suppose there is a rule stating that if you send any new message before you get the expected reply to your first message, you will be fined one thousand dollars. Keeping this image in mind encourages support staff to do whatever it takes to focus the individual on the effort required to make a successful reply. Give the individual positive feedback; then move on to the next step.

Acknowledge the inability to cope with abstract concepts.

Many individuals with developmental disabilities think in concrete or "black and white" terms. This may apply particularly to persons with autism or those affected by fetal exposure to alcohol. "Black and white" thinkers like rules. And, they like rules that are always applied the same way.

As a result, they do not cope well with "gray areas." They may struggle to understand the meaning of language that is ambiguous or abstract. They dislike "wishy-washy," "maybe," "if-then" and "either-or." They may frequently become quite frustrated when faced with "sometimes this and sometimes that," while "I don't know" can cause exceptionally strong, negative reactions.

Sometimes, a support person can ease these frustrations by trying to explain "black and white" (concrete and clear) versus "gray areas" (an abstract and ambiguous concept). For example, the staff person might explain, "Black and white means there is just one rule." She could include examples like

- A schedule with an exact time is always the same
- All the rules apply to everybody with no exceptions
- There is just one way to do things
- Events and expectations are predictable
- Rules seem fair and clear.

On the other hand, "gray areas" mean that the rule is sometimes one thing and sometimes another, so they seem unpredictable, confusing and unfair. However, illustrating the concept with everyday situations can clarify it. A support person could say, "'Gray areas' happen when…"

- Different rules apply to different people. For example, everyone at a party enjoys pop, cake and ice cream, but the person who is diabetic cannot. Or, everyone at the party can drink, but the person who drives her friends home afterward cannot.
- Different rules apply at different times of the day or week. For instance, people pay parking at meters until 6 p.m. but not at all on Sunday. Or, the hours you work at a job might be different on weekdays versus weekends.
- Different rules apply at different times of the year. For example, students go to school five days a week, except during spring break, Christmas, teacher discretionary days and summer vacation.
- Something is done one way some of the time, and another way at other times. For instance, some days your parents or friends drive you to play baseball, but other days, you have to take the bus because no one is available to take you.

When the people you support become confused about "gray areas" in their lives, it may help to explain in "black and white" terms. Identify situations as, "This is a black and white area," or "This is a gray area." By making this distinction obvious, they may become better able to handle their confused emotions. It may help them to have a better understanding of the reasons why some things are not always the same for all people at all times.

Acknowledge immediate attention span deficiencies.

Give only one small piece of information at a time, and explain the action required with every object. Use redundant cues–gestures, verbalization, a picture or completed model. Approach the learning activity each time as though it was the first time you ever worked with the individual.

Individuals with a short, immediate attention span tend to work completely in the present and focus on what they can see at the moment. They have great difficulty connecting a current action with that action's goal. In sight is in mind, and out of sight is often also out of mind. If the individual loses sight of cues for her immediate action, she may become anxious because she has, in essence, lost her place in space and time.

Trying to memorize a speech or a song provides an analogy. You can get pretty good at a few lines or bars, but then lose your place and forget what comes next. While you are in the early stages of learning, the only thing you can do is go back to the beginning and start all over again. The developmental learning of any young child clearly reflects this process.

> Approach the learning activity each time as though it was the first time you ever worked with the individual.

A dependent individual with a short attention span may freeze and resist when she loses her place. She may wait for a familiar person to give a familiar cue that will put her back in place or help her start all over again. Also, the individual may be very unwilling to trust an unfamiliar face, and will probably not respond to cues that signal her to do an unfamiliar action.

Driving in a deep fog on a dangerous road provides another analogy. When it is impossible to see where you are going, you pull over and stop (and pray you do not get hit by the person following too closely). In this situation, you remember the dotted line analogy. When it is possible to see just a little bit ahead, you drive very slowly, looking out the side window at the dotted line in the middle of the road. Then, imagine what it feels like when the fog momentarily thickens, and you lose sight of even the dotted line.

Be the dotted line for the individual who must have support to know how to focus her attention. Always allow her to know where she is. Show her that she can rely on you as a support person. Attend to her need to be shown where she is and what is going on constantly. Talk in a reassuring manner, explaining what you are doing and what is going to happen next.

Do not forget that new faces may evoke anxiety or panic in an individual because they represent the "deep fog" of unfamiliar cues.

Acknowledge a slower rate of thinking.

Allow many repetitions of small segments of task instructions, avoiding distractions and the practice of errors. Proceed only when the individual performs proficiently.

Imagine that she uses many different languages to communicate. Best practice would be to pick only one to communicate with her because you do not really want to force her to become bilingual or trilingual to learn what you are trying to teach. Teach one small thing at a time until she masters it.

For some individuals, assistance is not helpful. Your offer of help may so distract them that they forget what they were trying to do in the first place. They may need to be left alone to complete a task before they can consider any alternative thought or action.

Acknowledge that perseveration is not a "deliberate" characteristic.

Perseveration is an inability to initiate stop, slow down or shift behavior without assistance. The behavior does not reflect a difficult personality because the individual does not choose to be this way. She needs help to get out of the groove in which she is stuck. Do not correct a perseverated error; just start her on the next step or in a new direction.

Acknowledge the need for structure.

Structure is an important element in everyday life. Without some type of order, daily activities would generally become chaotic. Therefore, support staff should consistently consider ways to provide healthy structure for people with developmental disabilities.

In behavioral support, the concept of structure involves doing activities in the same order, with the same cues and prompts, and with the same expectations. These are the "rules." Structure of this sort anchors or stabilizes a person, by making routines and expectations predictable. It is like a sea anchor in rough weather that stabilizes a boat and prevents it from being blown over.

Structured support is neither restrictive nor intrusive. It establishes the framework needed to assist the individual to overcome neurodevelopmental disabilities and provides dignity by assisting her to achieve her goals. This framework provides a sense of dignity for the individual who requires intensive structure.

For a person with neurodevelopmental disabilities, structure has six main functions.

Structure provides predictability. Following rules gives the individual a viable alternative for understanding. Even if she does not know what to do, she can act in a manner that ensures success when she has a "rule" to follow. Using step-by-step guidance always allows the supported individual to know what is expected of her and/or what will happen next. This helps her overcome her neurodevelopmental difficulties in sequencing and organizing her actions.

Structure provides concrete guidance. Physical props give the individual a workable substitute for having to remember what to do, while also supplying an alternative for her inability to self-cue. Even if she does not remember what to do independently, placing physical cues and visual reminders in her environment allows her to "see" what she needs to accomplish in the moment, so she can act successfully.

Structure provides positive expectations. The support person's expectations supply an alternative for the individual's inability to organize her behavior. Even if she is unable to plan or analyze what she needs to do, a support person's positive expectations ensure that she always chooses the behaviors appropriate to the situation. Since the expectations are clear, explicit and set at her level of ability, she has the comfort of knowing she will succeed by following the routine.

> Using step-by-step guidance always allows the supported individual to know what is expected of her and/or what will happen next.

Structure provides continuity. Routines offer a viable substitute for an individual's lack of "time sense." Even if the individual is unable to understand how long a three-hour period is, habitual routines overcome memory deficits and difficulty with time concepts. Because the routines become automatic habits, she does not have to remember them, and they give her a way to connect prior actions to present and future actions.

Structure provides trust. Some neurodevelopmental disabilities lead to unsuccessful independence. But if the individual attaches herself to a reliable support person who guides her toward "right" choices, she gains a sense of security even when she feels that it would not make any difference whether she tried or not. Positive dependence overcomes an individual's lack of personal continuity and inability to orient herself in time. It also overcomes her sense that the world is a random, chaotic and overwhelming place.

Structure provides flexibility within a range of choices. Breaks in routine often cause an individual to feel anxious or fearful, discomfort that can result in disruptive behaviors. However, if she always knows that after an interruption in routine, the plan is to carry on with the established schedule, she learns a certain amount of flexibility. She does not lose her orientation completely because she can go back to where she left off and catch up.

Acknowledge deficiencies in handling abstract concepts.

Refer to concrete things in the here and now. Avoid referring to "when," "then," "where" or "there." Imagine that trying to have an individual respond to abstract concepts is like asking a person to lift a barbell twice his body weight. He might lift one end a little bit, and find it very difficult and frustrating to be continually requested to lift a weight that is too much for him to handle.

Acknowledge responses to the presentation of choices.

Helping a person with developmental disabilities respond appropriately when given opportunities to make choices requires paying attention to the subtle aspects of verbal interaction and personality. The support person's ability to read and adjust to an individual's characteristics can greatly enhance communication. Certain questions can be particularly helpful when support staff know an individual's reactive patterns.

Using open-ended questions. An individual may refuse any option or choice that was not her own idea because she feels that she does not have a real choice. In this case, it may be best to ask an open-ended question such as "What do you want to do?" This gives her the option to come up with her own suggestion.

For some people, this is the perfect way to offer a choice. It gives them the sense of having control, taking responsibility, and being expected to think and decide for themselves.

 Some individuals who interpret language literally construe an open-ended choice ("What do you want to do?") as permission to do anything that comes to mind at that moment. They may not understand that the question is a request for their preferences. In fact, they may become quite angry that the choice they made is not going to happen immediately.

Using forced-choice questions. Open-ended choices can cause some people great anxiety since they have no idea what is expected. For example, a person may not know what she wants to do or be unable to sort through her confusion about preferences. As a result, she may become disoriented, paralyzed, agitated, angry or aggressive towards the person asking the question because she experiences it as pressure.

If open-ended choices frustrate the individual, it may be better to offer forced-choice questions where the person asking the question defines the context. Forced-choice questions offer a choice between two options–"Do you want to do this or that?" The options are defined by the question, so the individual is always "right." She only needs to recognize the option she prefers.

When individuals are capable of coming up with their own alternatives, this approach still leaves them with the option to self-initiate, saying, for example, "I'd rather do something else."

Using closed-choice questions. Still other people may experience great anxiety when presented with forced choices. They may not know which option to choose, be unwilling to make a "wrong" choice, or want to do both activities and be unable to resolve the conflict. These individuals may respond better to closed, single-option questions.

Closed choice questions offer only one option–"Do you want to…?"–requiring only a "yes" or "no" answer. The person asking the question defines the context and helps the individual focus on the option available. It also still provides ample opportunity for a person who is capable to offer her own alternative–"I'd rather do…."

 Some people will always answer a closed question with "No!" This can lead to a support person's attempt to persuade, bargain with or confront them. An automatic "no" may be an answer that serves more than one purpose. Since a closed-choice question implies that one has the option to say no, that sense of control may be more important to the person than doing the activity offered. However, if you do not mean to accept any of her choices, do not use this question format.

Indirectly offering a verbal choice. If the individual does not know what she wants to do, giving an automatic "no" may simply be a statement about her uncertainty. If this seems to be the issue, it often helps for the support person to "talk to the atmosphere" before asking the question. This involves talking out loud about the options to be offered. State the positives and negatives that could go through one's mind before making the choice. Then turn to the individual and offer the choice. Since you will have already stated and resolved the uncertainties, she will know the "right answers" and only need to recognize which choice is relevant to her at the moment.

Indirectly offering a choice non-verbally. Finally, if the individual has language-processing problems or does not know what you mean, the automatic "no" protects her from getting into something that she may not want. The negative response also gives her time to think. However, she will often come along or participate if you simply start doing the activity yourself. The "choice" is offered non-verbally through your own actions, and the individual chooses by participating in or avoiding the activity.

Acknowledge that performance is variable.

The nature of learning any new task is inconsistent performance. Even when the person is able to do a task perfectly once, it may take a very long time before she can do it that well again. Think of the Olympic skaters or professional players in any sport who have slumps. Variable performance does occur with mastered skills, but it is more characteristic of skills during the learning process.

To deal with a slump in the learning process, remember to drop back to an easier level.

To deal with a slump in the learning process, remember to drop back to an easier level. It never helps to practice errors. Learning improves best by focusing on what you can do. When repeated errors delay learning, drop back to the level of competence where the person knows the required behaviors well. For example:

- Integrate the new learning into the context of proficient, previous learning. (For example, when learning a piece of music, you play the bars you know well, then tag on the next few notes.
- Focus intensely on the one thing that the person needs to learn next, and connect it with her well-known skill.
- Then have her practice it as a whole!

It is not very helpful to spend a lot of time practicing a skill with many errors that need constant correction. It is much better to spend a little time doing perfect practice, then go have fun!

In This Chapter

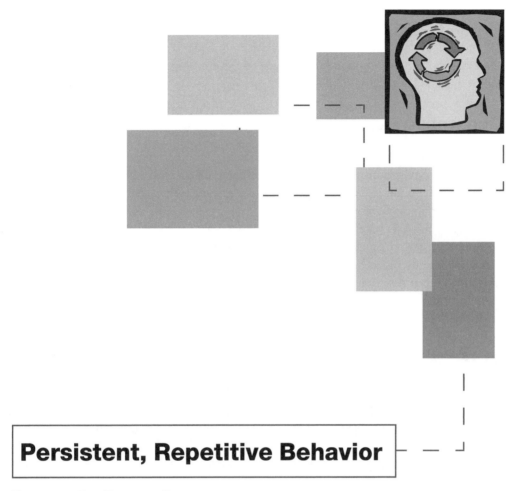

Persistent, Repetitive Behavior

Perseverative Responding

Definition: A person with persistent, repetitive behavior has difficulty initiating, stopping or switching the direction of an ongoing behavior, and gets stuck doing repetitive movements. Also described as perseverative responding, these persistent, repetitive behaviors reflect underlying brain dysfunction, are not purposeful and have no functional value. Perseverative responding reflects deficits in a person's ability to self-initiate, self-organize, self-sequence and regulate his own actions, thoughts and emotions.

The person is often able to move on if he is given an external prompt or if he is overfocused. Many with Tourette's syndrome fall into this category as do many with autism and fetal alcohol spectrum disorder. The perseverative behaviors do not present problems unless the person cannot "shift gears" when coaxed or prompted.

Issues Covered Elsewhere in This Book

Individuals who display persistent, repetitive behavior that is also attention seeking may do so as a form of self-activation, busying themselves when there is nothing else to do. (See Chapter 9: Socially Disruptive, Attention-Seeking Behavior.)

Individuals who display persistent, repetitive behavior that is also impulsive may do so as a means of controlling themselves, their environment or others. (See Chapter 6: Impulsive Behavior)

Individuals who display a mechanical, predictable, escalating cycle of emotional arousal may carry on until they go completely out of control. (See Chapter 9: Violent, Aggressive and Destructive Behavior.)

Generative Factors

All perseverative activity is "mechanical" in nature. Once the behavior begins to occur, the pattern of perseveration is highly predictable for each person. It is this predictable characteristic which indicates that the perseverative actions are not purposeful behavior; they result from brain dysfunction.

Because perseverative actions always follow a pattern, you can discover specific interventions that assist the person to initiate, stop or shift his perseverative cycle. Mechanical metaphors are useful to help support staff develop an instruction manual for managing the behaviors. If the support person can determine the person's pattern, she can alter it by following a mechanical procedure that will outlast or "out-perseverate" the person's repetitive action.

Typical Patterns of Perseverative Responding

Four patterns typify perseverative responding.

The person cannot initiate action until directed.

Some individuals are unable to start an action until told exactly what to do.

- One man with autism would sit looking at a blank television screen until someone asked him if he wanted to watch a show. He would answer affirmatively, but remain seated. Once the support person told him to use the remote control, he would flip channels until he found something interesting.

- Another man with a brain injury suffered during a car accident was squirming in his chair. When asked if he needed to use the bathroom, he answered, "Yes," and soiled himself on the spot. However, when told to go to the bathroom if he needed to use the toilet, he got up, went to the restroom and used it appropriately. If these individuals were cars, they would have a steering wheel but no accelerator.

The person cannot stop perseverative action until directed.

Some individuals who display persistent and repetitive behavior can switch immediately to another action when given an object or verbal direction to prompt them. If these individuals were cars, they would have a steering wheel and an accelerator, but lack voluntary control over their brake pedals. They could stop only when someone else applied the brakes.

The person cannot stop perseveration until completed.

Some individuals are able to self-initiate transitions only when they are ready. They can turn off what they are doing when they get to the end of their persistent, repetitive action. If these individuals were cars, they would have a steering wheel and an accelerator, but run on a set of fixed tracks. They could apply the brakes and change direction only at the end of the track at a round house. Once at the round house, they could shift into a new direction.

Captured by perseveration, the person cannot stop until rescued.

Some individuals may be completely unable to tolerate any external interruption in their persistent, repetitive actions. They are highly resistive to attempts to cause them to switch direction or make any sort of transition. These individuals are like runaway trains that have no brakes, no steering wheels and accelerators stuck at full throttle. They are only able to respond to external direction when a long, slow curve is created in their own track. This way, the change is hardly noticeable.

All persistent, repetitive behavior of this nature is also dependent behavior. A person stuck in a repetitive, stereotyped, response pattern may be unable to get out of it until a support person gives him the assistance he requires.

Five Types of Perseverative Behavior

"Stuck" or perseverative actions that are persistent and repetitive occur in a variety of forms. They include motor, verbal, sensory, emotional and mental perseveration. Once support staff identify the type of perseverative action, they can help the individuals they serve manage the behaviors more effectively.

Five Types of Perseverative Behavior

- Motor perseveration
- Verbal perseveration
- Sensory perseveration
- Emotional perseveration (leading to motor acceleration)
- Mental perseveration
  - Single-track mind; mental inflexibility
  - Perseverative thought; "obliged to carry it out"
  - Perseverative confusion (leading to motor inhibition).

Motor Perseveration (persistent movement patterns)

The following examples illustrate the behavior of individuals who are able to change actions when directed.

- One woman squeezes toothpaste onto her brush until the tube is empty. If someone reminds her immediately before going into the bathroom that she is to use just one drop, she will.

- When one young man washes his hair, he pours out the shampoo until the entire bottle is empty. He also uses the entire bottle when putting ketchup on a hot dog. Always giving him an individual portion pack solves these issues because it accommodates the reality that he will always use all of a container at once.

- When putting peanut butter on bread, one girl continues spreading it until the bottle is empty. She stops when told to put the lid on the jar.

- One man goes to the bathroom and uses an entire roll of toilet paper. Given direction to "count out four" allows him to follow a rule. For another man, support staff provide a box of tissues containing the required amount before each bathroom visit.

- A boy initially fills a sink to overflowing. Through hand-over-hand, rote guidance, he eventually learns to stop at a certain level. However, the learned behavior has not generalized to other areas. For example, he would continue to fill a wading pool until directed to turn off the hose.

- One man can sometimes be independent, getting himself ready to go to the pool in twenty minutes. At other times, after successfully completing one part of getting ready, he gets stuck and starts all over again, taking up to two and a half hours to finish. Support staff may be unable to interrupt until he has completed his sequence of actions. On other occasions, he becomes entirely dependent on being told what he needs to do next before he can move on.

Persistent/Repetitive or Ritualistic/Compulsive?

Persistent, repetitive behaviors are not the same as ritualistic or compulsive behaviors. Ritualistic or compulsive behaviors are functional or have personal meaning to the person. They may reduce a state of anxiety or be somehow reinforcing. While a perseverative behavior may be similar to a ritual, the person perseverating is willing and able to change his action if carefully guided out of the perseverative or "stuck" state.

The perseverative action has no personal meaning or deliberate function. The value of identifying a behavior as perseverative is that it allows others to recognize when the person may be stuck and require assistance to move on.

Verbal Perseveration

- One woman talks out loud. She strings out her thoughts in a never-ending associative train. Each new word in the train triggers other associated words or other associated thoughts. Not surprisingly, she loses the connection with her original intent. As a result, she becomes more and more anxious while trying to say what is on her mind. To assist her, it is necessary to write down her original statements, interrupt her, and read them to her when she goes off track. In this manner, she is able to stay on subject and not get lost in verbal perseveration.

- A man talks repetitively about the same topics. He is only able to change from his persistent topics when a support person introduces an alternative topic.

When not provided with an alternative, he immediately returns to his persistent topic. This seems to function as his "place keeper," providing him with something to do when he does not know what else to do.

Sensory Perseveration

- One man sometimes eats pizza until he vomits, or consumes an entire pack of hot dogs. Once started, he cannot stop. Attempting to take food away from him results in an agitated explosion. Support staff have resolved the problem by providing portion control and keeping out of sight whatever needs to be out of mind.

- For one boy with autism, the moment is everything, and it is sensory. He appears overwhelmed and trapped by his sensations. He perseverates any action that maintains continuous, sensory input.

- Another person engages in any repetitive action such as water play, picking up garbage or magazine flicking until redirected to some familiar, productive task. He will then competently work on the task.

Emotional Perseveration (leading to motor acceleration)

- One woman can follow any verbal direction and work competently with supervision. However, left on her own, she becomes anxious and engages in accelerated, random movements until someone tells her what to do.

- One young lady flicks her hair until she becomes agitated and begins to hit her head against the wall. She is happy to stop when a support person offers any alternative activity. Her agitation arises from frustration with her own inability to stop herself from flicking her hair. Furthermore, she becomes angry and aggressive with support staff who fail to save her from being stuck.

- Excess arousal in the environment overstimulates one man, who becomes increasingly more agitated. Once aroused, it is extremely difficult for him to stop any ongoing behavior, even in response to a direct cue. At the same time, he can easily change from one behavior to another when he is given explicit direction. He calms down instantly, given one-to-one guidance to do some familiar activity from his own repertoire.

- One man perseverates verbally on any word or phrases delivered with emotional intensity. He tends to repeat bad words that he has heard. For example, after seeing the movie "ET," he could not stop saying "penis breath," a phrase he had heard in one scene.

- When upset about missing a visit home, one woman displays emotional perseveration. Her behavior is similar to what might be observed in a distressed infant who, once upset beyond a certain point, is inconsolable and must cry herself to sleep.

Mental Perseveration

Single-track mind, mental inflexibility. Many individuals who display perseverative behavior are unable to consider alternatives. They are unable to see another point of view, stuck with their first impression and unable to shift their position. They are mentally inflexible.

- One man likes to wear his cowboy clothes. One Saturday, he dressed in his cowboy clothes for a family wedding. No one could get him to accept any alternative, and the continuing pressure led him to a violent outburst. This was not a ritualistic behavior. It was this man's perseverative response to his mental "rule" that when he takes off his clothes, he must change into pajamas for the night. Support staff resolved the problem by keeping clothes that he should not choose out of sight until an appropriate time to wear them.

- One person has learned how to cook but can only cook on high heat.

- One woman will accept instruction about menstrual hygiene from a public health nurse but cannot hear this from her support person.

These individuals do not learn from correction or their own errors. They are displaying a fixated approach to problem solving. (See "Accidental Learning of Perseverative Error Patterns" on page 120.)

Perseverative thought, obliged to be carried out. The person with this type of perseverative thought simply cannot make a shift, unaided, from the thought that is uppermost in his mind. When given a chance to talk it out or complete the thought, he *can* move on.

- Once a thought occurs to him, one man is unable to let it go until he has acted on it. For example, one time he was asked, "How is your sister?" He answered, "I don't know. I should go see my sister in Vancouver." Then, he had to leave his town and travel to Vancouver to see her. Attempting to interrupt him would escalate his behavior. Fortunately, support staff discovered that calling his sister for him, and having her describe to him how she is doing, would also allow him to be "rescued" from his imperative thought.

- A boy with autism watches a cat lose its footing by a pond. He wonders out loud what will happen if the cat falls in the water. He cannot stop talking about the question until he puts the cat into the water to find out. When asked, he now tells anyone that cats scratch when put in water.

Persistent, repetitive thoughts are different from obsessive thought. With obsession, the person "possesses" the idea and cannot get it out of his mind even with the opportunity to talk it out. Only when the thought-action is completed is the person able to move on.

Perseverative Confusion (leading to motor inhibition)

- A girl can carry out well-known sequences, but becomes physically frozen when she encounters the least bit of uncertainty about what to do. She requires assistance to move on to the next step in a sequence.

- One man displays no early warning signs when he approaches his emotional threshold. His actions are fluid and competent until he goes beyond his depth. Because he cannot adjust his approach, he will perseverate on whatever he had been doing. He cannot generate an alternative when under any stress. Presenting him with an easier task and "letting him off the hook" allows him to continue his other activities.

- Another man is able to perform all tasks in his repertoire when he can recognize what he is expected to do. But, as soon as unfamiliar material is presented, he begins to interact on a mechanical, sensory level. Re-prompted with familiar material, he instantly resumes performing in a competent manner.

- A young lady depends on the feedback of others to know how she is doing. She is very concerned about pleasing others and doing well. For instance, when a support person expressed concern about her eating habits, she stopped eating altogether! On another occasion, a support person expressed concern about her bowel movements. She then developed a disordered bowel and could not stop worrying about the support person's concern. This completely inhibited her actions.

Presenting him with an easier task and "letting him off the hook" allows him to continue his other activities.

- When this person is distressed by something, she demonstrates emotional perseveration. She cannot get a worry out of her mind, and persistently questions or repeats her opposition to whatever has distressed her. She appears unable to shift her focus or state of mind until she completes her thought and sorts out her confusion.

- One boy becomes verbally repetitive and cannot be distracted once he becomes upset. His normally poor language eventually disintegrates into inarticulate speech.

BEHAVIOR CHARACTERISTICS
- Perseverative action is mechanical or automatic in nature and reflects neurological deficits. The problem is in the brain, not in the behavior. Imagine that your television is receiving a bad picture from your cable company. Trying to address the problem by adjusting the television set does not work because the issue lies at the source of the signal. Switching over to direct cable input fixes the picture because you are

tapping into a different source. These are the types of results we try to obtain by switching environmental stimuli for a person who is having trouble with transition or is stuck.

■ Behaviors are all-or-nothing. Action sequences appear to have no beginning, middle or end. Once started, they have no self-stop mechanism.

Remember these metaphors to better understand and assist the person who displays perseverative behavior.

The person who has difficulty initiating action – a driverless car sitting and idling in neutral. It stays in one spot until it runs out of gas. The car moves only when someone puts it in gear.

The person who has difficulty shifting action – a car that keeps going in one direction until it runs into a physical obstacle. In other words, the person needs someone to put him into gear and guide his actions.

The person who has difficulty stopping action – a car that is in gear, beginning to move slowly, then accelerating down a hill. The more it gathers speed and momentum, the more difficult it is to stop or redirect. The person who becomes stuck in these perseverative actions needs someone to remain aware of his actions, intervene quickly, apply the brakes for him and redirect him if he starts to go the wrong way.

■ Perseverative action does not often occur during well-known motor routines. When the person knows what to do by rote, he tends to carry out well-learned sequences without becoming stuck.

■ The need to break through perseverative responding usually means that acquiring any new skills involves a lengthy period of hand-over-hand or backward chaining. In other words, the person learns new behaviors as rote movements.

■ Perseverative action is typically associated with repeated errors that never change, regardless of correction. The person makes a mistake, waits for the correction, then does it as corrected.

INDIVIDUAL CHARACTERISTICS

Many individuals who display persistent, repetitive behavior are autistic, while others are described as autistic-like. However, there is far more than perseverative responding involved with autism. This chapter only addresses perseverative responding.

■ The person is unable to stop making a prior response.

■ The person cannot organize his time or activities independently.

■ The person is unable to anticipate the consequences of his actions. He cannot see the connection between what he is doing now and anything that will happen more than an instant later.

  - The person may engage in one random action after another, appearing hyperactive if not occupied with a familiar action. When focused on a familiar task, he may be able to concentrate for long periods of time.

- The person may display a reasonable command of spontaneous, verbal expression that gives a misleading impression of the amount of information he can take in. For example, one person can repeat directions given to her, word for word, but cannot act on the meaning of those words. Another person has little or no sense of time, so he cannot process the meaning of "if-then," "when," or "not until."

- The person may be very motivated to do well, but without external feedback cannot tell how he is doing. This can make him very anxious about his performance.

- The person can hold only one concrete piece of information in mind at a time, causing him to appear very stubborn. The support person should always be aware that this person may be unable to go on to the next thought until he has complete the first one.

Interventions
Behavior Management Strategies

PREVENTION AND GUIDANCE

The general strategy is to help the person out of his perseverative rut by outlasting (or "out-perseverating him, so to speak). When a person becomes stuck, life needs to be taken moment by moment, one step at a time with consistent guidance from a support person. The following interventions should be used with two groups of individuals who display perseverative responses. The prevention, guidance and training techniques will work for individuals who are able to become unstuck in response to direction from a support person. The crisis management tech-

> **Key to Prevention**
>
> Use intervention with the environment and people providing support. Remember the six A's: Acknowledge, Anticipate and Avoid problem behavior. Have an Accepting Attitude; Accommodate the person's needs and deficiencies.

niques described on pages 117 to 120 provide ways of rescuing the second group, individuals who are unable to stop their perseverative responding.

■ When the person is attending to what is expected of him, he may be very responsive and interactive. Therefore, try to keep interactions emotionally light and happy to avoid introducing a motivation to resist. Once a person with a tendency to perseverate begins to resist, he may become stuck on the resistive movements themselves.

 The long-term goal is for the person to gain some sense of control over his perseverative responding. Do whatever will communicate that you know he is doing the best he can. Try to put a smile on his face.

■ Some activities always generate perseverative responding unless support staff anticipate the problem. For example, perseverative responses frequently occur with dressing. Children may want to put on the first items of clothing they lay eyes on and persist in wearing same clothes over and over.

  - Creating a routine such as color-coding clothes can prevent perseverative responding for many individuals. Support staff can code each day of the week on the calendar with a different colored dot. The clothes for each day can be hung on hangers of the same color. A cloth patch of the same color sewn into clothing provides additional coding.

- For further reinforcement, consider creating a single rule to govern all clothes-related behavior. For instance, all clothing goes into a laundry basket at night. Later, the support person can sort the clean and dirty clothes, and re-hang or refold wearable items for the next week.

- Also, support staff can prevent more difficult issues with clothing by keeping out of sight what needs to be kept out of mind. Certain clothes should only be brought out when they can be worn. Some individuals may require multiples of a favorite item so they can wear the same clothes daily without the need to wash them every day.

- A person will often begin a perseverative action when a trigger in his environment signals him to begin an ordinary action.
    - The person will endlessly repeat any action not defined by a concrete end point. For instance, asking him to wipe the counter does not offer an obvious end.
    - Define an obvious beginning, middle and end to each activity. Offer the person alternative responses with clearly identified triggers. Alternative activities should ideally have a built-in, natural end point. Also, a prop is very helpful.
    - Hand the person a small basket of flower bulbs, and ask him to place one into each hole you have dug in the garden.
    - Stack the dishes and ask him to load the dishwasher.
    - Hand the person a bowl of peanuts and ask him to shell them.

These activities provide good "teachable moments" for the person to learn the meaning of "all done" and "next."

- It can also be helpful to make a ritual, or clear signals for "finished." This serves as an end point that the person may eventually be able to generalize. If he can learn to use "Finished!" and "Next?" as a perseverative response, the difficulty with transitions can be greatly reduced. In some cases, you can just tell or show what is next!

 One major guidance goal is to redirect the person's intensely focused, perseverative responding without causing him to become confused, disoriented or angrily reactive. Start by treating him "normally." The moment this does not work, lower your expectations for any degree of independent, competent functioning. Raise your expectations for him to perform perfectly with whatever level of support he requires.

- Rather than approaching perseveration as a behavior problem, be prepared to help the person become unstuck. A number of approaches may prove helpful.

Get up and move. When the person is trying to work on a specific task, perseverative responding can sometimes be broken by putting aside the task at hand and changing physical location; for example, "Please bring that over here where there's better light."

Take a break. Sometimes, shifting momentarily to a different task can help; for example, "I'm tired of subtraction. Let's try addition now." Then prompt another familiar activity from the person's own repertoire.

Alter some sensory aspect. Changing the people involved in an activity, or some other aspect of the person's sensory surroundings can sometimes break the perseverative pattern. For example, close the blinds, turn on some music or call another person over.

Simplify the task. Bring your expectations down to single-step actions. Keep the person constantly focused on tasks in his repertoire.

- Sometimes, it is easier to reorient a person by being incidental, rather than direct, in your approach.
  - Talk to someone else about what you want to accomplish, and then ask the person if he wants to help. For example, "Cara, I'm going to need some help carrying these branches. Joe, would you like to join us?"
  - "Accidentally" remember something else that needs to be done.
  - Rather than say, "Get your shirt on," you could say, "Let's go get supper on the table—oh, you need your shirt on. Let me help you."

- Be indirect and make positive suggestions.
  - "I'll do my teeth before you do yours." Or, "I will open the door because you probably can't right now." The response may be, "I'll do it first!" or "Yes, I can!"

- Map out the person's activity for him and with him. This can be accomplished through a number of approaches.

Methods for Guiding a Person Out of Perseverative Responding

- Give verbal direction about what to do next.
- Offer a physical prop to signal the beginning and end of the next action.
- Allow or assist the person to complete what he is doing.
- Assist the person to mediate his own perseveration.
- Mediate transitions through personal involvement.

Give verbal direction about what to do next.

Saying "stop" is rarely enough for this person. Using this command is like attempting to change what you are hearing on the radio by pulling the wires out of the back of the speakers and stopping any sound from coming out. Even though you can no longer hear it, the original source is still producing the same program. Simply saying "stop" does not allow the person who is perseverating to move on. You must change the program by switching to another station. In other words, redirect the person by giving him a positive direction to help him proceed to the next action.

- A person who flaps his hands stops when told to put his hands on the table or to hold a pencil.

- One woman thinks out loud and gets lost in her verbal associations. She becomes extremely frustrated by people who "listen" to her because she can never get her point across. To be most helpful, a support person stops her as soon as she begins to trail off, writes down what she says in point form, and shows it to her. This kindly interrupts her with her own words. Then, she gets back on track immediately and can complete her thought.

- Another person engages in perseverative behavior whenever he does not understand what is expected of him. He is unable to respond to "Don't do…!" He does not understand "wait," "later" and "not until…" And, he cannot respond to correction. So, verbal explanations, questions and instructions diminish his ability to perform. It is necessary to show him what to do next.

- Support staff can help the person be "readied to be ready" to respond. They can tell him, "Ready now," then assist him in making a choice between two visual alternatives.

Offer a physical prop to signal the beginning and end of the next action.

Keep your language concrete and explicit, making sure the last two or three words of what you say contain the critical information.

- Describe the actions the person is to complete and the objects he is to use. Provide a description of the movements he is expected to make and have a physical prop for him to use to practice.
  - Give the person a key as a prop, and ask him to open a cupboard, unlock a car or enter the house.
  - Ask the person to set a channel changer on the table nearby while he is running the vacuum. This will keep him focused on what comes next.
  - Ask a child to hold the book you will read to her when she has finished changing into her pajamas.
  - Use lists or numbered picture sequences. Show them to the person and point to "next." Then, hand him a picture or activity depicted on a three-by-five index card and say, "Next!"

- One student carries out familiar tasks relatively independently, but if she encounters any complication, she comes to a complete stop! For instance, when she is working on a difficult math problem at school, she may insist, "I have to do this one." She is unable to skip it and go on to the problems she can complete.

  Sometimes, this pattern can be interrupted by using a visual stop sign, then showing the person a written rule such as "Go on to…" In other words, some individuals who get stuck need an "answer key for life," telling them what to do next to perform certain tasks correctly.

- One man was able to stop and move on when a support person showed him a stop sign with a happy face inside. This gave him the message that it was okay to stop.

- One woman talks endlessly to peers about pains in her body. She will also talk about anything else, if directed to do so. For her, a book of alternative topics or a photo album showing her doing activities with her peers can help. You cannot stop her verbal perseveration, but you can coach her to interact with peers, using a prop that evokes "good perseveration." (Good perseveration sustains relationships; bad perseveration interferes with relationships.)

Allow or assist the person to complete what he is doing.

Do not hurry the person. Allow him the opportunity to complete his present action.

Verbal perseveration. If the person begins to perseverate on a specific question like, "Where is the hamper?" try to get him off the hook. It may help to show him the answer to his question and have him repeat the answer. Then, signal to say, "Stop, we're done. That's finished!" Finally, redirect him to the next activity.

Sensory perseveration. If the person is physically involved in an activity that requires touching something at the time the support person makes a request, he may be unable to incorporate the request. He may be perseverating on his momentary sensory activity, which can lead to resistance.

Key to Guidance

Use positive intervention with the person. Use human relations techniques to engage him in other behavior without confronting him about problem behavior. Use suggestion, positive motivation and humor along with the three D's: Displace, Divert and re-Direct the person's behavior.

When asked, one woman would not let go of her personal audio player. However, she would join in a contest to find a special place to put it. She was told she could have it again when she was finished with the next activity. Joining in a stimulating game allowed her to let go of the sensory experience of the audio player.

Mental perseveration. Many individuals will persistently and repetitively ask questions about people who are not present. A person may be unable to get on with his day until someone answers this question, or until he sees or talks to the absent person. Helping him complete the thought may allow him to move on.

Instances of mental perseveration can cause difficulties, especially when parents or other relatives are out of town, or if someone the person is asking about no longer works nearby. When it is not possible for him to talk to or see the person he is asking about, it can help to provide photographs of him doing an activity with the absent person.

If the person in question is available at some point, he or she could sit and look at photos with the person, and make a video or audiotape of them. This way, the person can at least "hear from" the individual when he or she is absent.

For some individuals, this may backfire. Support staff must ensure that hearing the person's voice, or seeing him or her on videotape, does not produce more emotional arousal and perseveration.

Assist the person to mediate his own perseveration.

- Until taught a "toilet" sign, one youngster could not learn how to take himself to the bathroom. Support staff would find him soiled and then send him to the toilet. However, he quickly learned the sign, and was able to self-instruct to take himself to the bathroom.

- Another young man loves to be perfect and know that he is "good." He is motivated by routines, quickly learning and following explicit expectations. He actively seeks information about what is expected next by saying, "Then?" He can be overheard talking to himself, giving himself a running commentary of what he is going to do next!

■ It may help to provide a running commentary on what is going to happen next to the person who "talks out loud." After hearing the commentary enough times, he may "memorize the script" and use it to self-instruct, and possibly to guide himself out of a perseverative cycle.

Mediate transitions through personal involvement.

■ A support person can interrupt the perseverative response by inserting herself into the person's cycle.
   - If a person is stuck doing perseverative finger play, the support person could join in finger play with him. Once he is oriented to the new interaction, the support person has an opportunity to lead him out. She might do finger play with him while walking to the location of the next activity. She could then put a different object into his hands or engage him in the required activity.

■ The support person can provide a personal bracket.
   - She can give the person sensory orientation to herself with requests like, "Touch my arm," when introducing him to an unfamiliar situation. If the person becomes trapped in a perseverative response pattern at any point, the way out is always: "Touch my arm."
   - To conclude an activity, the support person again says, "Touch my arm," always allowing the person to know where he belongs and what to do when he becomes uncertain. In this way, the support person acts like the dotted line on the road that orients a person who is driving in a heavy fog.

■ Skill training with some individuals who display perseverative tendencies must be done in a manner that will refine and refocus this dysfunction because they are not able to respond to redirection. They remain stuck until the support person "out-perseverates" the perseverative action.

TRAINING

Teach single movements.

- Teaching strategies often need to be broken down into single-step, repetitive movements for the person because he is usually able to learn only one thing at a time.
  - In addition to relying on rote memorization of single steps, support staff may need to teach the person one-on-one, and constantly present him with the model from which to work.
  - Once skills are learned in this manner, a person will often be independent in carrying out a complex sequence of actions. Support staff can then correctly assess the person's learning potential.

- The person's ability to carry out complex action by rote memory can give others a very mistaken impression of the procedures required for him to reach that potential.

  In the initial stages of teaching, the person with perseverative responding should not be expected to follow a sequence of steps independently. Training should proceed at that person's unique pace. Introduce new ideas to him, one step at a time, only as he demonstrates readiness to acquire additional knowledge. For example:

  Learning toileting. Make the expectation for toileting part of a highly ritualized sequence of movements that can be memorized as part of a routine.

  The routine might include visiting the bathroom just before going out or coming in the door; just before or after meals; and just before going to bed. Support persons should provide visual cues to remind the person to cue himself, such as a picture symbol, the support person going to bathroom at that time, or sign language for "t."

  Key to Training

  Use positive intervention with the person. Employ motivation and skill development programs, and teach alternative coping skills over time.

  If visual cues are not enough, verbal cues can sometimes do the trick. These cues could, however, become an "accidentally" memorized aspect of the elimination cycle. Eventually, the person may not go to the toilet unless verbal cues are given. That is not the goal. Instead, support staff should work toward simply cuing the person to self-cue.

  Learning to cook. Using precooked portion packs, one for each meal, would provide an appropriate place to begin. "Boil it" is a single-step competency that can protect the person from getting stuck on one part of the food preparation sequence.

  Learning to launder clothes. Use visually distinct baskets—one white and one dark—with written instructions on each. This makes it "one step at a time," with a rule to help the person mediate his behaviors. This may allow him to interrupt himself should he begin to perseverate and put all the clothes into the machine at once.

Learning responsible money habits. Divide the person's money into separate budget item envelopes, with written instructions printed on each. You might also include pictures of what items the money will purchase on each envelope. This may interrupt his perseverative tendency to spend all his money in the first store he enters after payday.

■ Until a new routine is established, the person with perseverative tendencies requires monitoring to prevent and guide his excessive, repetitive responses. Support staff may find written and picture lists, or audio-recorded instructions useful. They may also need to check and remind the person frequently to ensure that the procedures benefit his learning process.

Use "errorless" and "incidental" teaching procedures.

It is a paradox that many individuals with persistent, repetitive behavior appear to build up an extreme inhibition against repetition that is prompted externally. Yet, if the person initiates an action, he may repeat it endlessly.

One woman could not respond to corrective feedback, and was unaware of how to generate any alternative strategies. While she understood that corrective feedback meant she had made an error, she quickly lost motivation when asked to try again or relearn a task.

■ Maintain the person's motivation by working from a known and familiar base. Use errorless procedures.

■ Recognize that it is often difficult for these individuals to learn from direct teaching because they have difficulty following external sequences and keep getting stuck. They often learn best by spontaneously doing their own, self-initiated actions. The trick is to prompt the person to do the correct, self-initiated action. Support staff can often accomplish this by giving the person the answer before asking the question.

This way, life can become a multiple-choice test where he always has the answer key and an open-book test. Then he can self-initiate what he recognizes as the correct thing to do!

■ Various "incidental" teaching methods can trick individuals into spontaneously doing the actions they need to learn.
- Show a sibling or peer what you want the person to attend to. Let him observe several others doing suggested actions, then say, "Want a turn?" or "You do it." This activity provides the answer before asking the question and allows him to initiate the action spontaneously.

- Take dolls or puppets through the motions, and ask the him to join in the play.

- Make a videotape of others doing the desired actions. Allow the person to view these repeatedly before asking him to do the same. This provides a picture of the whole to a person who has difficulty learning from parts.

When motivated with only positive feedback, the person is more likely to concentrate on rehearsing correct movements for an extended period of time. For this reason, do not "teach and test."

- Teach the correct movement patterns–approaching the person as though he is momentarily more dependent–in an attempt to teach him how to become less dependent. Take him through each movement, step by step, as though he were a marionette. Once he has thoroughly memorized the movements, ask him to do the action. Do this using backward chaining, asking the person to do the last step you know he can perform.

- Many individuals do their best when they spontaneously self-instruct from a memorized rule. The person makes automatic responses to his own, familiar, verbal self-prompts. If this is the case, identify common words to which the person has a specific, attached response, and use them to cue him consistently. In other words, rely on his ritualistic, perseverative motor responses to verbal cues as a learning strength. In every area where it is important for him to learn the correct movements, create a specific verbal cue and use it with him.

Teach self-advocacy.

It may be possible to coach the person to self-advocate in situations where perseveration is his response to uncertainty and confusion. For example, support staff may teach him to perseverate verbally on a response, such as "Tell me again," or "Show me a picture," causing him to receive the direction he requires. Or, if a person is impulsive he may be able to learn to perseverate on the verbal question, "Is it okay?" Train him to rely on social feedback and permission.

Special Techniques for Teaching Receptive and Expressive Language

Perseverative responding can greatly interfere with learning speech and understanding language. The person may become so involved in perseverating on the rhythm and sound of language that he fails to focus on the meaning.

Giving Directions

Persons with perseverative tendencies often have significant auditory sequencing difficulties that disrupt the ability to process language. So, verbal explanations, questions and instructions meant to be helpful often function to decrease the person's ability to perform. It is essential to focus on one thing at a time, orienting the person to the very next action.

- When giving directions, present the person with only one-step directions, letting him complete each step before giving the next short direction. For sequential actions, help the person memorize a verbal sequence that allows him to mediate his actions, such as, "hands, face, towel."

- Keep all verbal directions to four or five words. The person may perceive a "word soup" if directions are longer. He may retain only four- or five-word bites that are out of order and do not reflect the meaning of the sentence.

- Do not say, "Please go get your coat, then your backpack." Instead say, "Coat, backpack!" This may sound extremely directive, but it may be precisely the explicit language the person needs to function at his best.

■ When making requests longer than four or five words, use repetition as though you were sending repeated telegrams. Send the first four words, then the first six words. Next, send the first eight words and finally the complete ten-word message. With repetition, the person may be able to process more information and better understand what is expected.

- "Clean up" may not be explicit enough. Say, "We need a cloth. Go get a cloth. The cloth is in the sink. Bring the cloth here." If the person still does not know what to do, say, "Here is the spill. Take your cloth. Take your cloth and wipe the spill. Wipe the spill with your cloth."

■ Do not expect the person to respond to words like "when," " next," "after," "or," "if," and "except." Conditional phrases are usually contained in sentences longer than four words. He may not have the ability to put the first part of a sentence together with the second. This may arise from difficulty in remembering an entire direction. Or, it can result from the person's difficulty in understanding the sequential or conditional nature of the direction.

Teaching the Meaning of Language

"Incidental" teaching methods can be used to give the answer to individuals before they are expected to respond to the meaning of language.

■ It may be easier for some individuals to track on language if the words follow the actions being described. To help this person focus his attention on language, show him an object, and get him to taste, touch or smell it. Then, say the name of the object and get him to say the name. Also, model what is expected by using pantomime, and then label the actions.

■ Another person will benefit from having someone "telegraph," or describe ahead of time, the movements that will occur next. To do this effectively, make sure that when you have the person's attention you communicate only what is important and relevant to him.

- Offer the person control over his world in the form of choice between two alternatives, such as food items, clothes and play activities.
- If a person attends well to the content of pictures, show him pictures of himself doing two activities. Describe them to him as though you are reciting a script and performing the action. Then, ask him to perform the one he chooses.

■ Other individuals benefit from describing their momentary experience as it is taking place. A constant, running commentary may assist them to focus and stay connected with the actions they are performing.

- Language that is concrete and of immediate consequence to the person will be easier to grasp. Present everything as a choice: "Orange cut or peeled?" "Red or blue shirt?" This offers a person control through language!

- With some individuals, you can help them focus by describing their actions as though someone were reading off subtitles, explaining the step-by-step actions of their lives. ("Here is your shirt. The shirt goes over your head. Here is your head. Here goes your shirt over your head. Now, you are wearing your shirt. Here are your pants…" and so forth.) It seems as though they are visually "blind" to the actions in their world, but capable of mediating and interacting with others through the explicit, verbal description of those actions.

■ When giving verbal directions, using rhyme or rhythm in vocal patterns can be helpful. This may make it easier for the person to track and repeat the "movements" of the language you are trying to prompt. For some, it helps to tap out a physical rhythm on his leg that mimics the rhythm of the language you are using.

■ For some individuals, an audio recording of short phrases of instruction, repeated twenty or thirty times, can help. This allows the person enough repetition to integrate the meaning of the words being used.

All of these techniques are designed to help the person integrate the meaning of language with actions and objects in his world. They also make visual and continuously present an example of what he is expected to learn and imitate.

CRISIS MANAGEMENT

Some individuals cannot stop perseverating regardless of prevention, guidance or training procedures. The inability to respond to redirection can create a crisis, when physical interference with their perseverative response leads to an explosive outburst. These individuals need to be *rescued* from their stuck response patterns.

In a crisis situation, support staff can attempt a hierarchy of approaches, each of which may work with the person in question. To be most effective, adapt the following methods to the person's individual needs.

■ To de-escalate resistance to transitions, communicate expected events clearly to the person. It may be helpful to have photographs of the place he is going next, especially ones that depict a person doing the things planned for him there.

Key to Crisis Management

Use direct intervention with the problem behavior. Remain calm and always use guidance techniques first. Accommodate the person's special needs and disabilities. Respond to chaotic behavior with a prearranged plan for surviving the crisis while bringing challenging behavior to a stop! Interact positively with the person as soon as she exercises a degree of self-control. Have a plan for how to re-enter normal life.

- Depending on the degree of anxiety and uncertainty, it may be helpful to detail step-by-step the required movements–getting into the car, traveling, arriving, getting out of the car, entering the building through the door, and so on. This same approach can be used for moving from room to room.
- When telling a person about what is going to happen next, always give him time to think about what you have said. Bring a prop to assist him in making the transition, and tell him again while he interacts with the prop.

Imagine it will cost you ten dollars a word if you use more than three or four words to talk about what is next.

- Read the person's signals so you can ascertain when it is time to back off. He may stop paying attention to the content and goal of action, and turn an activity into a sensory-motor, autistic-like activity. This is an early signal that the person is becoming disoriented. Change the task to an easier, more familiar, sensory-motor piece of his repertoire. But, before removing anything from the person, bring in the next thing he may want to do. Once he becomes interested in the new item, remove the first item.
  - Make a long list of sensory activities in which the person will sometimes become involved. (For one child, this included play dough, squeezy items, keys, coins, silly putty, beads, Legos, dolls, plasticine, baking activities, water play, playing the organ, working on a computer and listening to music.)

For some individuals, behavior management approaches are counterproductive. Use of positive or negative consequences may cause them to perseverate resistive behavior. For many individuals, saying, "Don't do…" functions as an instruction to do the very thing you do not want.

- Avoid having to interact constantly with undesirable, perseverated behaviors by establishing routine activities that the person can always be directed to do as an approved alternative. Once these become part of a routine, he will tend to expect and to perseverate on the approved activities.
  - Offer the person a choice of any two of the activities he enjoys. Put the related object(s) in or near his hands so that it will be more likely to capture his sensory attention. For instance, give him a cup as a prop, and assign him the job of getting a drink or other activity that involves using the cup.

The problem with some individuals is getting them to focus on exactly what is expected. The key is to stop any perseverative movement first by capturing the person's attention, then focusing his attention on what you expect.

If the person is unable to transition when given a new direction, ask him to transition to an old, familiar direction. Rescue the person by redirecting his tendency to make a perseverative response.

For a person who is stuck in some maladaptive, repetitive action, it may assist him to "get ready to be ready" to respond. Give him a calendar for the hour, day, week or month, a picture list of daily activities, printed rules for action, and/or cartoon stories.

- It is helpful to identify a repertoire of "good" perseverative behaviors to replace "bad" perseverative behaviors. These could include sensory-tactile activities with scratch and sniff items, water, nail polish and hair brushing. Auditory-visual activities might include looking at a digital camera slide show, watching bubbles in a fish tank and looking at a talking picture album. Cognitive-social activities might include playing cards, flicking channels on the TV and playing a game box.

■ For lower-functioning individuals with perseverative behavior and/or for persons with autism, the following methods can sometimes interrupt the perseverative cycle.

1. Try to remove any interfering distractions, avoiding any emotional or negative interaction with the individual's behavior.

2. Offer the person an opportunity to engage in a sensory activity that is almost certain to distract him.

3. Deliberately use a strong form of sensory stimulation as an interrupter or distracter. It should be something that can be used very briefly and totally under the support person's control.
   - Call the person's name, whistle part of a favorite tune, give a quick tickle, or offer a quick sniff of an interesting smell like aftershave or some spice.
   - Hum a favorite tune, then hand the person an audio player with a tune playing.
   - Once the person is briefly reoriented, gain eye contact and direct him to respond with an aspect of his own familiar repertoire. If necessary, guide his attention, movement by movement, with the use of a powerful reinforcer. Do this until the alternative perseverative response pattern is well established.

4. Always make the person aware of a desired activity that will follow his positive response to the support person's direction to get him "unstuck."

■ A higher functioning person with more repertoire to draw on can make a written inventory of every acceptable behavior that he knows how to perform. When there is not enough time to interact continuously with him, direct him to do one of the approved behaviors in his own repertoire.

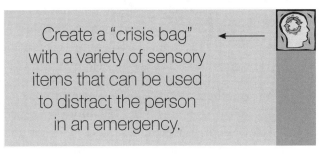

Create a "crisis bag" with a variety of sensory items that can be used to distract the person in an emergency.

■ It is frequently helpful to take pictures of every approved activity the person does and place them in an album, one per page. The album can be used to assist him in choosing what to do during down time. Often, just sitting and looking at the pictures is a good activity.

■ In a crisis, a support person can often help to mediate a transition through personal involvement. By "inserting" herself into the perseverative response cycle, she can sometimes capture the person in a mutual sensory activity (such as finger play). Her most important task is to act like the dotted line on the road that people always look for when driving in a heavy fog.

- Create a "crisis bag" with a variety of sensory items that can be used to distract the person in an emergency. This will be especially helpful when the person is in the community. Include items known to capture his attention, such as a skipping rope, cards, a video game, bubble gum, or photographs.

- Try to establish an "escape procedure" to bring the crisis to an end. Identify a ritualistic behavior that can be "triggered" and used as a "way out" of the problem behavior.

- One man responded positively when support staff handed him a box and several unorganized items. He was told to "put them away." "Put away" was one of the most perseverative responses in his repertoire.

- Support staff found an "escape route" for one girl by providing her with paper and something to copy. Putting the pencil in her hand would immediately end any escalating crisis.

- With one child, crises immediately de-escalated when a support person said, "Race you to the car!" The child always made a perseverative response.

- The "way out" for another person was, "Come play with me!"

Some individuals become "stuck in emotion," captured by emotional perseveration and disinhibition. We are all sensitive to the emotions expressed by others in our environment. For instance, some people cry when someone else in the room is crying, or they become carried away by a piece of emotionally evocative music. But, a person who becomes stuck in emotion is *extremely* vulnerable to the distressing emotions of others.

When support staff recognize this in a person, they can take steps to protect him from the presence of those who are experiencing emotional distress. Since this person functions like an "emotional sponge," it can be very helpful to assume the role of an emotional cheerleader. This allows his to absorb and reflect the cheery emotions to which he is exposed.

- Another metaphor for the person who is unable to attenuate or regulate his emotional responses is an "emotional magnifying glass." Not only does he reflect the emotion to which he is exposed, he cannot control the intensity of that emotion. For instance, if he becomes excited, his giddiness escalates out of control. If he begins to roughhouse, it turns into a "rumble." If he becomes distressed, he slips quickly into deep depression. It is very important for support staff to recognize the impact of their own emotions on the persons they serve. They must remain consistently low keyed and pleasant around a person who is like an emotional mirror or magnifying glass.

Special Case: Accidental Learning of Perseverative Error Patterns

The person with perseverative responding tends to have a narrow focus for his attention. Once he forms an intent, it is quite difficult to distract or redirect him. Typically, the person requires several repeated, insistent interruptions before he will abandon his perseverating and reorient to the support person's direction.

Unfortunately, this person and his support person will often learn together a pattern of interaction that is counterproductive. He makes an error, then the support person corrects it. The support person is unaware of–or is ignoring–a basic fact: *Individuals with a tendency to become stuck in repetitive patterns of response do not learn much from correcting their errors.*

■ Giving this person constant correction does not teach him how to self-correct. From his point of view, a repeated pattern of error and correction is exactly what is supposed to happen. (I do something, and you make me do something else.) The support person becomes constantly caught up in correcting persistent, "error" behavior.

■ The key is to turn the dysfunction of perseverative responding into a training asset. Focus the person on an errorless, routine pattern of expected behavior and *cause him to perseverate the correct response.*

    - Imagine, for example, that the person's behavior is like a picture he draws repeatedly, and one you wish to change. You have to paint a picture of the behavior you want to see on top of his picture. You have to use deeper colors and make more brush strokes on your picture than he makes on his.

    - You must *out-perseverate* him. This means motivating and guiding the behavior you expect him to use before he has an opportunity to practice the error.

Error-Free Training Procedures

The person may be cue-dependent and unable to organize his own time. However, he still has to be given an opportunity to become as independent as possible.

■ To establish error-free training routines, all training should take the form of backward chaining. In this procedure, the person is expected to do only the *last step* in a procedure that he has first seen demonstrated. Then support staff can slowly shape his skills at any task.

■ To build potential for independent action, support staff must allow the person with a disability to do as much as possible for himself. We should avoid doing for the person what he is perfectly capable of doing for himself. With a person who displays perseverative responses, however, support staff must be sure to do as much for or with him as is necessary to maintain error-free practice.

    - With any learned motor skill, such as toileting, dressing, feeding or a social-verbal habit, the support person must assume that the person with perseverative responding could be unaware of what exact behaviors are expected. And, we assume that he will remain unaware until these become part of a well-defined routine.

    - The support person must also assume that, for several months after any routine procedure is established, the person will frequently forget parts of it and require assistance at a more dependent level. Whenever this occurs, the support person simply reinstates the earlier, error-free practice for several days. It is only necessary to do this for the specific parts of the task where errors occur.

- The support person must also remember that, until tasks become part of well-established routines, the person may continue to require the use of special procedures to capture and motivate his attention. He may show lack of awareness, forgetfulness or a need for special motivation. Support staff may need to guard against the tendency to interpret this as resistant or stubborn behavior.

The Need for Assistance and Respite

Creating and organizing error-free response patterns for the person always requires dedicated effort at home, at school and in the workplace. In fact, developing new routines for error-free practice and training often calls for skilled assistance. Furthermore, support staff must constantly think several steps ahead of the person with a disability.

The intensity of essential care can easily lead to support person burnout. Preventing this almost always requires predictable, frequent respite. This can be a significant challenge since people who perseverate well-learned patterns of behavior are usually quite dependent on their well-established, familiar cues. A new support person usually requires several training opportunities with the person's established support staff to become familiar with him and his routines. For these reasons, respite is sometimes best delivered in the person's own home environment with minimal disruption to his familiar routines.

In This Chapter

6 ■ Impulsive Behavior

- ■ Definition
- ■ Generative Factors
    - *Behavior Associated with a Young Developmental Level*
    - *Reactive Behavior*
    - *Behavior Due to Cognitive Disability*
    - *Functional Behavior (functional impulsivity)*
- ■ Interventions
- ■ Special Prevention Procedures for a Person Who Is Unusually Sensitive
- ■ Special Cases

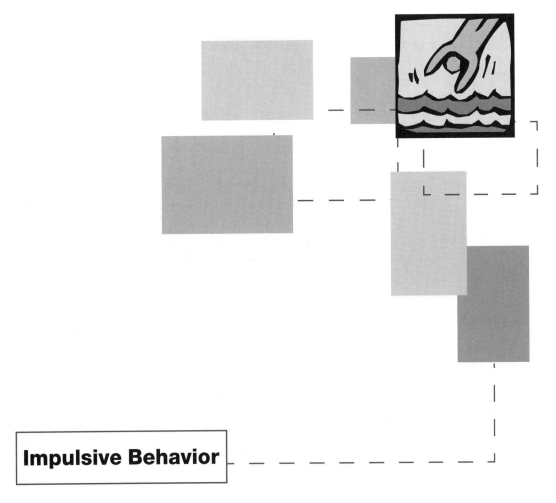

Impulsive Behavior

Definition: Impulsive behavior is rapid, goal-oriented behavior, occurring without consideration for the consequences of an impetuous action. (Acting before thinking.) It is directed at obtaining the goal object. Impulsive actions include lunging; grabbing and snatching; bolting and running; touching; mouthing; and hugging.

Three Categories of Impulsive Action

These three types of action can be generated by any of the four generative factors described later in this chapter.

Impulsive action that occurs upon initial perception of a goal object. ("In sight is in mind" leads to "I have to have it right now.") A person who displays this type of behavior may be easily angered.

 On the basis of her writing skill and ability to answer questions, a woman with mild developmental delay appeared able to function independently in the community. She could explain all the rules about stores, and about having to pay for food items before eating them. However, when in the presence of food or objects she wanted, she could not remember to act on the rules. She needed a companion to remind her. Otherwise, she could only act on the uppermost thought on her mind, her immediate desire. While support staff called it stealing, she never stole if she was reminded of the rule just before entering the store.

Impulsive action that is based on the first thought that comes to mind. The person's perception is: "If I think it, I have to do it right now." (Idea equals action.) People with such actions have difficulty putting on the brakes.

A young woman with moderate developmental delay was in the schoolyard when it started to rain. Since her raincoat was at home, she left the schoolyard immediately and impulsively crossed the road in heavy traffic to go get her coat. While focused on her immediate intent, she "misses the whole picture." Her impulsiveness is due to her difficulty in thinking about the possible consequences of her immediate actions. Seeing the "whole picture" would require her to put two or three thoughts together for herself at the same time, a task beyond her abilities.

Impulsive action that may not occur until the person is denied access to a goal object. In this instance, the person never paid attention to the goal object or activity until she was told she could not have it or do it.

A fourteen-year-old boy with moderate developmental delay was walking by the doorway of the computer room at school. He looked in and immediately wanted to work at a computer. In sight was in mind! Since another class was in session, this was not possible. When prevented from entering the computer room, he bolted and ran out of the school toward a busy road. Support staff knew that trying to stop him physically when he was running led to aggressive attacks, so a support person ran beside him and said, "Let's go get the computer." He stopped, returned to school and accepted a new directive: "First, have a drink. Computer next!"

Does Impulsive Equal Challenging?

If a person accepts external direction to inhibit her behavior, the impulsive behavior may not be challenging. But, impulsive behavior can be extremely challenging when the person has a cognitive (thinking) disability that causes her to be unable to inhibit her impulsive actions. She constantly "gets into trouble" for breaking the rules.

One normally intelligent child with brain damage can formulate goals for himself, but cannot organize the sequence of activities that allows him to reach them. During any task, he jumps immediately to the final step because he can perceive the conclusion. He can only complete a sequence of actions if someone guides him verbally step by step. While others see him as a bright fourteen-year-old based on his apparent strengths in expressive language, in reality he must receive the guidance ordinarily given to a three- to four-year-old child.

Impulsive behavior can become extremely challenging when a direction to inhibit causes the person with impulsive behavior to escalate. She "gets into trouble" for her oppositional behavior and get labeled as "conduct disordered."

A young man functioning in the mild-to-borderline range of intelligence would impulsively attempt to engage in whatever job caught his eye when he arrived at his workshop. Trying to redirect him led to episodes of explosive violence and destruction. However, when a support person met him at the door and asked him to read the workshop rules, he behaved in a cooperative and productive manner because the first rule stated, "Follow directions."

Impulsive actions, because they can occur with little to no warning, often raise significant safety concerns for the individual and her support person.

At an intersection with a visible rule, such as a "walk" and "do not walk" sign, One young lady can display good road safety practices. But, she impulsively crosses the street without looking if no signs are present.

Generative Factors

A single factor or multiple factors can generate impulsive action. Typically, an impulsive behavior will reflect more than one factor. Each factor is summarized below with suggestions for intervention. Typical examples and interventions may overlap.

Four Generative Factors in Impulsive Behavior

- Behavior associated with a young developmental level (spontaneous attraction to an experience)
- Reactive behavior (instinctive avoidance of an experience)
- Behavior due to cognitive disability (subtle thinking disability)
- Functional behavior (a learned coping response).

Behavior Associated with a Young Developmental Level

Individuals with intellectual disabilities are developmentally young. Their thinking is extremely concrete, making it impossible for them to imagine themselves in the abstract, such as in other times or places. ("What might happen later" is an abstract concept.) These individuals function in the here and now, and their comprehension of explanations is extremely limited. They act on the first thought that comes to mind and cannot consider alternative actions. They cannot keep an idea or a goal in mind while also evaluating the pros and cons of various ways to achieve it. Moreover, they may have limited comprehension of the future consequences of their current actions. The following examples demonstrate four types of impulsive behavior in individuals with a young developmental level.

- *An underactivated state:* "Something to do when there is nothing to do." A seven-year-old girl with a severe developmental disability appears to relate to her world on a primary-sensory level. If she is not continuously directed and kept engaged in activities within her repertoire, she regresses to sensory self-stimulation behaviors. This includes rocking firm objects against her groin, or putting any object within reach into her mouth. The more the support person reacts emotionally to these behaviors, the more the girl engages in them. However, she does respond well to a matter-of-fact diversion, such as the support person handing her a favorite toy.

  A nineteen-year-old man with moderate delay always wants to be part of the action. He observes others doing things, and takes any opportunity to do the same. This includes turning on the stove, throwing switches, cutting branches, putting away dirty dishes with clean dishes, moving things from place to place, and poking things into plugs. He requires constant supervision and continuous positive direction to keep from getting into trouble.

- *In sight equals in mind: Primitive communication and an inability to understand "wait."* A woman with profound developmental delay screams for her meal as soon as the serving tray is within sight. Diverting her to an activity at the other end of the living area just prior to mealtime prevents this. (For her, out of sight is out of mind.)

- *Lack of alternative means of communicating desire.* A woman with profound developmental delay would lunge impulsively and grab at the support person's arm from behind, pulling her to the ground. Support staff had to teach her to use touch to communicate. They started by training her to grip the support person's hand firmly in her own.

  After making a list of her typical desires, support staff then approached her with "Show me," and led her to each item on her list until she accepted one (that is, a coat, the bathroom, a kitchen cupboard, and so on). Then, they gave her what she desired. When she "forgot" and grabbed at body parts other than the hand, she was taken to a semi-isolated area (behind a Dutch door) where she could observe, but not contact the support person for a few moments. When her time-out ended, the support person approached again with "Show me," and modeled the hand grasp, repeating the initial training procedure.

- *Attention-seeking behavior.* Some individuals with a developmental disability use physical contact with their support staff in a socially disruptive and impulsive manner. Behaviors include demanding a handshake or hug; tickling or poking; waving a hand within a few inches of someone's face; intrusively following the support person around; or asking repetitive questions. (See Chapter 7: Socially Disruptive, Attention-Seeking Behavior.)

Impulsive actions reflect either the person's lack of understanding that alternative methods for obtaining goals exist, or a lack of skill necessary to achieve goals in any other, more acceptable manner. She may or may not be capable of comprehending an explanation or acquiring skill through training.

 The implication for some is that counseling and training in decision making is an interesting exercise. But, the ability of a person to apply counseling and training at a later time may only occur in the presence of a person who is coaching her to remember to "follow the rule."

Behavior Characteristics

- The behavior is a clearly purposeful attempt to obtain a desired object or outcome.

- The behavior may be an exaggerated attempt to have instantly what cannot be provided until later. Once heard, or in sight, the idea is in mind. Once in mind, it must be acted on immediately.

- The behavior is often associated with hyperactivity and a high level of distractibility.

- Without constant supervision, the person may touch or mouth everything in sight.

- The behavior may be accompanied by a significant degree of perseverative responding. (See Chapter 5: Persistent, Repetitive Behavior: Perseverative Responding.)

Individual Characteristics

- The person lacks the experience base required to exercise good social judgment. This characteristic is very common in individuals who are deaf or severely language impaired.

- The person does not understand the possible consequences of her actions. Typically, she lacks the physical or cognitive ability to communicate in an alternate manner.

- She sees what she needs or wants, and perceives it as an instant need. Imagine a blind person stranded in a field. She will grab desperately at the first person who comes by. Any offer to come back later and help her is irrelevant because she feels desperate. She would have to learn to trust that her needs would be met before she could relax her grasping, impulsive plea for help.

Reactive Behavior

These impulsive actions tend to be a reaction against an immediate event or feeling that the person experiences as aversive. Highly impulsive individuals tend to lack alternative coping skills. Even if the person has communication skills, she seems unable to access them in moments of distress or frustration. And, her impulsivity is typically associated with uncertain or inconsistent expectations. All of these factors contribute to confusion or disorientation, leading to increased levels of stress, anxiety and loss of self-control.

 Explosive and reactive behavior is sometimes more than just a temper tantrum in a person with developmental brain dysfunction.

It is normal to experience emotion when we are thwarted from achieving what we want right now. We experience frustration and perhaps distress and disorientation. The ordinary temper tantrum of a young child may last for a few minutes until she cries herself out or forgets what she was crying about. For many people with developmental brain dysfunction, the associated emotional arousal is more than they can handle.

A large part of what the brain does when we learn is to inhibit inefficient neural pathways and enhance efficient connections. We know what it looks like when the brain does not do a good job of inhibiting unnecessary neural activity because we see this when a person has a seizure. This is called *disinhibition*.

A person with little ability to self-regulate emotion will often find that stress, anxiety and emotional arousal will lead to an emotional or behavioral disinhibition. There is nothing at all "normal" about a person who can cry for hours because she is unable to calm down. The same is true if, the longer she remains upset, the more upset and agitated she becomes, finally losing all control.

■ Reactive, impulsive behavior is not panic behavior. (See Chapter 2: Agitation, Distress and Panic Behaviors.) The reactive behavior described here is a distressed, momentary reaction that may instantly subside when the person obtains the goal object or an acceptable alternative. Following are several examples.

- *Low tolerance for frustration: Behavioral learning.* A woman with profound developmental delay would lunge and grab at support staff to get into the entire box of snacks whenever edible rewards were being offered for completing household chores. Some staff would allow her to reach into a pouch on an apron to take out a box; others would pour the snacks into her hand; and still others would hand snacks to her themselves.

  The varied forms of delivering the rewards led the woman to take matters into her own hands. The solution was to give her a "self-control" cue before giving out the reward. Furthermore, all support staff gave the reward in the same manner and in the same place. After prompting the woman to go to her favorite chair, they would follow up with the verbal and gestural cue, "hands down." Then, the reward would be placed on the table beside the chair for her to pick up.

- *Arousal-disinhibition when told "No," leading to aggression: Emotional learning.* A woman who is developmentally infantile is full of energy, and may try to touch or put in her mouth anything she sees. Telling her "No" or "Don't" causes her to throw the object and attack the person who tries to stop her.

  Physically taking the object from her requires two people at whom she invariably strikes. However, she is so highly distractible that offering her almost any other item causes her to drop the one in her hand to accept the new one. When no alternative object is available, support staff divert her by clapping their hands, causing her to clap her own hands. And, singing a song with her gets her to dance to some other area with a support person.

- *Disorientation leading to agitation and emotional escalation (arousal-disinhibition).* A fifteen-year-old boy with autistic features and intelligence in the borderline range was watching television one day. The movie channel temporarily stopped broadcasting, while other channels continued unchanged.

He became hysterical and fell into an inconsolable, crying rage. However, when the channel began operating again, he instantly calmed down and became responsive.

Another, older man with cerebral palsy would become similarly aroused and disinhibited when his pencil broke while he was writing a letter. He could not calm down until a support person brought him another pencil.

BEHAVIOR CHARACTERISTICS

- Impulsive action is characterized by an exaggerated effort to overcome any obstacle that thwarts the person's intent. This may involve communicating the intent or taking physical action to carry it out. It may also include attempts to get others to obtain the object or perform the action.

- The person may not display exaggerated or excessive behavior until she is denied an object or activity she has requested. To her, the words, "No," "Don't" or "Stop" may function as an instruction to do the action with higher intensity.

- When a support person prevents an impulsive action, the person displays a wide range of agitation and emotional escalation (arousal-disinhibition) behaviors, including aggressive biting, flailing out, screaming, banging her head, biting herself, and so on. These "temper tantrum" behaviors escalate until she is out of control.

- A person displaying impulsive behavior may also exhibit emotionally fragile behavior. (See Chapter 8: Emotionally Fragile and Reactive Behavior.)

INDIVIDUAL CHARACTERISTICS

In the general population, reactions to frustration vary widely. However, they all fall into three categories: coping, acting out, and withdrawing. (See Behavioral Responses to Distress, page 23.)

- While it is normal to experience emotion when frustrated or disoriented, many people with disabilities find the associated emotional arousal more than they can handle. They disinhibit.

- The person may be unable to respond to "Wait!" "No," "Don't" or "Stop." Some individuals with disabilities have no sense of future time so do not understand when told they can do or have something "later." Often, they cannot process the meaning of the word "not" in the phrase "not now!" and only respond to the word "now."

- The person may suffer from an organic brain dysfunction that affects her arousal-disinhibition, that is, a seizure disorder, cerebral palsy or an organic brain syndrome. She might also exhibit an identified metabolic, physiological or psychiatric dysfunction; that is, a mood disorder.

- Whether the problem results from an identified cause or not, people with impulsive behaviors all have a very low threshold for tolerating frustration or any inhibition of their immediate intent.

- Support staff who have to cope constantly with impulsive-reactive behavior patterns may label the person as "demanding, impatient, irritable, moody, jealous, possessive, immature and/or inflexible," implying that her behaviors are purposeful. But, this limited ability to regulate and control one's emotions is a characteristic of brain dysfunction and is often more disabling than the person's level of intellectual dysfunction.

- The impulsive and reactive action typically escalates when a support person attempts to stop it.

- The person is often able to remain focused and oriented on just one thing at a time. She may show impulsive behavior only when confused, disoriented or faced with complexity, Excessive actions occur as soon as she feels lost and out of control. This behavior is often seen in a person with fetal alcohol spectrum disorder (FASD or FAS).

- The person may be greatly affected by fatigue. Behavior that she can normally keep somewhat under control may cycle rapidly out of control when she is tired or ill, and feeling very irritable.

- The person may be emotionally fragile and reactive. She may show the same type of affect that is seen in Post-Traumatic Stress Disorder (PTSD). Each experience of confusion and disorientation has the potential to cause her to relive previous experiences where she has been confused and disoriented. She may react as though this is a traumatic association. This is why the reaction to the current situation can be so excessive and extreme.

- The person may be unable to focus, sustain and organize her attention. Typically, her short-term memory is impaired, and she has significant problems understanding and following sequences, and comprehending time-ordered explanations. She is most likely at her best in places with few distractions.

Behavior Due to Cognitive Disability

Some individuals with developmental disabilities may appear to be quite sophisticated. The person's area of relative strength, such as verbal or mechanical skill, may give the false impression of her ability to function independently in areas that are quite disabled. In other words, to the outside observer her strengths cover up her subtle but disabling areas of thought and function.

When the person is calm and focused, she may seem to understand that there are consequences to her actions. That is, she can repeat the correct rule for appropriate behavior. But, while she is acting impulsively, she may be unable to think about or consider what she knows.

The person's impulsive behavior is not the result of functioning at a young developmental level (as discussed earlier). Her impulsive behavior is not the result of "concrete thinking." In the case of subtle thinking disabilities, the impulsive behavior reflects organic brain dysfunction and disabilities in cognitive processing. The impulsive action is a reflection of an internal state, and the person is coping the best she can.

Subtle thinking disabilities will often include perseverative features. In these cases, once a behavior begins, the person may find it impossible to stop what she has started until she has completed her initial action or thought. Also, behaviors may appear to be under the control of specific environmental triggers. (See Chapter 5: Persistent, Repetitive Behavior: Perseverative Responding.) Following are several examples of behavior due to cognitive disability.

- *Perseveration: all-or-nothing response and lack of independent judgment.* Arriving home after school, one girl will impulsively raid the refrigerator and eat anything, regardless of what she was told before leaving that morning. She might find the ketchup and drink the entire bottle. However, she does not eat impulsively when support staff leave her a prepared snack in the refrigerator.

- *Dependence on explicit, familiar cues and few distractions.* One girl with mild developmental delay was highly impulsive, distractible and dependent because she lived in a foster home with other children with physical disabilities and did not receive the structure and constant guidance she required. Once moved to a home where she was the only child with a disability, she constantly imitated the behavior of her peer siblings and ceased to display impulsivity and high distractibility.

- *Dependence on familiar environment; overwhelmed by unfamiliar sensory input.* In her familiar home environment, one woman can organize her time and activity meaningfully: write letters, do artwork, watch TV or clean the house. In loosely organized social settings, she is captured by her impulsive responses to her immediate sensory environment and displays autistic behavior patterns.

- *Inability to organize attention to or effort at tasks.* Asked to do a page of math, the student works impulsively without attending to the details of each question. Asked to do only one at a time, she focuses and demonstrates her math skill very well.

- *Inability to independently self-regulate, requiring continually imposed external boundaries.* One man with moderate delay would impulsively get off the bus on the way to work each day and hang out, bumming cigarettes from the workmen at various construction sites. If he was directed, just before getting on the bus, to call his support person as soon as he

> While she is acting impulsively, she may be unable to think about or consider what she knows.

arrived at work, he invariably made it to work and stayed all day. Support staff also stipulated that he call before leaving work so he would come directly home. His problem was not an issue of noncompliance; it was an inability to self-regulate without an externally maintained expectation for him to exercise self-control.

- *Inability to resolve conflict.* A twenty-five-year-old man with mild delay would run away from his support person's home whenever he did something that he thought was going to create conflict. His placements were continually breaking down, and he would try living on the street until arrested by the police for assault. Then authorities would place him in yet another setting. But, if he had a probation order that required him to live at his placement setting, he would remain and work through conflict until the probation expired.

BEHAVIOR CHARACTERISTICS

- The impulsive behavior occurs every time the person is in a situation where it can occur. It is "stimulus bound."

- Impulsive actions appear to be triggered by a specific visual or auditory cue. When the impulsive response is triggered by the thought of a goal object, the action cannot be interrupted until the action has been completed. It is as though there is no "off switch."

- Lower-functioning individuals learn some skills, such as movement sequences, without awareness of the goal of their actions. Their established repertoire of behavior demonstrates a stimulus-response, conditioned learning quality; it appears memorized and mechanical. If the person sees an opportunity to use the skills she has learned, she does so spontaneously. There is an all-or-nothing quality to the behavior.

- The person may be impulsive only towards an object or people within arm's reach ("in sight equals in mind").

- Impulsive behavior may be associated with anxiety and uncertainty about what to do in an unfamiliar social setting. For example, when a person is around young children, her anxiety may trigger impulsive and excessive behavior.

- The person's behavior may constantly catch the support person by surprise. The support person who finds it hard to believe that a person can react so strongly to such "small things" is likely to develop resentment toward her. These reactions create a feeling of constant pressure and helplessness because the support person feels that he must constantly be on duty, monitoring the individual for any sign of impulsive behavior.

- A person may demonstrate skilled behavior in specific settings where she has received explicit training. However, individuals with impulsive behavior typically show little ability to generalize a skill from one setting to another.

- The person's behavior may be highly focused toward specific goals. Under these circumstances, she shows very little distractibility or impulsive action. In fact, her behavior is most predictable and self-regulated when she focuses on activities *she has chosen*.

- The person's behavior occurs during unstructured time. At these moments, she becomes momentarily unfocused and/or disoriented, and acts without thinking on the first thing that comes to mind. Unorganized down time may lead to highly impulsive actions.

INDIVIDUAL CHARACTERISTICS

Most people determine their next actions by thinking about how to best achieve their goals. For a person with subtle thinking disabilities, the occurrence of a thought may instantly lead to action without thinking. (Even very intelligent people can display this functional characteristic.) They act on the spur of the moment. This characteristic of being "able" to think, but not thinking before acting can be very confusing to support staff.

Thinking in the Moment

Thinking that is characterized by functioning "in the moment" leads to:

- Poor organization about what to do "later"
- Poor planning to attain goals
- Poor strategy because the person cannot or does not shift approach
- No inhibition and easy distraction
- No multi-step actions because the person cannot plan the "next" step. She completes one thing and then stops until the next instant impulse.

Whatever is most salient to the person in the present moment is what "organizes" her actions. It seems as if she only responds to the oil that rises to the top of the water of her consciousness. The observer sees the person acting in the instant, but sees nothing of the "iceberg" of brain dysfunction that is "beneath the surface."

- The person often has severe deficiencies in her immediate attention span. Unless externally focused, she may be extremely distractible. As a result, she often has great difficulty understanding the sequence of actions in time and organizing her own actions over a period of time. This is what leads to "living in the moment."

- The person tends to function on the basis of "in my sight, on my mind." She tends to be visually oriented to the "here and now" and relates to the world in linear, concrete terms.

- The person may have little experience of continuity between the events of her life, and make almost no connection between previous and present experiences.

- The person may have little ability to plan for or remember more than one or two things at a time. She also has difficulty considering alternative actions.

- The person may not attend to detail unless directed to do so in an unfamiliar setting.

- The person may be able to learn only from moment-by-moment direction since she does not possess the ability to respond constructively to correction.

- The person may tend to display significant anxiety in novel situations and show great reluctance to participate until she is comfortable.

- The person may be unable to sustain momentum at tasks independently. (See Chapter 4: Dependent Behavior.)

Functional Behavior (functional impulsivity)

Impulsive actions are considered functional behavior if the person has acquired them through experience as a means of coping with her disability. Also known as functional impulsivity, these behaviors function to allow the person to control herself, her environment or the actions of others.

- *Coping strategy for a short attention span.* One man with borderline intelligence has a severe, relative deficit in his short-term memory. Whenever an idea occurs to him that he perceives as important, he acts on it immediately to avoid forgetting it. He does this at the cost of leaving any other task undone so he can achieve his new, immediate goal.

- *Coping strategy when threatened by direct confrontation or challenge.* One man with mild developmental delay and autism would change the place where he did his banking whenever someone standing in line at the bank urged him to hurry up. He felt too threatened to return to that location. Another man had fetal alcohol syndrome and mild delay. Whenever he experienced any rejection or confrontation about his performance at his support person's home, he would run away on impulse and turn up later at his parent's home.

- *Coping strategy to control others.* One young woman has temporal lobe epilepsy and a mild-to-borderline intellectual disability. She can be "talked through" almost any confusing situation if she is approached quietly and rationally. But, she will impulsively and violently attack the person helping her if she is confronted, blamed or approached bluntly. (See Chapter 8: Emotionally Fragile and Reactive Behavior.)

- *Coping strategy for feeling angry.* Individuals sometimes express juvenile thinking when they become angry. It takes the form of, "I want this, now!" or "My way, not your way" or "If I don't get my way, I'll make you pay for it." (See Chapter 9: Violent, Aggressive and Destructive Behavior.)

BEHAVIOR CHARACTERISTICS

Every person who displays functional impulsivity has a unique combination of disabilities and learning history.

- Impulsive actions are often a reflection of a subtle thinking disability.

- A very wide discrepancy frequently exists between areas of functioning in which the person can do very well and those in which she is extremely impaired.

- These individuals can frequently say the right thing, but cannot act on what they say.

- Unless focused on a specific goal, these individuals often have great difficulty organizing their time beyond a few minutes. But, they display a significant degree of self-control when given careful guidance.

- Without guidance and structure, the person may demonstrate no conscience and have no internal inhibition at all about impulsive actions. Yet at the same time, when given guidance and structure, the person accepts this and cooperates as directed. It is as though the function of the out-of-control behavior is to cause someone in her world to take control of her behavior for her and tell her exactly what to do. It seems that she "goes out of control in search of control."

- The person may experience a mental health disorder or emotional disturbance when she is not being externally focused. Disturbed thoughts or emotions may overwhelm her during unorganized down time.

Interventions
Impulsive Behavior

For most individuals with challenging, impulsive behavior, two or more factors are typically operating at the same time. Intervention techniques overlap across all generative factors. It is best to use an intervention hierarchy as outlined below. If methods arranged at the beginning of the hierarchy are not successful, gradually include more structure and planning to support and protect the person from her disabling conditions.

PREVENTION
- Observe the person closely, and attempt to identify a pattern in the impulsive behavior. The behavior is often stimulus-bound, or specific to a unique set of circumstances.

- Control the visual, environmental factors that you have identified as typical triggers for impulsive action. In the same way that you would "childproof" a house by putting covers on the electrical outlet, keep out of sight what needs to be kept out of mind.

- Arrange circumstances to prevent the experience of frustration. Try to anticipate and meet the person's needs so that frustration due to avoidable delays will not occur.

Key to Prevention

Use intervention with the environment and people providing support. Remember the six A's: Acknowledge, Anticipate and Avoid problem behavior. Have an Accepting Attitude; Accommodate the person's needs and deficiencies.

- Maintain continuous control of situations where the person tends to be impulsive. Give continuous orienting comments and directions to keep her focused on what she can do. For the lower-functioning person whose impulsive actions are associated with developmental immaturity, provide direct physical guidance. For example, keep one hand on the item you guess she will lunge for.

- Keep down time organized with planned activity to eliminate most of the impulsive demands and associated tantrum behaviors. Keep the person alternatively occupied, diverting and distracting her with aspects of her own pre-existing repertoire. In this way, all down time becomes organized, pre-arranged down time.

- Create a list of activities to engage the person when you and she do not know what else to do. Stay several steps ahead of her, and always have the next activity option organized and ready to offer her.

- Activity options might include:

- *Table play:* "play" dough, bubbles, scissors, ceramics-style "mud," glue, paint, familiar puzzles, connecting blocks, books, musical toys, catalogues to tear, and water to play in.
- *Outside and inside tasks:* feeding ducks, carrying wood, carrying laundry, pushing a lawnmower, riding a bike, going for a walk, swinging on a swing set, climbing on any playground equipment and any helpful chores in a person's repertoire.
- *Passive moments:* sitting in a moving vehicle, sitting passively beside a familiar person touching hands, sitting and listening to others read aloud, listening to music, holding a vibrating object or doing another activity.

■ Ask the person to focus on what is next. Always stay three steps ahead of her by knowing what will be next. Be prepared to keep her continually aware of when she can do what she often impulsively attempts. Have a visual schedule available to show her the next activity.

■ Provide the person with a picture album of alternative things she could do "right now." This gives her a choice. Put one picture on each page that shows someone doing an activity that is immediately available. Combine this with a daily schedule of predictable activities that happen on an hourly basis. Have a picture for each, and use this to divert the person's attention, so she can always focus on what is next.

■ Provide continuous focus for the person who cannot maintain a sense of continuity.

How to "Set Up" a Person for Success

Do not look for unsuccessful independence.

- Look for acceptance of, and successful dependence on, external structures.
- Look for independent functioning within these external structures.

Lower expectations for how much the person will "independently" accomplish.

- At the same time, raise expectations for the person to become successfully dependent in "set up" situations.
- Structure environments to provide the person with successful experiences and slowly build her memorized routines for living.

■ Provide the person with a daily schedule that reminds her of the rules. Coach her to check her list of rules just prior to going into any situation where there is a repetitive display of impulsive behavior.

■ Remind the person to check her list when she does not know what to do. Coach this behavior verbally. Try having a printed note with the comment, "What next?" to cue her to keep focused and oriented.

Reinforce good self-control with a smile chart. Give continuous, positive feedback for following the rules.

■ Some individuals experience agitation and emotional escalation (arousal-disinhibition) when they become disoriented. In addition, they may experience a startle reaction if a support person attempts to physically assist them. In this situation, verbally prompt every mechanical action, step by step, and support the person with an external focus.

 A woman is unable to organize her belongings independently. Support staff name each item and where it goes while she cleans up. (This may also work for each action required to get into a car and put on a seatbelt.)

■ Protect the person from distractions. For those who become behaviorally excessive when in crowded or unfamiliar places, always structure the environment. Pre-correct the impulsive action by having a pre-organized, meaningful role for the person with an identified, physical prop.

 A young man displays impulsive behavior when he must wait for his meal at a monthly pancake breakfast. Support staff always give him a responsibility near the start of mealtime—serving the tea, or putting out the chairs.

■ Sometimes, what the person wants and cannot have is the support person's attention. People with impulsive behaviors are not primarily attention seekers. They are more interested in the immediate; that is, "I want what I see in front of me right now." If that happens to involve someone else getting attention, the person wants attention, too. While support staff tend to call this "jealous" behavior, it is more likely "something to do to fill in the down time" behavior.

 A woman with moderate intellectual and physical disabilities would throw a screaming tantrum during cleanup and care procedures. She continued screaming the entire time she observed others getting their physical care while she had nothing to do but watch. The behavior stopped when support staff put her into her stand-up walker so she could walk her physiotherapy circuit independently during cleanup time. Afterward, support staff rewarded her with one-on-one attention, tea and cookies.

Special Prevention Procedures for a Person Who Is Unusually Sensitive

■ Some individuals are quite reactive to what they see and hear. Confusing images can distract them and exaggerate irritability. Monitor the person's exposure to distressing images from television or movies.

■ Consider the possibility that the person is fatigued, in pain or ill. For example, a naturally good-natured young child may become impulsive and demanding when overtired. The level of irritability may escalate with the child wanting, and grabbing at, everything in sight. Yet, she accepts nothing for more than a few seconds. The more a support person tries to placate the child, the more the child may demand, her voice rising into a whine. The message is, "Please put me to bed. I'm overtired (or sick)." The child will often complain at first, then cry herself to sleep within a few moments.

■ Be sensitive to any exaggerated level of irritability and lower frustration tolerance associated with a physical state. Pay attention to patterns of heightened impulsivity during a certain time of day or comments like, "You can tell by the look on his face when it's going to be a bad day." Anyone who is fatigued or experiencing some other stressful physical state will find it harder than usual to control her temper when required to wait.

■ Organize physical space in the home or work setting so the person can have a place to go for quiet when she needs to rest and calm down. Do not wait for excessive levels of irritability before giving her a rest. Offer a choice if you think she might accept it.

GUIDANCE

Individuals with developmental disabilities who display impulsive behavior require a sensitive reaction from people who support them. This includes extra feedback to guide their behavior, and positive redirection in the form of extra choice or activation to keep them from losing control. Unfortunately, support staff will sometimes feel that a person is a "bad actor" and does not deserve such special treatment. They would rather "teach a lesson" to the person who is reactive and impulsive.

■ Attempt to treat the person "normally." The moment this does not work, lower your expectations for the person to function with competency or self-control. On the other hand, expect her to perform perfectly in response to whatever level of support is required. Rather than approaching the behavior as a problem to control, be prepared to guide her to focus on an acceptable action. Do not attribute to malice what can be explained by disinhibition and stimulus-bound behavior.

■ Some impulsive actions cannot be anticipated or prevented, so be prepared to move very quickly. Have a pre-established, immediate alternative for the person to come back to, such as, "Take my arm." Give positive guidance without causing her to feel thwarted. Consider taking a quiet moment to sit and "veg out" with her, perhaps humming a friendly tune, until she appears settled and ready to move to the next prepared activity with you.

■ Keep unfamiliar information short and sweet. Give only one idea at a time. Individuals who respond cooperatively when they are focused will often respond impulsively to the first part of a verbal communication that is too complex. It is their way of coping with too much information.

■ Deal with the person in the "here and now." Avoid explanations that are lengthy, and give her the cues she needs to get what she wants right now! ("Do this first!" or "Do this now!") This can focus her on the next action and allow her to make the transition without impulsive action.

■ The person may not be able to filter out and organize her own approach to multiple requests. Wait for one action to be completed before asking her to do the next action. This tends to diminish distractibility.

Key to Guidance

Use positive intervention with the person. Use human relations techniques to engage her in other behavior without confronting her about problem behavior. Use suggestion, positive motivation and humor along with the three D's: Displace, Divert and re-Direct the person's behavior.

- Find a way to provide the person with a non-impulsive way of obtaining what she is impulsively seeking.
  - If a person wants the pen you have in your hand and grabs for it, focus her attention on what will work. "Do you want a pen? Get one from the drawer!"

  - When a person who has no money wants an object in a store immediately, say, "Let's go get more money!" This is much better than a "No" that will lead predictably to frustrated agitation.

  - Interrupt by giving the person the option of getting something that she can have and usually is happy to accept. For instance, replace impulsive grabbing at a rack of bus schedules by giving her a schedule you have brought along for this purpose. And, replace lunging at the fruit stand by offering her an apple from your backpack to eat while walking by the fruit stand.

- When a person cannot respond to "No" or "Wait," offer her the choice to reorient her attention. Say, "Yes," "Do," and "Come here!" Distract her from what she was trying to get but cannot have at the moment. Give her the option to do something that she knows and likes to do.

 Following a trip to the grocery store, one man always wants to tear open a box of cookies and start eating them. The support person shows him the car keys and says, "Come and help me open the door."

- Use powerful diversion/distraction techniques to capture the person's attention and displace her focus on the impulsive action you are trying to interrupt.
  - Provide items from the person's repertoire list. (See the prevention section.)
  - Have her focus on what comes next.
  - Try picture sequences or a printed schedule of daily, predictable activities.
  - Provide her the option to do something she is proud of, or offer meaningful, helpful tasks.
  - Use strong, sensory diversions (gum, food, water play, cat, etc.).
  - Interact with a doll or puppet to capture her attention, or do something wrong that she will recognize and impulsively want to correct.
  - Do something silly to evoke a laugh.
  - Use some favorite phrase or song to evoke a repartee, or offer her reassuring physical contact.

■ Some people are very slow to process their immediate experience, so give the person several seconds (up to thirty) to process your visual or verbal suggestion. In addition, start doing something you want to distract her toward. She may stop what she is impulsively doing to involve herself in the activity with you.

■ Some individuals "run by the clock," doing exactly what is on a schedule unless they encounter unstructured time. For this person, displace impulsive action by inventing an intermediate activity.

 A woman has down time from 11:30 a.m. to noon when she leaves her worksite. Support staff created a schedule for her, so she has no opportunity to act on impulses. The schedule includes activities such as:

11:30 a.m. - Clean up sawdust
11:40 a.m. - Stack wood
11:50 a.m. - Wash hands
11:55 a.m. - Get coat and go to front door
12:00 noon - Leave on bus

The support staff could also provide a wait-for-the-bus activity, such as looking at a magazine that she should then deliver to the bus driver when the bus arrives.

TRAINING

Normally, most young children begin to take food and eat as soon as they sit down at the table. We accommodate very young children by feeding them separately or feeding them immediately. As they become old enough to sit with adults, we begin to establish good manners by asking children to wait for a specific cue.

Cue options could include waiting for everyone to be seated, waiting for the mealtime prayer to be over or waiting until the food is offered to them. In this manner, we train and coach children to inhibit their impulsive tendency to take what they want immediately. If they forget, we remind them of the cue and ask them to put the item back and try again. If they refuse, we may send them from the table to convince them that it is an important family rule.

To apply these common sense principles to a person with developmental disabilities, you must establish a ritual. Teach the person what is expected and have her follow a routine consistently. (See Chapter 1: Introduction to Values and Methods.)

■ Coach and motivate self-control until it becomes a reliable response. Then you can reasonably expect the person to exercise self-control in a structured setting that maintains these expectations. Otherwise, there is no way out of the cycle of impulsive action > restriction on the person > frustrated blow up > punishment of the person > escalating blow up, and so on.

■ Specify verbal and physical cues that support staff can use to motivate and reinforce self-control. Establish clear, consistent expectations for how the person can get what she desires. Make her an offer she cannot refuse, saying, "You may have what you want if you wait or ask politely." The offer should always include the exercise of some form of self-control.

■ For a person with a communication disability, try to teach appropriate, alternative communication. When she reaches impulsively, attempt to gain eye contact and make her aware that a request will gain her the goal object. Prompt her to point, sign or vocalize "Please" or "Show me." Help the person make the request, and then give her the goal object. Rehearse the correct action to focus her attention on how to satisfy her desire.

■ The person may not have a communication deficit, but might not know any other way of obtaining the goal object. Constantly provide her with a "right answer" to her unasked question: "When you do not know what to do, come ask!" "When you do not know what to do, go look at your list!"

Key to Training

Use positive intervention with the person. Employ motivation and skill development programs, and teach alternative coping skills over time.

■ Teach the person that asking works! Model the desired behavior for her in a teachable moment. In each of the areas of impulsive behavior, show her that she needs to ask, "Is this okay?" Do not just say, "No." Demonstrate a) how to get permission, b) when she can use that behavior, and c) where she can use that behavior.

 Place a visible stop sign on things you want the person to avoid touching without permission. Put a buzzer by the back door with a picture of her pushing the buzzer. When she starts out the door impulsively, the picture might remind her of the expectation to push the buzzer to ask permission before leaving the house.

■ Teach self-control over impulsive actions by cuing the person to stop and think. Also, cue her to make the right choice.

 For the person who hugs impulsively and throws you off balance, then gets upset at "rejection," start by accepting his need for contact. Then, teach him to stop and think, "How do I get a hug?" Finally, praise him for pausing to think and "finding the right answer all by himself."

■ The person's lack of repertoire may cause impulsive action. To expand the number of alternative actions to which she can be diverted, expose her to a variety of activities with high personal value.

■ If the person does have a large repertoire of alternative behaviors, but does not particularly like doing most of them, the support staff must teach her to enjoy other things.
  - Use the behavioral principle of conditioned secondary reinforcers. By association with primary reinforcers, train her to value stars, tokens, praise and check marks.
  - Use the Premack principle to reinforce a less desired activity by allowing a more desired activity immediately following. (Refer to the extensive behavior modi-

fication literature for skill training procedures; for example, *Behavior Modification: What It Is and How to Do It* by Garry L. Martin and Joseph Pear [Prentice Hall, 2006].) The Premack principle is often referred to as "Grandma's rule": You can have dessert just as soon as you eat your vegetables.

■ The person's failure to focus on expectations may be causing her impulsive actions. People providing support need to ascertain whether they can expect her to establish any degree of self-control. Find out if there are any circumstances in which she uses self-control over her tendency to impulsively react. For instance, can she only maintain self-control in the continuous presence of support staff who are offering all the necessary visual, verbal and physical cues?

■ If control can be maintained during direct supervision, try to bring the behavior under the control of external reinforcement. And, once her repertoire includes some degree of learned self-control, you can gradually expand expectations for self-control while your supervision gradually becomes more remote.

■ Contract with the person that if she controls her impulsive behavior, she will receive a special desired outcome. Use powerful reinforcers to establish her expectation of reward for having self-control over impulsive behavior. Develop a pattern of self-control under some circumstance even if it seems highly artificial. Maintain a high frequency of positive feedback for periods when she exercises self-control.

A man would receive a special treat at each snack or meal when he was calm and self-controlled during the period just before mealtime. If he acted impulsively when the serving tray arrived, he still received his meal or snack, but not the special treat. Offering stars for good behavior and for following the rules works the same way.

Often, the person with disabilities will offer suggestions for what will work to help her exercise self-control. If you explain the need to exercise self-control to someone who reacts against the control of others, she may figure out the best ways for others to remind her to avoid impulsive behavior. One person suggested using a stop sign with a happy face inside. Another suggested using a sign that said, "Come see me when you are ready!" Using suggestions given by that person allows her to inhibit her impulsive actions.

Using discipline or punishment before it is verified that self-control can be demonstrated under any circumstance does not aid the development of self-control. It only causes the impulsive person to resist the support person's exercise of power. In fact, the support person will become a part of what increases the person's frustration, rather than a helper who decreases her frustration.

■ Once external cues establish cooperation, it may be possible to shape and fade them. Support staff can remind the person to self-cue, with a reminder like, "Remember the rule." The rule might be, "Finish this first. That next!"
Coach the person until she develops the habit of exercising self-control in the

presence of explicit prompting. Everyone knows how hard it is to break a habit, so create a good habit of exercising self-control in the presence of a cue.

■ The goal is to make the person more dependent temporarily to ensure her comprehension of, and adherence to, rules for appropriate social behavior. Over-rehearsing self-control is essential. For all impulsive circumstances, we teach one rule: "I must have permission." In other words, the goal is to train the person to ask, "Is it okay?" or "What can I do?" so that the rules govern her behavior whether support staff is present or not. This applies everywhere the person happens to be. Effective teaching may include direct instruction (stating the rules to her), role-play, using visual guides or lists, and group participation.

■ Do not assume that teaching self-control skills will be successful for persons who have a long history of using impulsive actions as a functional means of controlling themselves, their environment or others. Nor should you assume that discipline or punishment procedures will have an effect on functional, impulsive behavior.

■ For some people, the nature of their disability combines with their learning history to render them unable to learn self-control. In this case, assume that you cannot teach the concept, and the person cannot learn from the positive or negative consequences of her behavior. But, you can teach the required movements! Create a series of automatic movements that will allow her to reliably achieve what she has been obtaining impulsively.

 Imagine yourself to be Geppetto, the father of Pinocchio, the fictional marionette. Imagine how you would like to see the impulsive "scene" played out differently. Think about how you can pull all the strings to assist this person to appropriately achieve what she wants. Start by defining the exact movement sequences that she can use to do this. Next, coach and lead the person with disabilities through the desired movements repeatedly. Describe the actions in the here-and-now. Eventually, hand the strings to her and let her pull her own strings. Prompt her to prompt herself. This is training by rote association, leading eventually to development of a functional skill.

CRISIS MANAGEMENT

When prevention, guidance and training techniques repeatedly prove unsuccessful, respond to the chaos with a predictable ritual. In addition, follow these procedures.

- Do not reprimand the person during an impulsive behavior crisis.
- Do not forget to remind her what action she should take to get what she wants.
- Do not try to show her who is in control.
- Do not take the behavior personally.

Key to Crisis Management

Use direct intervention with the problem behavior. Remain calm and always use guidance techniques first. Accommodate the person's special needs and disabilities. Respond to chaotic behavior with a prearranged plan for surviving the crisis while bringing challenging behavior to a stop! Interact positively with the person as soon as she exercises a degree of self-control. Have a plan for how to re-enter normal life.

- Do not begrudge the person your time and effort. She is stuck with her emotional reactivity and needs assistance.

■ Be consistent about how you react to impulsive behavior. Even if this is artificial, come up with some rule about how support staff should react to these behaviors. For any situation where there is repeated conflict with impulsive, demanding behavior have a rule that everyone applies, such as, "Never give in," "Always give in," or whatever rule support staff have found effective in the situation.

 A child might see a candy machine and want to get sweets. Have a rule such as one piece of candy per day, only on Saturday, only after meals, never, or always. You might also keep candy in your pocket, and give the child a piece once shopping is completed and you are leaving the store. Consistency is the key. Inconsistency increases frustration and impulsive, demanding actions. Know the answer to the question about candy "ahead of time," and rehearse it with the child.

■ Some individuals with disabilities will act impulsively every time the triggering situation occurs. They cannot be expected to exercise self-control in a situation where they are exposed to a conditioned stimulus. Unsupervised interactions with the conditioned object should be prevented. Whenever the person is going into a triggering situation, be sure to keep her very busy doing helpful, meaningful tasks.

 For a person who cannot demonstrate self-control under any circumstance, it is necessary to maintain continuous, protective supervision to prevent escalating behavioral crises. This is especially true when the impulsive action is a challenging sexual behavior. (See Chapter 10: Challenging Sexual Behavior.)

■ Safety issues permitting, try to avoid directly engaging with impulsive actions. We do this by providing protective supervision. Think of the person who would follow the directions on a road sign, but would dart into traffic if there were no road sign. Such a person is unable to generalize training in one set of circumstances to a slightly dissimilar circumstance. She tends to be so distractible that she cannot be expected to safely exercise independent judgment. This person is *dependent* on the support staff's external guidance. It is not a question of waiting for support staff to help her. She is *unsure* or *unable* to act safely without a support person's assistance.

■ Help the person to reorient herself by visually cuing or verbally prompting a favored activity. Keep at hand an "emergency backpack" full of high-value sensory stimulus items that evoke a familiar, impulsive action from the person's own repertoire.

Special Cases

With some individuals, having someone interfere with their impulsive action only increases their levels of arousal and agitation. For instance, a person may react to a support staff's attempts to stop her from harming herself. It seems as though she is reacting to an implied criticism or rejection. For this person, a symbolic intervention may work to safely signal her to inhibit self-destructive behavior. But, you must pre-establish the symbol with her.

- • For one man, "Rescue 9-1-1" functioned as a code word. When a support person said it, he accepted it as meaning *danger*, an intervention that did not upset him.

- • One woman was able to respond to a visual stop sign with a smiley face on it. But, a verbal intervention always escalated her behavior.

■ In an unsafe situation where the person has a tendency to bolt or run, always avoid raising your voice. It may escalate her oppositional, impulsive actions. Try speaking slowly and lowering the pitch of your voice.

■ When possible, do not engage in chase behavior. Make your presence known in an unobtrusive manner, but be involved in some innocuous activity so that the person can register your presence and perhaps calm herself down. If this occurs, you may not need to intervene at all.

■ Some individuals react negatively to any attempt by support staff to intervene in their impulsive actions. When nothing will divert the person, it may be necessary to help her to safely complete the impulsive action she is attempting.

On occasions when a person's rapid, impulsive, unpredictable movements could endanger her, a support person may need to remain in continuous physical contact with her. This may require extra one-on-one assistance. A support person may have to walk or run beside the person, and maintain her safety. If she is running, avoid chasing her if possible. Instead, try to help her "go with the flow" of her momentary impulse, then redirect her once she becomes responsive.

■ Create a ritualistic procedure for "re-entering" interactions that are no longer crisis-oriented. This procedure can ease both the individual and the support person back into the normal, daily routine. One easy method is to interact with the person on familiar ground. Use an item from your emergency backpack, objects that can capture her attention on a comforting, sensory level.
  - For a lower-functioning person, these items might include balloons, special books, a piece of fruit or a favorite music recording. For a person who is higher functioning, the backpack might include picture albums, audio recordings, musical instruments, activity lists, copying exercises or letter-writing materials.

Once the support person and the person displaying impulsive behavior are re-engaged on a comfortable level, the crisis management is complete. It is then okay to proceed with prevention, guidance and training techniques.

In This Chapter

7 ■ Socially Disruptive, Attention-Seeking Behavior

■ Definition
■ Generative Factors
   Functions of Attention-Seeking Behavior
   Forms of Attention-Seeking Behavior
   Identifying Attention-Seeking Behavior
■ Special Case: Seeking Attention for Nurturing and Affection

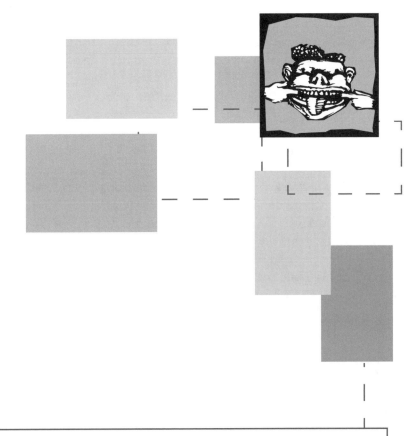

Socially Disruptive, Attention-Seeking Behavior

Definition: All attention-seeking behaviors communicate, "Interact with me!" They are maintained by the social response they receive and become socially disruptive when individuals with intellectual disabilities present the behaviors as their main form of social interaction. For them, socially disruptive, attention-seeking behavior is functional.

Generative Factors

 Functions of Attention-Seeking Behavior

- To gain acknowledgement, recognition or acceptance
- To gain feedback, assistance or information
- To explore issues of control and curiosity
    - a) attention seeking to test limits
    - b) attention seeking to avoid tasks
- To self-activate (something to do when there is nothing else to do).

Functions of Attention-Seeking Behavior

Attention-seeking behavior serves one or more of at least four purposes. All of the following are legitimate functions of attention-seeking behavior.

To gain acknowledgement, recognition or acceptance

"Look at me!"   "I'm feeling left out!"

"Look at what I did!"   "I'm feeling rejected!"

"I'm not getting enough attention."

To gain feedback, assistance or information

"Did I do this right?"   "Is this okay?"

"This is too hard for me."   "You do it for me."

"When are we going?"

To explore issues of control and curiosity

"Can I do this?"   "Do I really have to do this?"

"What are the expectations or limits?"   "What am I allowed to do?"

"Can I distract him and get out of doing it?" "Who is in control here?"

"Can I get a 'rise' out of my support person?"

- *Attention seeking to test limits*

  It is as though the person is exploring the question, "Who is in control?"

  - If the person only uses attention-seeking behavior with someone new, it clearly functions as a way of testing limits.
  - If the person only uses attention-seeking behavior with support staff who are not in a position of authority, it functions as a way of testing limits.

- *Attention seeking to avoid tasks*

  The person's attention-seeking behavior appears to communicate: "If I get you focused on this, then I won't have to do what you've asked me to do."

To self-activate: Something to do when there is nothing else to do

"What do I do now?"   "What do I do next?"

This behavior is a "time filler" while the person waits for support staff to provide external structure, cuing or redirection. These individuals tend to be "sticky," following you with their "clinging" behavior. They usually cannot focus their attention on any task unless there are no distractions. They go "where the action is." Individuals looking for cues about what to do can become excessively clingy or intrusive if they do not get some kind of direction. They may not know what to do unless someone else helps them focus.

Forms of Attention-Seeking Behavior

Individuals with intellectual disabilities may seek attention by using a broad spectrum of behaviors that range from ordinary, social behaviors to maladaptive ones. Their disruptive actions may be the only skills they have for satisfying their needs. Any of these behaviors may be used to communicate one or more of the functions listed above.

Forms of Attention-Seeking Behavior

- • "Ordinary" social behavior
- • Excessive social behavior
- • Misbehavior or "bad behavior"
- • Maladaptive behaviors.

"Ordinary" social behavior. This behavior includes eye contact, smiling, waving, conversation, proximity (entering another's physical space) and physical contact (handshake, touching, hugging). Any of these done repeatedly or inappropriately can be socially disruptive.

Excessive social behavior. This type of behavior falls into two categories: physical and verbal.
- - **Physical**: Grabbing at arms or clothes, tickling, poking, following someone around right underfoot, smiling within six inches of a person's face, repeatedly trying to shake hands or sticking a hand right into someone else's.
- - **Verbal**: Repeatedly asking "What's your name," repeatedly saying, "Hey, come here!" constant jabbering about "nonsense," asking questions incessantly with no interest in the answer and constantly asking questions to which the person knows the answer.

Misbehavior or "bad behavior." Disruptive, misbehavior can also be dangerous to the person and/or those nearby. These behaviors include throwing or dropping items, pulling fire alarms, climbing up drapes, flooding toilets, stripping off clothes, "bumping" others, "stuffing" themselves with food and similar actions.

Maladaptive behaviors. These behaviors include:
- - Helpless, dependent behavior: Whining and complaining
- - Purposeful, minor self-injury: "Suicide" attempts in the nature of "jumping out of the basement window"
- - Avoidance of responsibility: Arguing over trivial issues, which can escalate into swearing, threatening, and violent, aggressive and/or destructive behavior

Issues Covered Elsewhere in this Book

Attention-seeking behavior can involve a number of issues. This chapter addresses those considered functional to the person with disabilities. See other chapters for the following.

- ■ Some individuals engaging in socially disruptive, attention-seeking behaviors can be very impulsive. (See Chapter 6: Impulsive Behavior.)

- ■ Many individuals depend on others to organize their time and focus their attention. (See Chapter 4: Dependent Behavior.)

- ■ Some attention-seeking behaviors are sexual in nature. (See Chapter 10: Challenging Sexual Behavior.)

Identifying Attention-Seeking Behavior

How do we determine if disruptive behavior is really motivated by a desire for attention and not some other motive?

- Attention-seeking behaviors are very difficult to ignore.
  - If the support person is feeling "bugged," it is likely attention seeking.
  - If the support person is feeling worn down and frustrated by the persistence of a behavior, it is likely attention seeking.

- Depending on the support person's reaction, the individual either persists in the behavior or gives it a rest.
  - The more the support person reacts to "feeling bugged" or to her own frustration, the more the attention-seeking behavior is displayed.
  - It seems as though the attention-seeking behavior is "feeding off" (reinforced by) the support person's emotional reactions.

Fortunately, there are ways to respond to the person without responding to the disruptive behavior.

One woman with a profound intellectual disability responded well to "programs" designed to diminish her excessive misbehavior, but she would create a new disruptive behavior every two weeks. Providing new activities for her every time she invented a different misbehavior was reinforcing her excessive actions. Support staff finally resolved the problem by designing a highly organized, but variable sequence of daily activities. She was "kept too busy to misbehave."

Sometimes, a person appears to work just as hard for negative as for positive attention. The person may stop the behavior momentarily when he is corrected, then quickly increase it.

One woman would cycle through a number of maladaptive behaviors over a year's time. These included soiling herself, then only wetting herself and finally scratching her face. The behaviors appeared to be under her own control because she would do them only when she was alone in a room. The more self-injurious she became, the more nursing care she required. But, the more nursing care she received, the deeper she scratched herself. Support staff resolved the problem by handing her a washcloth each time she scratched herself and asking her to go wash her face. Nursing care was done only in the bathroom and only for a clean face. In addition, support staff required her to sit where she could always observe them so she was never in a room by herself.

Some behavior functions to hook the support person into interacting with the individual. Behavior like this can get under a person's skin so effectively that the staff member may actually feel the pull of the emotional hooks. Every time the support person responds to what appears to be one legitimate question or concern, the person comes up with another.

Besides the repetitive nature of the questioning, there is another good clue that the person's excessive questions are attention seeking. The questioner does not have an explosive reaction when denied what he appears to seek. The interaction with the support person satisfies his momentary need.

 A child repeatedly asks, "When are we going to the park?" When told that she cannot go the park because it is raining, she easily accepts the alternative activity of helping make cookies. Companionship and interaction were what she needed.

Some individuals are looking for structure when they employ disruptive, attention-seeking behaviors because these are their only means of marginally satisfying needs. Whenever their time is not structured, they misbehave by "coming at you" for attention. If a person accepts and remains focused on any job the support person assigns, you can assume that he is looking for structure.

 A man who attends a workshop will hang around the support person, standing close and physically touching whenever he can. But, as soon as he is focused on an assignment, he loses interest in physical contact.

When support persons ignore a behavior that has been functional, it will either increase in frequency or become more intense. Both scenarios are difficult to manage, so ignoring is never adequate. Prevention, guidance and training are necessary.

Interventions
Attention Seeking for Acknowledgment, Recognition or Acceptance

Attention-seeking behavior can be managed if the support person identifies the apparent function for the individual, then applies intervention techniques that are *appropriate to the function*.

PREVENTION AND GUIDANCE
A common sense approach to "ordinary," attention-seeking behavior that becomes disruptive is to acknowledge the person the first time he seeks social contact. Give him the recognition he seeks and then redirect him to another structured activity.

A high need for structure. Some people need more attention and/or structure than others. When this person's "nurture cup" is one drop below full, it feels empty. He may be unable to feel a strong sense of self or identity unless he is in close contact with others.

■ Both the individual and the support

Key to Prevention

Use intervention with the environment and people providing support. Remember the six A's: Acknowledge, Anticipate and Avoid problem behavior. Have an Accepting Attitude; Accommodate the person's needs and deficiencies.

person will find it helpful to schedule sufficient opportunities to give the person regular recognition and attention. This way the person avoids struggling to get his needs met, and the support person avoids struggling with disruptive behavior.

- Set aside time when the person has permission to express acknowledgement, recognition and acceptance-based attention seeking. For example, have a "what's up with Ben" (using the person's name) period at regular intervals throughout the day or the week.
- Schedule appointments to "fill up the person's cup," making sure they are on terms the support person can meet consistently. For example, have a "high five" time before lunch for reviewing the positive events of the morning.
- Increase recognition by increasing non-contingent, positive contacts with the person. For example, use his favorite phrase, hand gesture or nickname as often as possible.
- Catch him "being good" or neutral–especially when he does not expect it–and reward him with attention.

Repetitive questioning. For the person who asks repetitive questions as a means of gaining recognition, it is not enough to explain better or to correct the behavior. Support persons must be consistent and intentional about how they give the person recognition.

- A woman with a mild intellectual disability understood that when she said, "I am going to the store," support staff would say, "That's nice." She also discovered that when she asked, "Am I going to the store?" support staff would stop what they were doing to find out or explain what was going on. They resolved the problem by answering the question one time and then saying, "Did I answer that?" followed by, "What did I say?" and "The subject is closed!" The woman was then asked to participate in helping out with a meaningful activity.

- One man would say, "Hey, come here!" to any new support person and then begin to tell the "story of his life." Typically, the well-meaning support person would reinforce his behavior by saying, "That's nice." Or, she would reinforce it by telling him, "That's not the right way to call someone." They resolved the problem by saying, "Sit down, and I'll come see you as soon as I'm free."

Negative misbehavior. For the person who seeks recognition with "negative" misbehavior, try to make a non-issue of the behavior. Build the person's image of himself as someone who gains recognition by cooperating and being a do-gooder! Do this through organized periods of exercise, sports, work, chores and other activities.

One woman would grab at other residents only when a support person was looking her way. Any reprimand escalated the activity because she gained recognition. Support staff resolved the problem by giving her a favorite object to hold in her hand (a stuffed toy) and providing her with special recognition for having the toy in her hand. They also scheduled opportunities for her to "shadow" a support person and participate in frequent, structured activity.

Negative self-talk. Some individuals seek social contact with maladaptive behaviors such as negative self-talk. They might make comments about being a bad person, going crazy, being unlucky or unworthy of what others have, or committing suicide. In these cases, support staff should acknowledge the person but not over-attend to the content of his talk.

Key to Guidance

Use positive intervention with the person. Use human relations techniques to engage him in other behavior without confronting him about problem behavior. Use suggestion, positive motivation and humor along with the three D's: Displace, Divert and re-Direct the person's behavior.

■ Interrupt "suicidal," "pity me" and "I'm a bad person" talk with reality, and replace it with appropriate content for social communication. Offer to talk about reality–things that are visual, concrete and immediate such as clothes, food, the weather and other real world subjects. Respond to negative self-talk as a request for nurturing, recognition and acknowledgement.

Self-injurious behavior. Be aware that there is always a possibility that self-injurious behavior (SIB) is the person's only means of getting acknowledgement or recognition. Some individuals with profound intellectual disabilities may not know any other way of getting a support person's attention. Always delay your response to SIB. Wait for a few seconds, and respond when the person is not engaging in self-injury.

TRAINING

Teach better communication. It may be that few people spend time with the person unless he first approaches support staff with excessive behavior. Teach him an alternate, acceptable method of communicating his need for acknowledgement.

• A non-verbal woman with a moderate intellectual disability and multiple physical disabilities would pinch support staff while they were doing care tasks with her. The behavior ceased after teaching her over a period of years to use a picture communication system. She showed support staff that she had quite a lot to say and pinching had been her only means of communicating this.

• Another person who was engaged in this behavior was prompted to take a support person's hand and show him what she desired. (See Chapter 6: Impulsive Behavior.)

Key to Training

Use positive intervention with the person. Employ motivation and skill development programs, and teach alternative coping skills over time.

Teach self-control. Train the person to control attention-seeking behaviors. It may be necessary to teach the person how to wait for acknowledgement. Give him recognition and rewards, such as tokens, following any period when he displays no socially disruptive behavior. As soon as he collects a few tokens, allow him to trade them for a time of special one-on-one attention. (See Chapter 9: Violent, Aggressive and Destructive Behavior.)

When out in public with a support person, one woman would walk up to any stranger and begin to "tell her life story." The support person trained her to control the behavior by reminding her just before going into a store, "Remember the rule?" The woman would answer, "Don't talk to strangers." Each time she was successful in controlling her acknowledgement-seeking behavior, she would have tea alone with the support person as a special reward at the end of the outing.

Use positive modeling. Allow the person to observe a support person paying attention to another person involved in a positive action. Then, invite him to participate.

 One man repeatedly put too much food in his mouth. When reprimanded, he would stop for a moment but stuff his mouth even more as soon as the support person was not looking. To resolve this, the support person would turn to a nearby person who was eating properly and praise him for taking small bites. Then, she would tell him how nice it looked to see him eating with such good manners. The man got the message and began taking smaller bites. The support person made sure to praise him as soon as he did.

Expand the person's repertoire. Expose the person with a limited repertoire to a more expansive one. Create options for diverting his attention to alternative activities with support staff. For example, sensory activities such as rubbing hand lotion, blowing bubbles or playing with balloons are appropriate options for a very low-functioning person.

Build on existing strengths. Focus on skills with the person who has a larger repertoire. Build his self-confidence and competence in areas of personal competence.

Structure learning. Avoid the tendency to counsel the person during a crisis. Instead, train him to indicate, "I need help" more appropriately. Practice this skill on a structured, non-crisis basis.

CRISIS MANAGEMENT

- Do not try to correct the person's disruptive behavior. Pay as little attention as possible to the negative behavior, while attempting to divert him by asking him to do a meaningful, helpful activity. Once that is accomplished, give him acknowledgment and approval.

- Be as neutral as is humanly possible. Do not show that you are angry, disgusted, disappointed, or otherwise upset.

- It may be helpful to imagine yourself wearing "invisible glasses" about this disruptive behavior. Look at the person and respond to his need for recognition but do not interact with his disruptive behavior.

Maladaptive, negative self-talk. Do not get caught up in the person's crisis talk!

- Use a stoic, structured response aimed at reducing the person's arousal. Remain as unemotional and non-reactive as a computer! (For recommendations, see the Crisis Management section of Chapter 9: Violent, Aggressive and Destructive Behavior, and the section titled Essential Approaches to Emotionally Distressed Behavior in Chapter 1: Introduction to Values and Methods.)

- Focus on the positive. Coach the person and model ways he can gain positive attention from others.

- Use reality therapy. Do not pay attention to the negative self-talk. Help the person focus on "what you can do about it" and "what you are doing to make it better."

Self-injurious behavior. Remember that SIB is frequently an accidentally (adventitiously) learned request for physical contact. Therefore, always try to delay your reaction. The minute the person has quit injuring himself, make contact and attempt to meet his needs.

Function: To Gain Feedback, Assistance or Information

INDIVIDUAL CHARACTERISTICS

- The person may be seeking attention because he is unable to focus his attention and/or stay on task. He might also have memory problems or be highly distractible.

- The person may have little ability to occupy his time. He may be unable to function outside of a predictable routine or without one-on-one guidance because he depends on specific prompts and cues.

- The person may have much time-related anxiety about what activities come next.

- The person uses expressive language that often exceeds his language comprehension.

PREVENTION

- Reduce surrounding distractions, and ensure that the person is paying close attention to the support person before giving him information.

- Use routines and rituals for communicating information. Also use concrete, visual references such as calendars.

GUIDANCE

Common sense suggests giving the person the feedback he requests, helping him or answering his question. However, if he asks the same question repetitively, his behavior can become socially disruptive.

- Repetitive questioning typically occurs during down time. Answer the person's question one time, and then provide a "sit and wait" activity to occupy him.

- One young man would come in the door from school and ask his support person a barrage of questions about mail he was expecting. Each answer led to another question. Providing him with a newspaper to look at and putting on his favorite music gave him something better to do.

- A man with a mild intellectual disability and physical disabilities would come in the door and demand to know the plan for the evening. He became much less intrusive when support staff set up a "meet and greet" ritual. It included joining a support person for tea, cookies and a talk about the evening schedule.

- Some individuals respond well when someone advises them prior to each activity what will happen immediately afterward, such as, "Next, we're going to eat a snack / return home / get dressed." Always let the person know what is coming up next!

- Repetitive questioning typically occurs with a very anxious person. Answer the person's question one time. Then when he asks again, respond with, "Did I answer that already?" "Do you know the answer to that question?" "Good for you! You answered it all by yourself."

- Repetitive questioning generally occurs with a person who is distractible and forgetful. Answer the person's question one time, but also write the answer down for him if he can read. If he cannot read, make an audio recording for him. The next time he asks the same question, remind him where he can find the answer by saying, "Look in your book," or "Listen to your CD."

TRAINING

The person may be unaware of personal space, those invisible social boundaries that exist around every one of us. Teach this person about the "bubble" that people have around them. But also, keep in mind that the idea that personal space is about an "arm's length" may be too abstract for some people. Demonstrating it with a hula-hoop may be much more effective.

Function: To Explore Issues of Control and Curiosity

PREVENTION AND GUIDANCE

Limit seeking. Some people work hard to discover expectations or find out who is in charge. In an uncertain situation, they may be deliberately disruptive to find out, "what the rules are around here." Common sense suggests setting out expectations and rules ahead of time, making it unnecessary for them to search for the limits.

- Have printed expectations posted for everyone to see, and always inform the person with a tendency to test for limits who is in charge. Also, every support person should have the authority to maintain expectations, and the ability to do so with consistency and fairness.

- Many socially disruptive individuals also have difficulty organizing their time and actions. This is an additional reason to provide clear, consistent limits and social expectations. Keep their time structured and directed, using lists and schedules for organizing activity. Always have the next thing ready to do.

Limit testing. Some individuals test to see if they can get a rise out of a support person. For verbal attention-seeking behavior, it may help to pretend you are wearing a hearing aid that turns off when any person engages in the disruptive behavior. And, have a rule for responding to limit testing that becomes repetitive.

- A woman with a profound intellectual disability would come up close to a support person and grin right in her face. Saying "Stop that!" or pushing her away led to extreme escalation of this and other intrusive behaviors. When the support staff were able to "act blind" for a moment, she would cease. Once staff began engaging her in a stimulating activity schedule, these behaviors were greatly reduced.

- One man would "nitpick" with support staff about the rules of his group home. When a support person negotiated with him, his episodes of nitpicking escalated to twenty per day. Staff resolved the problem by asking him to write down any concerns and bring them up at 6:30 p.m. That after-supper appointment provided him a chance to present all his concerns.

- One person who engaged in socially disruptive, attention-seeking behavior required positive redirection. When prompting him to respond to positive direction, support staff learned not to expect an immediate response. They used the "dit, dit, dit" method, and gave him three opportunities to respond.

The Dit-Dit-Dit Method

- The first positive direction allows the support person to gain the individual's attention.
- The second provides him with a reminder and lets the direction sink in.
- The third is for good will. It allows the individual time to save face and get ready to respond.

■ Giving three positive directions accepts the person's right to test the support person. It also establishes the support person as one who knows the limits, is able to communicate the expectations, and is willing to persist and pass the test.
  - If the function of a person's behavior is to seek attention, this method provides the attention in a directed manner. Remembering to give three positive directions limits support staff's tendency to say, "Stop that!"–a response that pays attention to the negative behavior.

■ What about a fourth dit? A person's disruptive behavior may gain momentum and persist beyond three prompts to positively respond. He is likely to be either "stuck" in perseveration and needing more help to shift focus, or trying to control a situation with disruptive actions. A greater degree of structured intervention may be required.

Task avoidance. Task-avoiding, attention-seeking behaviors can prove very functional for a person who experiences anxiety.

■ Acknowledge the possibility that the person feels threatened by the task, and work to reduce his anxiety.
  - Make the task relevant.
  - Break the task down into simpler components while increasing positive feedback.

- Expect less performance, while rewarding effort at the task, not accuracy.

■ Recognize that the person may have a very short attention span and high distractibility. First, focus him briefly back to task (up to thirty seconds with assistance). Then focus only on the positive, task-related behavior while giving him more personal attention.

TRAINING

There are many ways to motivate a person to exercise self-control over his own "control seeking" behavior. Some key elements are clear expectations for behavior; understanding the factors that motivate a particular individual; and using those factors to create rewards. (See more on motivating a person to use self-control in Chapter 9: Violent, Aggressive and Destructive Behavior.)

■ Have support staff reinforce self-control. Provide regular praise and approval for task completion, including additional recognition as often as possible with "Thank you" or "I like the way you did that all by yourself!"

■ Ask the person to self-monitor. Being the one to give the reward can be very motivating. Provide checks, stickers, stars, or other rewards that the person can earn, but also help to administer them for time spent on task or following the rules.

■ Enlist other people to help monitor and motivate him. For example, make arrangements with the driver of public transportation to give him a star or token for "acting like an adult" on the bus.

 Avoid unhelpful responses to attention-seeking behavior. For instance, taking away something the person values because of his loss of self-control can lead to an attention-seeking power struggle that no one wins. Address the behavior as follows:
- Do not react immediately.
- Do not give an emotional response.
- Do not reprimand, or use the words "no" or "stop that."
- Do not give warnings or struggle with the person.
- Do not let the person see a support person repair any of the damage he has done.
- Do not be inconsistent.

CRISIS MANAGEMENT

Minor testing behavior. Respond minimally to minor testing behavior, such as flicking a light switch.

■ Do not exactly ignore it. Instead, act like you are wearing invisible glasses, so you can be indifferent to the behavior while you direct him to do a helpful, meaningful chore or activity. (This is a good approach to take during non-agitated episodes of "testing" behavior. It is an essential approach when the person is in an agitated state.)

■ Minimize any demanding, time-pressured, or task-oriented aspect of your positive directions. Accept participation at any level.

Excessive behavior, such as grabbing and poking. Try to "see it coming," and avoid the inappropriate contact.

■ Keep the person at arm's length. If you are unable to avoid the inappropriate contact, try to outlast him by waiting it out and denying the reaction he is seeking.

One man would wave, call a support person's name and reach out. If close enough, he would grab the person's arm. Any reprimand would increase the strength of his grip. (It was as though he was thinking, "Aha, I have a live one here!") This became excessive and limited his involvement in the community. The safest way for him to go out in public was to have someone warn others to remain out of reach and limit themselves to verbal interaction with him.

■ If you cannot get away in time, you may still be able to salvage something from the negative interaction.
  - Try to turn away and "go stone cold." Or, simply delay your reaction.
  - Then, after counting to ten, maintain an indifferent manner and turn inappropriate contact into a training exercise. For example, you might say, "Hold me like this!" or "Shake hands like this!" Or, direct the person to an unrelated activity that occupies his hands (for example, something to hold and eat).

Function: To Self-Activate

INDIVIDUAL CHARACTERISTICS

■ The person has limited ability to learn sequential skills. He has a short attention span and may be highly distractible, so he tends to learn only single movements.

■ The person has little ability to organize his time and activities.

■ The person has little sense of goal orientation. He does not see the purpose of tasks in which support staff ask him to participate.

■ The person does not learn from his mistakes or correction.

■ The person requires direction from another person to know what to do next.

BEHAVIOR CHARACTERISTICS

■ The person tends to display a variety of socially disruptive behaviors that have been adventitiously (or accidentally) reinforced. This occurs when his behavior generates an immediate response. He perceives an instantaneous connection between his most recent action and the support person's response.

■ Interacting with the socially disruptive behavior is also reinforcing to the support person. Why? Because any easily distracted person who is prompt dependent will stop what he is doing momentarily when anyone interacts with him. Any interaction gives the support person temporary relief from the unwanted behavior.

■ Often, an accidental opportunity will turn a simple behavior into a powerfully motivated, attention-seeking behavior. This is particularly true with prompt-dependent individuals whose behavior is actually "structure seeking."

A woman with a profound intellectual disability would pull lightly at the hair of other residents in her group home. Assuming that she needed to learn the limits, support staff told her, "Hands down." This escalated the behavior. When the support person would act "blind" to the behavior and keep the woman's time more occupied, the hair pulling diminished.

- Sometimes, seeking attention is the only game in town! The person resorts to these behaviors to avoid boredom.

An elderly man with a mild intellectual disability often displayed attention-getting "trouble" chewing his food, allowing food to drop out of his mouth. Support staff would tell him to eat properly or ask him, "Why can't you learn to chew your food properly?" He was able to eat properly but used this as a way of gaining extra attention during mealtimes. They resolved the problem by giving him a small spoon and smaller portions of food at a time. In addition, they began paying attention to another person any time he took too much food. The minute he took small bites, attention was refocused on him, and he was acknowledged for "good chewing."

PREVENTION

- Give the interaction and direction that the person seeks. The key is to do this non-contingent upon disruptive behaviors. Support staff must make no direct response to any of the socially disruptive, attention-seeking behaviors to avoid reinforcing them. For example, avoid the instinctive response to say, "Stop," or in any way interact directly during the seconds that the person engages in any of the disruptive behaviors.

- Imagine that you are wearing invisible glasses so that you can see the person, but do not see or hear any of the inappropriate behaviors.

- Wait for a momentary pause (about ten seconds) in the person's behavioral display, and then interact immediately with him by giving a direction, such as "Touch your nose," "Come with me," "Hold this for me," "Have a drink of water," "Let's go wash your face," "Let's go brush your hair," or other directives.

- Get involved in something else the person may enjoy doing and then invite him to join you, (for example, "Let's go pack your bag for the fishing trip" or "Let's go get out the bingo board").

GUIDANCE

- To prevent being forced to interact with socially disruptive behavior, it may help to keep the individual by the support person's side as a "shadow." Constantly direct his attention and actions. If that is not possible, at least keep him in sight. Watch for a period of neutral behavior, and give him positive direction.

■ Make sure there is other meaningful activity for the attention-seeking person to do besides interacting with a support person on a one-to-one basis. Have a repertoire of activities available to occupy him. Keep a cupboard full of materials that can be used to direct his actions. For instance, in community settings, have an emergency pack full of materials and activities that can be handed to him as positive diversions.

TRAINING

■ A person with lots of energy may be eager to do an activity but unable to organize his time. Socially disruptive, attention-seeking behavior is really structure-seeking behavior that asks the support person, "What's next?"

■ Create a long list of alternative activities that the person is able to perform. Every disruptive approach to someone earns him a job! Draw his attention to a picture list or schedule of activities.

■ Divert the person to a behavior or task that you can give attention for doing! If none exist, create some. Train him to do those things. Pay attention to any appropriate behavior. (This is discussed in detail in Chapter 6: Impulsive Behavior and Chapter 4: Dependent Behavior.)

■ Train the person to wait for a support person to initiate interaction. Reinforce passive behavior by giving a positive interaction, a change in environment, or an activity in response to any period of passive, non-disruptive behavior. For some individuals, this means interacting every fifteen to twenty seconds. For others, giving direction every fifteen minutes by handing them various self-activation objects will be sufficient.

CRISIS MANAGEMENT

Some structure-seeking individuals can become extremely excessive and demanding. This behavior may require extra measures.

A "time-out" is not recommended for the person who cannot organize his time. The attention given to him in the process of directing him to take time out may reinforce the very behavior the support person wishes to extinguish. For the same reason, asking a person to repair damage or apologize may backfire when applied to one who uses attention-seeking behavior.

Key to Crisis Management

Use direct intervention with the problem behavior. Remain calm and always use guidance techniques first. Accommodate the person's special needs and disabilities. Respond to chaotic behavior with a prearranged plan for surviving the crisis while bringing challenging behavior to a stop! Interact positively with the person as soon as she exercises a degree of self-control. Have a plan for how to re-enter normal life.

■ Any procedure such as overcorrection can also backfire with a structure-seeking, attention-seeking individual. Instead of taking the structure-seeking person to a time-out, remove other people from the vicinity. In addition, lead the structure-seeking person to some other location while any damage is being repaired or those who have become upset are being consoled. With structure-seeking, attention-seeking behavior, less is more!

■ Do not correct the disruptive person. Instead, redirect him. Engage him in an activity that the two of you can do together. Focus on minimally verbal interactions to calm him down. For example, get a broom and hand him a dustpan. Get out the silverware tray and begin setting the table. Hand him the plates that need to be put on the table.

Special Case: Seeking Attention for Nurturing and Affection

Everyone needs to share nurturing and affection with significant persons because it sustains growth, development and involvement. Therefore, seeking physical contact and nurturing is an ordinary form of attention-seeking behavior. And, while any physical display of nurturing and affection is open to interpretation by others, it is unreasonable and contradictory to manage or program that affectionate interchange.

For the person with a disability in a residential placement, this is his home. And, too often, support staff comprise his only family. Therefore, the questions for any placement setting are, "How do we allow nurturing and affection to be offered to residents while also protecting them and support staff from risk?" and "How do we respond to a resident's display of affection toward support staff?" These questions often arise with individuals who present attention-seeking, challenging behaviors. Unfortunately, inconsistent support staff responses to a person's spontaneous display of affection will often sustain inappropriate physical contact.

Consistent interventions require that support staff have agency support, and feel personally comfortable with sharing spontaneous nurturing and affectionate contact with residents. However, planned interventions do not reduce the requirement that support staff exercise good judgment at all times. The following are proposed to assist agencies and support staff in developing a reasonable and consistent approach to these issues:

- A definition of safe, appropriate and acceptable expressions for nurturing and affection.
- Guidelines for the giving and receiving of affectionate contacts.

Proposed Definition
In a residential setting, the support staff's expressions of empathy, caring and acceptance provide safe, appropriate and acceptable nurturing and affection for individuals. These interactions cover a wide range of behaviors, including:

- Physically comforting individuals while doing care procedures
- Throughout the course of the day, brief physical contacts, such as a brief hug or kiss on the cheek while tucking in at night; a pat on the back; a shoulder rub; a handshake; and vigorous body contact in the context of physical activities such as floor hockey, wrestling, soccer and other sports
- A wide range of encouraging verbal comments, and the use of vocal inflection and facial/gestural expressions.

Proposed Guidelines

Recommendations for support staff's giving nurture and affection, and responding to expressions of nurturing and affection.

Guidelines for support staff offering nurturing and affection to individuals

Actions should be:

- Natural and spontaneous in the manner of one loving family member to another
- Considerate of the individual's age and physical maturity, but appropriate to his or her functional level and emotional needs
- Relevant to each situation, while regarding each person's specific requirements
- Considerate of individual differences between support staff. (In any family, not everyone likes to spontaneously give affection in the same manner.)

Guidelines for responding to an individual's expression of affection toward support staff

- Support staff should acknowledge an individual's desire to express affection.
- The person receiving services should be given guidance to make his response in a form that is most acceptable in a community environment. (For example, some mature individuals will offer a full-frontal, standing hug. One alternative could be to provide nurturing physical contact by sitting beside him with an arm around his shoulder.)

Every agency and its support staff should reach their own consensus about issues of affection when programming a response to this type of attention-seeking behavior.

In This Chapter

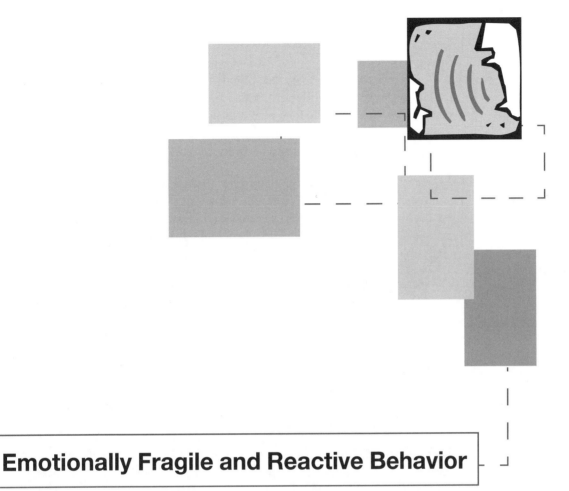

Emotionally Fragile and Reactive Behavior

Definition: Extreme vulnerability to emotional distress, with an inability to tolerate experiences of frustration, failure, non-acceptance or lack of control.

While this person is emotionally reacting to her experiences, she may be quite unresponsive to the support person's common sense attempts to offer assistance. Traditional behavior modification techniques are usually ineffective. Correcting, instructing, ignoring or using consequences all typically escalate the disruptive behavior rather than reducing it. In trying to manage or control the emotionally fragile person's behavior, the support person often becomes trapped in a spiral of increasingly negative interactions.

The person is more functionally disabled by her emotional reactions than by her intellectual deficits. Her *excessive reactivity* to the experience of confusion, uncertainty, inability to meet self-expectations, or perceived rejection is what causes such concern.

Difficult Concepts and Situations

The nature of her subtle thinking disabilities sets up the emotionally fragile and reactive person to experience a great deal of frustration with her world and herself. The following concepts and situations typically present a difficulty for this person.

- *Difficulty with choice.* One man who lived with all women support staff enjoyed a new male volunteer for two visits then violently attacked him on the third. On the first visit, the volunteer had asked the man if he wanted to go bowling or to a movie. On the second visit, he had asked him if he wanted to go for a walk or out fishing. On the third visit, he simply said, "What do you want to do tonight?" He punched the volunteer in the face. This problem disappeared when the volunteer was careful to ask only closed-ended questions that require a yes or no answer or a choice between two options.

- *Difficulty with the concept of time.* One man sent away for a record club membership on Monday. When the records did not appear in his mailbox on Tuesday, he became hysterically upset and trashed his bedroom. The support person could not get him to calm down or understand that some things take time.

- *Difficulty with the concept of rules.* A man with disabilities was late getting out the door to go to work. When he realized this, he returned to his room weeping, and remained there until late afternoon when he would have normally returned from work.

- *Difficulty with rejection.* One woman was invited to a cousin's home for a holiday. The cousin had to cancel due to illness in the family. The woman with disabilities ran screaming to her room, destroyed everything in it, and would not come out for twenty-four hours.

- *Difficulty due to misinterpretation of, and overreaction to, social communication.* A student's math teacher was showing his good work to another teacher. The student punched the math teacher. He later said it was because "they were talking about me behind my back." In another instance, a support person reminded a woman with disabilities to do her hair when she had already brushed it. Her response was to run away from home for several hours.

Common Sources of Emotional Distress

There are many circumstances that can cause a person to experience emotional stress and distress. For the most part, they fit into a few general categories. (See section titled Sources of Emotional Distress in Chapter 1: Introduction to Values and Methods.)

Unknown or unfamiliar social expectations. Any action that another person demands in a situation where expectations are unknown or unfamiliar will set the person up for fear of criticism.

Unrealistic or unachievable social expectations. Time pressure, quality pressure or quantity pressure may create demands that are unachievable, or beyond the person's current level of competence. The person is set up to feel incompetent and inadequate.

Unrealistic personal expectations. Self-imposed, unrealistic time limits or quantity/quality standards sets the person up for constant self-criticism.

Common Responses to Emotional Distress

In Chapter 1, normal responses to distress circumstances are outlined in the table titled Behavioral Responses to Distress. In this chapter, we address why some individuals respond to emotional distress with *extreme* acting out or withdrawal.

- When faced with the inability to meet expectations that are unknown, unfamiliar, unrealistic or unachievable, the person may respond with feelings of frustration, anxiety, confusion or dependency.

- If the person thinks her inability is her fault, she may feel embarrassed, ashamed or very inhibited.

- If the person thinks her inability to perform is someone else's fault, she will likely be angry, disappointed or demoralized.

 Working with emotionally fragile individuals without acknowledging their disabilities continuously places them in extreme distress situations. It forces them to face demands and expectations that are beyond their coping abilities.

When inadequate responses to distress are observed, the support person's task is to teach the person with disabilities alternative coping responses. It is important to recognize that coping behaviors are often difficult to practice, even for people with no disabilities. Support staff must work out protocols to assist the emotionally fragile and reactive person to "survive" her feelings of being overwhelmed. At the same time, it is necessary to *assist those supporting her* to survive and recover from her explosive outbursts.

Generative Factors

Emotionally fragile and/or reactive behavior is generated by two main factors: *personality* and *cognitive characteristics.*

Personality Factors

When people feel confused, criticized or rejected it is normal at a certain stage of development to try to "save face" and give themselves a feeling that they are okay, and in control of a distressing situation. Normal children eventually acquire more appropriate means of expressing their emotions and coping with their frustrations.

The following are maladaptive patterns that assist persons who have not been able to develop more adequate coping responses.

Self-blame: "I can never do anything right."

Constant, unresolved conflict: "Nothing is ever right for me."

Self-shame/abject humility: "I'm sorry, I'm sorry." Burying her head in her shoulder; pleading; promising; guilt-laden apologies

Hypochondria and/or apparent malingering: "There's something terribly wrong with me."

Oppositional debating: nit-picking and looking for "legalities" and loopholes in every comment

Extreme competitiveness: "I can never do anything wrong." "You can never do anything right."
Righteous indignation: "It's all about me. It's always all about me."
Victim response: hysterical crying tantrums; self-injurious behavior; "No one listens, no one cares about me. I'm mortally wounded."
Negative bragging: "Look how bad I am. Listen to the story about how I hurt someone. I could do it again!"
Emotional quicksand: huffing; cursing threatening suicide; "I don't care" response
Emotional minefield: "I have nothing else to lose" response.

BEHAVIOR CHARACTERISTICS

The person is unable to tolerate frustration, failure, lack of control or loss of control, lack of choice, or rejection.

■ The person is highly vulnerable to stress and distress, and is highly sensitive to emotional stimuli. As a result, she has poor regulation of her emotional states. It does not take much to set her off, and she experiences a slow return to her baseline level of emotional arousal (a poor recovery time) after becoming over-aroused.

■ She has an extremely limited ability to inhibit her behavior related to strong emotions, either positive or negative. Her actions are *mood dependent* rather than goal dependent. She acts in the emotional moment, finding it extremely difficult to refocus her attention *in any way* in the presence of strong emotion.

INDIVIDUAL CHARACTERISTICS

■ The person is extremely emotionally sensitive, and very dependent on her mood. The emotional experience of the moment seems to be everything to her.

■ The person often performs well when asked to help out, or is able to perform in an area of strength. However, she becomes upset and disruptive when she finds herself faced with demands for performance in a situation that taxes her intellectual or physical capabilities.

■ The person is unable to tolerate the feeling of not being able to perform, or not being able to control a situation. She is often hypersensitive to any attempt by others to control her, and reacts immediately and intensely. She tends to be a perfectionist in her expectations for herself and for others.

■ The person will rarely accept or acknowledge her own disabling condition.

■ The person easily picks up on the support person's mood, detects even an insinuation of dissatisfaction with her, and is sensitive to even the smallest emotional slight.

 Some individuals become "stuck in emotion." Unable to attenuate or regulate their emotional responses, they become "captured" by emotional perseveration and disinhibition. If the person with this behavior begins to roughhouse, it turns into a "rumble." If she becomes distressed, she quickly slips into deep depression. We are all sensitive to the emotions expressed by others. Some people will cry when someone else is crying or when they hear emotionally evocative music. The person who becomes stuck in emotion is *extremely vulnerable* in this way. Her "emotional radar" spots every feeling and absorbs it like a sponge. Then, she functions like an "emotional mirror" or "emotional magnifying glass." Staff must protect her from the presence of those who are experiencing emotional distress. And, they must remain low-keyed and pleasant around her–the emotional cheerleaders who supply her with cheerful feelings to "absorb" and "magnify."

- The person is eager for acknowledgment or acceptance by others, and feels hurt when she does not receive it.

- The person often displays jealousy or becomes very unhappy unless she is the center of attention.

- The person often misinterprets a simple comment or benign action–such as an offer of help by the support person–as an implied criticism. Instructions or directions, then, are often misinterpreted as implied criticism that she is unable to perform adequately by herself.

- The person is often confused about personal space and what is appropriate physical contact. When given corrective instruction in this area, the person reacts.

- The person often has unachievable and unrealistic self-expectations. She is intelligent and self-aware enough to be able to see that she is not performing well enough to meet the expectations of others or herself. And often, she has well-established procedures for punishing herself when she does not perform to her personal standards. For example, she may say, "If I can't do it perfectly, I won't do it at all."

Interventions
Personality Factors

PREVENTION

- Give the person emotional acceptance, taking care to avoid negative emotional expression. Focusing on the negative sets up emotional confrontations that cause interventions to fail.

- Always have clear, consistent, before-the-fact agreement among support persons about limits, rules and expectations. For example, everyone puts a seatbelt on before the car starts.

- Leave no room for confusion or ambivalence in communicating expectations for positive interactions, successful participation, cooperation and self-control. Do this with kindness and without anger.
    - Be certain without being angry.
    - Be explicit without being mean.

- Eliminate the need to exercise control. Reduce challenging behavior by planning daily routines and non-routine events around the person's disability (also known as person-centered planning).

Key to Prevention

Use intervention with the environment and people providing support. Remember the six A's: Acknowledge, Anticipate and Avoid problem behavior. Have an Accepting Attitude; Accommodate the person's needs and deficiencies.

Mealtime Behaviors and Issues of Control

Mealtime is a typical area for "correction" and external control. The following are prevention methods that eliminate the need for a support person to feel that he may have to control the emotionally fragile person's demanding behavior.

- A person will not ask to leave the table before the meal is over to watch a favorite TV show if the meal is held earlier, or if the show is taped for later viewing.

- A person will not eat before meals if nothing edible is accessible to her or left within sight.

- A child cannot become agitated by the behavior of others at meals if she eats first, or last, or behind a divider.

- Children cannot disturb each other by making faces if they are not seated facing each other.

- A person cannot snatch food off someone else's plate if there is extra distance placed between her and others at the table.

- A person cannot reject eggs if she is never served eggs.

GUIDANCE

■ Strive to be as non-confrontational as possible. Do not pay attention to negative behavior, if possible.

■ Follow the "less is more" guideline when individuals get caught up in the emotion of the moment. The less you do in direct response to the person's emotional reaction, the more satisfactory your results.

 Manage your own emotional states. Remember the "emotional mirror" and "emotional magnifying glass" effect. Work with this as a positive asset, projecting only positive emotions.

■ When giving any direction, comment or correction to the person:
  - Monitor your tone of voice, posture, volume and speed of speech
  - Attempt to keep the person calm and relaxed by being relaxed and calm yourself
  - Ask yourself what you might be feeling in a similar situation. How would you want someone to respond if you were in distress?

■ Use *invisible glasses* to help you avoid focusing on undesired behaviors. This is different from simply ignoring undesired behavior. Ignoring suggests an active emotional turning away, communicating dislike to the person one is ignoring. Putting on "invisible glasses" suggests a lack of emotion, and a focus on some aspect of the situation other than the undesired behavior.

Key to Guidance

Use positive intervention with the person. Use human relations techniques to engage her in other behavior without confronting her about problem behavior. Use suggestion, positive motivation and humor along with the three D's: Displace, Divert and re-Direct the person's behavior.

■ Interrupt inappropriate behavior without paying any attention to it! When the person is displaying minor "testing" behavior, or simple disregard for the presence of others, use gentle, indirect reminders that someone is watching and there are expectations. It often helps if the support person simply gets physically closer to the person who is upset and remains calm the whole time. Dr. Randall Sprick is a proponent of this technique, known as *proximity control*, and its use with younger children.[1]

Use humor to stop a disruptive behavior when the person has the ability to do an appropriate behavior. Gently tease the person out of a sulk, or out of resistive or bugging behavior. Get across the friendly, non-confrontational message that cooperation and positive participation are expected. This is especially useful with younger children.
- "Where did you hide that smile?" Reach your fingers behind the person's ear and say, "There it is!"
- "Those peas look so lonesome on that plate all by themselves. They want to keep those potatoes in your tummy company."

■ Set it up so that the person can be helpful. Give her the opportunity to cooperate or correct the situation without feeling coerced or criticized.
    Poor: "Get your hat and coat."
    Better: "We'll be leaving in five minutes. Can you find everyone's coat?"

■ Always ask the person a question to which you are sure she knows the answer. *Set it up so that she can be right.*
    Poor: "Set the table."
    Better: "Whose turn is it to set the table? Go look at the list!"

■ Stay two steps ahead of the person. As you see her heading for a predictable conflict, divert her into a positive, accepting interaction. Ask her to assume a valued, helpful role either with you or with a less competent person.
  - "Come and help me peel the carrots," or "Help Katie reach the cleaning supplies."

■ Do something totally unexpected—a response or activity totally unrelated to the negative emotional behavior.
- The person slaps your backside. Instead of telling her, "No hitting," turn to her and say, "Give me a high five."
- The person comes in the door muttering and in a bad mood. Instead of backing off or being confrontational, be ready with tea on the table. Invite her for tea

and cookies before she can start off on a bad note. Talk about completely irrelevant topics, rather than responding to the complaints.

■ Interrupt by distraction with a more appropriate activity.
- Set out an art or craft project, or just get busy somewhere else.
- Begin to sort socks.
- Get your coat and ask if anyone wants to go for a walk.
- If she is sitting at a table, interrupt with: "Please pass me the salt," or "What did Tom do today?" or "That was some hockey game. What did you think about that last goal?"

■ Interrupt by distraction with a more positive emotion.
- Hum a favorite happy tune. Then, ask the person how the rest of the tune goes.
- Take out a picture album with things the person has done that contain happy memories. Invite her to remember the happy time with you.
- Put a smile on your face by thinking about a really pleasant, personal memory. Then, talk to the person about something while you still have the good feeling and the smile.
- Communicate respect and encourage the person's self-control.

■ Imagine the person you are talking with has held a position of ultimate respect and regard in your eyes. Think of how you might state your message to the queen, the pope, your parents or some other respected authority figure.

■ How would you give your message to a person who had a stroke or has Alzheimer's disease and suddenly began to behave with exaggerated, emotional reactions to their own disability and confusion? You would know it was due to brain dysfunction. Would your reactions be different from the way you are talking to this person right now? You would certainly not say, "You have been warned for the last time." Nor would you say, "Stop fooling around with me and smarten up!" or "Behave or you will be sent to your room."

 Think of yourself as a special agent who could somehow magically live inside the head of the person with the stroke, gently reminding her of what she needed to do to achieve whatever she is attempting successfully.

TRAINING
■ Teach the person to maintain emotional equilibrium and self-control in a distressful situation.

■ Teach the person how to accept her own anger. It is essential to acknowledge the person's anger and her right to have emotions, whatever they may be. But, we must also teach the important distinction between having emotion and acting it out.
- "I know you are angry, and that's okay. But it's not okay to hit." Role-playing alternative expressions of anger may be helpful here.

■ Teach her how to express emotion.
- Help the person to locate the emotion in her body: "Where do you feel it when

this happens to you? In your chest, heart, throat?"
- Encourage the use of direct "I" messages: "I feel mad!" "I feel sad."

■ Teach her how to use emotional outlets that will work in different situations.
- Help the person do the following: Use a diary to write out feelings. Paint a sad or angry picture. Go for a walk to cool down. Punch a pillow to vent anger. Request time for counseling to talk out feelings with the support person.

■ Teach the person how to slow things down. Teach her how to use self-relaxation, humor and visualization.

Key to Training

Use positive intervention with the person. Employ motivation and skill development programs, and teach alternative coping skills over time.

- Have the person blow on a hand-drawn picture of a cup of coffee to cool it off.
- Have the person put her hand on her forehead and say, "Thought, get out of my head. Go into my hand." Then, have the person throw the thought away.

■ Teach the person how to handle correction without exploding. Use role-playing to practice accepting correction.

■ Teach the person that she can ask for help, and that it is all right for her to ask for help as a way of controlling distress situations.
- Teach *when* to ask for help. This starts with learning to recognize one's own tension then using it as a signal to ask for help.
- Teach *how* to ask for help. This starts with saying, "I cannot do it by myself." Then, teach the person how to assert herself using her most effective way of asking for help.
- Create a written explanation that the emotionally fragile person can hand to a support person who does not understand her limitations.

The goal of these training techniques is to develop more frequent positive emotional interactions between the support staff and the individual. She requires a great deal of positive interaction so that negative behavior is not the only means she has of obtaining intense contact with the support person.

■ Pay a lot of positive attention to naturally occurring behaviors that are cooperative and responsive. Catch the person "being good." Reinforce every such behavior.

■ Make sure positive feedback–for whatever the person is able to do–far outweighs negative feedback or corrections for inadequate behavior.
- Create daily opportunities for positive interactions so they occur at least four times more often than negative interactions.

■ Increase the amount of positive feedback the person receives simply for "being in the game of life." The person will likely receive this attention like manna from heaven.

Imagine that you are the banker in a game of Monopoly. Your job is to hand the players two hundred dollars each time they pass "Go," just for being in the game. Your job is not to send players to "Jail" for landing on the wrong space.

■ Make positive feedback visible and concrete. Positive feedback is not something the person should have to earn. It should be given regularly, in a way that it cannot be taken away. When feedback is set up as a recognition and acknowledgment system, it shows the person that others are focusing on her spontaneous, positive behavior.

 Think of yourself as a mayor trying to develop good citizenship training, not a police officer trying to enforce the laws once they are broken.

■ Schedule special time to spend with the person on a totally positive and non–demanding activity. For example, skip stones on the water, pick flowers, or listen to music together. Make it an expected part of each day, not just when the person has an especially good day.

■ Keep her so busy doing things that a support person can regularly acknowledge and approve of the fact that she has little opportunity to engage in disruptive behavior.
  - A blank sheet of paper that features an additional happy face each time the person with a disability makes the support person smile. This marks special moments, and reinforces the idea that you can never take away those memories or the fact that the individual made them happen.
  - A line of stars that just keeps getting longer. The number of hours or days between stars does not matter. What matters is that there are no unfilled spaces that communicate to the person, "You didn't earn one this time." Instead, the message is, "No matter how often or how seldom you do it, this behavior is great and others appreciate it."
  - A positive report book, featuring a one-page description of each positive action or interaction. The person can keep the book as a personal tool for seeking attention for behavior.

CRISIS MANAGEMENT

The emotionally fragile or reactive person displays a wide range of behavior when in crisis. She gets caught up in the moment and perceives little else besides her own emotions. Typically, she has great difficulty stopping her agitated behavior, which can be very upsetting to the support person.

How the support person chooses to respond stems from learned skills, but also from his own emotions and attitudes. Responses will vary by the individual or the situation, but they should always serve the needs of the person with fragile behavior and reinforce long-term goals. Some helpful questions to ask are:
  - Whose problem is this?
  - Who has to accommodate?
  - Who has to learn something new to be able to solve these problems?

Cognitive Factors

INDIVIDUAL CHARACTERISTICS

■ The person often has a wide range of strengths and weaknesses. Intellectual abilities in the person's profile may fall in the four- to twelve-year mental age range. On cognitive testing, she may score from the first percentile in areas of weakness to the eighty-fifth percentile in areas of strength. For this reason, these individuals often present in public as "normal," and others often underestimate their true disabilities. Support staff will mistake areas of strength for indicators of a person's general ability level if the person's areas of weakness are only partially understood or acknowledged.

■ Paradoxically, these individuals are sometimes able to spontaneously *express themselves better than they are able to comprehend* the same language being used by others. This can be very confusing because usually the opposite is true; that is, most people can understand more than they can say.

■ Often, the person can only work on one thought at a time. It seems as if she has a one-track mind. As a result, she often reacts with an emotional outburst if requested to change her mind once she has one idea about something. For example, if someone suggests different clothes to wear, or a different activity to do, she interprets the request as a criticism.

■ The person is often confused about rules and issues of control. She can become extremely preoccupied with whose rules to follow and who is in charge. Once she has accepted one leader, that becomes the only person to whom she will respond. Once she has become comfortable with a rule, she will have great difficulty accepting any alterations, regardless of the circumstance.

■ The person is often quite slow in working through a thought. She is often distracted, and loses her thread of thought if interrupted while trying to think about what someone is telling her. She will typically have an emotional outburst if someone talks too fast for her, or gives her too many things to think about at once.

■ The person is often confused about time concepts, such as how long it takes things to happen. She seems to expect nearly instantaneous results in response to plans or ideas.

■ The person is often confused about the consequences of her actions. She has little or no ability to conceive of something that will happen later as a result of what she is currently doing.

■ The person often has difficulty organizing her own time or activities, though to the casual observer she does not appear to have this difficulty.

■ The person is often confused about how to make choices, though she seems to know what she does not want to do.

A Note about Interventions

In general, when giving directions to a person who might be emotionally fragile and reactive, the usual assertiveness guideline of directness must be modified. Instead of ordinary communication, appropriate in situations with others, we must use especially diplomatic requests, indirect directions, and special, low-risk responses to her requests.

Following are interventions for both cognitive factors and personality factors. Separate guidance and training techniques are described for each factor, but the same counseling and crisis management techniques are suggested for both factors.

Interventions
Cognitive Factors

PREVENTION

■ Reduce or eliminate expectations for the person to independently complete anything that is a source of difficulty for her. Arrange to have extra assistance, structure, and positive feedback for every area of difficulty.

■ Beware of having expectations that are too high for a particular task or activity just because the person is really good at some other tasks or activities.

■ Provide the person with extra information to overcome areas of weakness.

■ Always make the person aware of what is going to happen next. *Do this before she has an opportunity to engage in an activity for which you may have to correct her.* She should never have to ask or wonder what you expect her to do. She should never have to be told that she is making a mistake because she did not understand what you wanted.
  - Communicate all expectations clearly in simple phrases, lists or picture sequences. Keep a model of the correct or desired response continuously available to the person.
  - Provide the person with the answer or response that is expected before she has a chance to make a mistake. That way, all she is required to do is recognize the correct answer. Use backwards chaining and errorless training techniques. (For more discussion of these techniques, see Chapter 5: Persistent, Repetitive Behavior: Perseverative Responding.)
  - Prevent misunderstanding about things such as the sequence of daily activities or the appropriateness of clothes for that day or that activity. Use pictures to make a daily calendar of activities. Color-code hangers and clothes and days of the week. Remove from sight or access any items that are constant sources of conflict.

What about the expectations imposed on support persons by others? People will say, "She has to learn" or "That's enabling her" or "The world won't always provide that level of protection. She has to get used to failure." The reality is that the long history of this person has shown that she cannot learn to compensate for certain areas of cognitive weakness. In these areas, she requires extra support and protection.

We give specific foods to individuals who have diabetes and do not insist that they learn how to process insulin better. Diabetes is a biological fact and a part of Mother Nature's impact on that person that must be accommodated. Similarly for these individuals, the accommodations that must be made should respect the organic and neurological facts of life—part of Mother Nature's impact on them.

GUIDANCE

When counseling individuals with developmental disabilities, support persons must keep in mind several typical deficiencies. The following approach is especially helpful when the person displays emotionally fragile and reactive behavior.

A Four-Step Counseling Response

To resolve the person's emotional crisis, it is essential to overcome communication challenges due to disability; overcome communication challenges due to distress; overcome social skills challenges; and maintain a focus on relationship goals.

1. Overcome Communication Challenges Due to Disability

Expressive language ability and receptive processing is often deficient, so the support person must help the person clarify her thoughts and express her legitimate concerns as accurately as possible.

- Focus and ground the person in present reality.

- Speak the person's language. Use her own key words (parrot talk) to keep her focused. Do not interpret.

     Poor: "Cushion. You want me to adjust your cushion?"
     Better: "Cushion. Can you tell me more?"

- Listen actively. Assist the person in voicing her concern by feeding back your interpretation of what she is trying to say. Double-check your interpretation with a question. This lets her know you are listening and you are understanding what she is trying to communicate. You might say, "You sound really upset. Is that right?"

- Help the person find the words. Sometimes it is necessary to suggest to the person what she is feeling and what words she wants to use. Once you have found the right words, ask her to tell you, using the words you have just given to her.
  - Work out a list that has every concern written down, with an answer for every concern, and every expectation clarified. This way, you do not have to repeat that counseling session. Just refer to the list.
  - Be highly literal and specific.

  - An individual was told by the support person, "You got it right from the horse's mouth." Later, the woman was upset and told another support person, "He called me a horse!"

  - A person was asked, "Did you change your sheets?" He replied, "Yes." On checking, the support person found nine sheets on the mattress! She had never specifically said, "Take off the top and bottom sheet. Then, put on a new top and bottom sheet."

- Make clear reference to earlier discussions. Individuals with cognitive disabilities often have difficulty making connections between events. Say: "Remember when we talked about...," or "Remember what we did when...?" Then add, "This is like that. Let's try the same thing!"

2. Overcome Communication Challenges Due to Distress

When emotionally aroused, some individuals with developmental disabilities lose much of the verbal processing ability they have when they are calm. Typically, the person can only handle a single thought or concern at a time. Often, even that concern is overwhelming.

■ Break down the topic of concern for the person. Show her how to focus her attention on one concern or complaint at a time. Then, show her how to seek a resource and work it out.

■ Do not get caught up in the person's anxieties, fears or fantasies. Stick to the facts.

■ Move on to the next complaint. Let her know you will look into it and get back to her. Do this at a time that you have set aside just for that purpose.

■ Never attempt to negotiate or renegotiate major concerns in the midst of a crisis. Save that for later!

3. Overcome Social Skills Challenges

Individuals with intellectual disabilities often cannot perceive or acknowledge another person's point of view because it is too abstract. Since social awareness is very nonspecific, it must be put into concrete terms for the person to make sense of it and act on it.

■ Take "feelings of others" from the abstract to the concrete for the person. Break social awareness down into step-by-step behaviors, using specific cues to help the person pay attention to relevant details. Social stories and cartoon stories can be very helpful to many individuals.

■ Assist the person to focus on the social problem situation. Then, help her work her way through alternative actions.
   - How did she act?
   - How would she feel if someone acted like that toward her?
   - Does she want to make others feel that way?

4. Maintain a Focus on Relationship Goals

Emotionally reactive persons are often very difficult to build a relationship with, and are often poor at keeping in touch with the goals of their behavior.

■ Using the activities described in the Reality Therapy counseling approach of Dr. William Glasser will help you meet the person's need to feel emotionally secure. These interactions create positive involvement between the individual and the support person.[2]

Special Case: When Not to Counsel

While intellectually limited in some areas of performance, many individuals are quite proficient in the ability to recognize what is wrong about a situation. The person may bombard the support person with a never-ending stream of problems and complaints about what is wrong with her world. She appears to be in constant crisis. Attempting to solve one problem only leads to the expression of another problem. So, responding to the content of her complaint only reinforces her complaint-making activity. Because the individual is caught in a trap of knowing no other way to interact with others, nothing you do will elicit a better emotional response.

■ Acknowledge the person on a constant basis without responding to the content of the complaints.

■ Set aside one time of day for all complaints. At that time, set a timer and only work on one problem at a time, for a set amount of time. Throughout the rest of the day, direct the person to write down complaints, or make an audio recording of them, to air only at "complaint time."

■ Prevent the person with disabilities from going from one support person to another with complaints. Assign only one support person the role of complaint responder.

Goals in Working with Emotionally Fragile, Reactive Behavior

• Help the person to feel secure and accepted, and assist her to calm down.

• Help the person accept a limitation on behavior without causing her to feel emotionally rejected.

• Help the person accept counseling about how she is handling a situation inadequately, without becoming demoralized by the implied criticism.

• Help the person to accept positive guidance about expectations for self-control.

• Goal 1 > Have the person peacefully enter the box of positive expectations.

• Goal 2 > Have the person come out walking and looking for a positive direction and acceptance, not a fight.

• Avoid giving the person any reason to burn bridges behind her.

TRAINING

■ Give the person time to respond. Always make sure she has received and incorporated one message before you make any additional comments. The person often needs time to mull over what was said. Giving a second direction too soon may cause her to feel criticized for not moving quickly enough.

   – Never underestimate the value of waiting for a response. The support person should always count to ten before giving any direction a second time. This helps to eliminate any negative emotional tone, or any sense of nagging.

Imagine you are sending the person a telegram from Australia. It costs five dollars per word, and your budget is twenty-five dollars. The telegraph office cannot send another telegram until you get a reply to the one you sent. You are allowed to send the same telegram as many times as you wish at no extra charge, but if you try to send anything before you get a reply to the first one, it will cost you one hundred dollars per word!

■ Offer comments or directions in the form of choices between specific options that you provide. (See section titled Acknowledge Responses to the Presentation of Choices, pages 94-95.)

■ Make use of positive modeling. Offer comments or directions to others whom the person can observe responding. These methods take the pressure off the person to respond directly.
  - Catch someone else "being good." For example, you might say, "And look at Mary. She ate all her peas, too. That's terrific, Mary."
  - Teach someone else what you want the person to be doing.
  - Work with puppets or dolls.

This can backfire if you do not immediately follow up with praise for any cooperation you observe from the person who was not cooperating earlier. The goal is to use praise to point out desired behavior, not to set up rivalry between two or more individuals.

■ Write down or make an audio recording of anything that is said to the person so she can read or listen to it at her pace and figure out what is being asked.

■ Use *nonverbal methods* to communicate expectations for self-control and voluntary cooperation.
  - Use a picture of a stop sign with a happy face drawn inside for the individual who has trouble stopping herself, and who reacts to corrective comments. She can use this as a prompt to stop while still feeling good about herself.

■ Use *indirect methods* to communicate expectations for self-control and voluntary cooperation.
  - Let the individual overhear the support person telling some other person how proud he is of her when she is so helpful and cooperative. Set it up so the individual does not know that the support person knows she is listening.

Using Consequences for Excessive Emotional Reactions

Behavioral contracts involve the negotiation of clearly stated behavioral limits and consequences for overstepping those limits. This approach teaches the person that cause and effect exist, that she has choices, and that she is responsible for her choices and behavior.

■ Make sure there are sufficient positive opportunities in the person's life so that some of them can be used as special privileges in behavioral contracting.

- According to the behavioral contract, a special privilege is lost when pre-established rules have been broken.

- The support person must avoid giving the emotionally rejecting message: "This is me, giving you what you deserve." The support person is just a worker doing his job. There should be nothing personal about the administration of consequences. Do not threaten or warn, "Now these consequences are happening." Let the consequences speak for themselves.

- Later, at the moment when a privilege would have occurred, and only if questioned about it, say, "Next time, when you earn all your stars," or "Tomorrow, when you have followed the contract, you will get another chance."

Use consequences and contracting for excessive emotional reactions only with great care. Beware of the inconsistent use of consequences, or jumping from one consequence to another. This may inadvertently teach the emotionally reactive person to avoid any external direction or control, or to avoid responsibility or concern for the rights of others. In addition, a person's cognitive dysfunction, such as the inability to process language, may make it impossible for her to learn from consequences or to grasp the concept of behavioral contracting. If so, the support person must rely on prevention and guidance techniques.

Responding to Verbally Abusive Behavior

- Recognize and acknowledge the person's emotion. ("You're really upset, aren't you?")

- Realize that fear is often involved in the generation of anger. The support person should respond to the fear rather than the anger. For example, "I know you're afraid, but the scratch must be cleaned." (not "Calm down! You're a big girl and that little scratch doesn't hurt you.")

- Acknowledge that when people are frustrated, it is "normal" for them to experience a strong emotion.

- Allow emotional ventilation. Accept the person's non-directed expression of anger as emotional venting as long as it does not lead to anything more disruptive. Do not take it personally. Do not feel the need to confront every inappropriate emotional expression. Ignore it for the moment then assist the person to find a better way of expressing her anger.

Let the person know she has the right to all of her emotions, but that there are limits on how she may express them. "You can ventilate, but you cannot perforate!"

- Once things have settled down, it may be useful to help the person who is feeling remorseful to "make up" for hurting others' feelings. For example, the person can do something helpful for them, or send them a card or a flower.

Using Give and Take to Overcome Resistance

The emotionally fragile person will immediately become resistant when she feels she is being corrected or criticized. The support person can take several measures to alleviate those feelings.

- Eliminate time pressure.
- Do not require that the requested behavior happen immediately.
- Schedule extra time for the activity to occur so that there is no time pressure.

 One man always dresses before he eats, so he will not have to hurry to get dressed after breakfast just to get to the bus on time.

Keeping the Focus on Rules

■ Negotiate rules, then do things by the rules!

■ Let the person negotiate in setting up a structured routine for doing undesired tasks such as brushing teeth, bathing or getting dressed. Then, let the person perform them according to the rules that have been negotiated.

■ With plenty of advance notice, let the person know what must occur *before* a preferred activity can take place. Then, let her exercise some choice and control over when she complies with expectations.

Keeping the Focus on Ritual and Routine

■ Create a ritual or routine for individuals who tend to resist all requests or directions.
  - Have the person exchange clothes at night for the clothing she will wear the next day.
  - Have the child brush her teeth or do homework before she watches TV.

■ Use statements of fact–including known specifics on who, what, when and where– to tie any unwelcome instruction to the ritual or routine. This prevents having to say no in a way that implies that the support person is personally denying the individual's preferences.
  - "It's 10:30. We always meet with Kelly out front at 10:30."
  - "I can't hear the dishwasher, can you? Jason needs your help in the kitchen when the dishwasher turns off."

CRISIS MANAGEMENT

The better the support person monitors and minimizes his emotional response, the more likely he is to facilitate an agreeable resolution to the person's crisis. This requires a strategy. First, let go of the confrontation and back off from the precipitating issue. The issue can be dealt with later, under circumstances where the person is protected from the experience of failure or nonacceptance. Next, help the person move forward. Following are: a summary of goals, the emotional responses that will or will not support those goals, and specific methods for responding during a crisis.

Counterproductive Support Person Responses

- *Exasperation:* yelling, sharp tone of voice, facial display of anger

- *Self-blame:* taking it personally, feeling responsible, pleading (that is, "She really doesn't like me," or "Oh no! I should have known this would happen," or "Please, honey. Do it for me.")

- *Helplessnes*s: believing the individual's behavior is the support person's personal failure (that is, "I've tried helping her, but nothing I do makes any difference.")

- *Becoming punitive*: acting on the desire to hurt the person

- *Over-controlling*: attempting to compensate for feeling out of control by taking too much control (Consider saying, "She's eating all her potatoes. Let's let her leave the peas.")

- *Apathy about goals:* not caring anymore what is being modeled by the support person's reaction; just wanting control over the person at any cost

- *Abuse of authority:* using the personal power of the role of support staff to try to overcome emotional reactions and resistance (Raising your voice or threatening to take away a pre-arranged, positive activity.)

- *Making "heavy weather":* treating situations as though they are more difficult, serious or urgent than they are.

Key to Crisis Management

Use direct intervention with the problem behavior. Remain calm and always use guidance techniques first. Accommodate the person's special needs and disabilities. Respond to chaotic behavior with a prearranged plan for surviving the crisis while bringing challenging behavior to a stop! Interact positively with the person as soon as she exercises a degree of self-control. Have a plan for how to re-enter normal life.

Productive Support Person Responses

Imagine attempting to sail a boat during a sudden storm and against a changing tide. What do you do? Reduce the amount of sail; that is, change the pressure of confrontation. A sailor headed for the rocks must tack–change direction, change focus and steer for calmer waters. You cannot solve the problem if your boat is smashed on the rocks.

- *Defuse.* Think about anything you might be able to do with the person, momentarily, to defuse the emotions of the moment.

- *Keep your head.* Become balanced, relaxed and totally precise in your response. Be cool, neutral and certain about what you will do to handle each situation.

- *Do nothing.* Recall the Rudyard Kipling poem "If" that states: "If you can fill the unforgiving moment with sixty seconds worth of silence…" Think of that distance as silence, and say nothing for one minute.

- *Stay close.* Do not over-isolate. Tell the person: "Let's sit here and calm down together," or "Let's get a drink of water and calm ourselves," or "Sit here and get relaxed for a minute. I'll be able to talk with you as soon as you stop crying."

- *Remain friendly.* Interact positively as soon as possible after the person has accepted an instruction to accept guidance to calm her emotional reaction.

■ *Maintain normal expectations.* Accept the person's temporary emotional withdrawal and nonparticipation. Do not chase the person to try to make her feel better. Do not rub it in. Do not indulge in put-downs or asking why! Do not hold a grudge after an emotional outburst.

■ *Tap into the person's strengths.* Refocus the person physically, emotionally and mentally on some other activity. Make sure it is something that is likely to make her feel happy, strong, proud, confident, approved of, accepted, secure and in control. For example: "Let's get out the pictures of your birthday party and look at them."

Chapter 9, which describes violent, aggressive and destructive behavior, is an extension of this discussion. It offers more detailed suggestions for preventing crises and managing emotionally fragile individuals who become violent.

In This Chapter

9 ■ Violent, Aggressive and Destructive Behavior

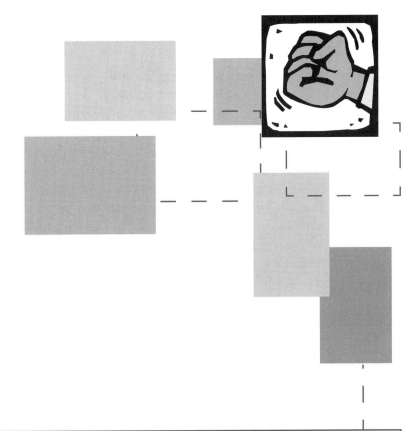

Violent, Aggressive and Destructive Behavior

Definition: Violent, aggressive and destructive behaviors are socially inadequate coping responses. A person's fear, anger, and/or frustration may be aroused by any perception of danger, due to a threat or loss of control. Accompanying the emotional experience, the body prepares to defend itself against the perceived threat or loss on a biological level, pumping adrenalin into the bloodstream and increasing activity in the autonomic nervous system.

Arousal of the autonomic nervous system can energize a person to apply his repertoire of adequate coping responses to a situation, or act out in a socially inadequate manner. The explosively violent person is frequently aroused to the level where fight behavior is displayed, sometimes directed at a target. This behavior poses a danger to support persons and others in his environment. (Coping responses to distress are described in detail in Chapter 1: Introduction to Values and Methods.)

Issues Covered in This Chapter

This chapter focuses primarily on individuals with a persistent history of explosive, violent actions. The discussion includes specific behavior analysis of generative factors that evoke violent behavior in emotionally fragile persons along with detailed procedures for preventing and managing violent behavior. Impulsive or resistive issues are different from the violence described here. And, the behavior of a person who is emotionally fragile may or may not be violent. Issues covered in other chapters include:

- Violence or aggression stemming from an impulsive attempt to obtain a goal object (Chapter 6: Impulsive Behavior.)

- Power struggles that stem from the individual's need to be ritualistic and maintain control over his own behavior (Chapter 3: Resistive Behavior.)

- Power struggles that erupt when the individual becomes oppositional and driven to avoid support persons who are attempting to control his behavior (Chapter 3: Resistive Behavior)

- Violence that results when a support person ignores the individual's initial communication of resistance to the support person's control (Chapter 3: Resistive Behavior.)

- Personality and cognitive characteristics of an emotionally fragile and reactive person, who may or may not display violence during an emotional crisis (Chapter 8: Emotionally Fragile and Reactive Behavior.).

Generative Factors

Violent actions are typically generated by one or more of the four factors. They may be developmentally normal, but exaggerated, reactive-defensive behaviors; be learned, functional, coping responses; reflect a level of emotional disturbance in the person; or be fear/anger responses exacerbated by a physical or psychiatric condition that lowers the person's arousal threshold.

Generative Factors in Violent, Aggressive and Destructive Behavior

- Reflecting developmentally "normal," exaggerated responses
- A learned, functional coping response (for this person)
- Behaviors reflecting a "disturbed" emotional state
- Behaviors reflecting a physical or psychiatric condition.

By the time a person with violent, destructive and aggressive behavior is sixteen years old, he usually has a record that is several inches thick. The documentation generally describes the many behavioral incidents and repeated professional interventions that have been sought.

- Things do not get better for these individuals until those who are providing them with services and support finally come to accept that some are not able to learn from "correction" or "ordinary" behavior modification approaches. In other words, it is essential to identify and accommodate the mentally and emotionally disabling conditions that underlie violent and aggressive behavior.

- Usually, many factors coexist and contribute to violent outbursts. Everything–not just one thing–will lead to extremely disruptive episodes. Therefore, accommodating approaches must be comprehensive and support the person in multiple areas of dysfunction.

For the majority of individuals described here, a large proportion of their violent episodes are preventable by the use of adequate preparation, structure and communication. Episodes that could not be prevented can be managed with guidance, training and crisis intervention procedures.

- Unsuccessful behavior management approaches simply react to the person's reaction to his environment. The approaches suggested here use techniques to protect the person from circumstances that will invariably lead to violent episodes. For episodes that are not preventable, the goal is to "survive" the impending crisis and keep the person positively involved in relationship-sustaining activities.

 The consistent, underlying belief that connects all of these approaches is that no person should be expected to cope, unassisted, with circumstances that will overwhelm him.

BEHAVIOR CHARACTERISTICS

■ The person appears unable to live up to expectations for self-control and self-management.

■ The person may give no previous indication that he is going to become violent. The outburst may be a spontaneous reaction to an immediate, threatening or highly arousing circumstance, such as slamming a finger in a drawer or hearing a loud noise.

■ Typical, physical signs of stress-arousal may appear prior to the outburst.
  - The person may show confusion and anxiety with rapid breathing, reddening of the face, a rise in voice tone, or increased muscle tension in the jaw, neck, shoulders and hands. These are signs that the person may be preparing to attack or defend himself from a perceived threat.
  - The individual may present the support person with a significant problem that requires an immediate solution. Then, he may immediately present another one as soon as the first one is solved.

■ The person may be physically, emotionally and mentally overwhelmed by the flood of stress-threat hormones in his body. He may respond as though he is experiencing a catastrophe that is sweeping him away or drowning him. He uses exaggerated and desperate attempts to maintain some sense of control, and may seek to engage others as an outlet to express these emotions.

 Once a person becomes threatened, agitated and/or angry enough to lose control, he may direct his violent behavior toward a selected target. The target will often be the support person who has been unable to protect him from the initial, distressing emotions. Or, the target may be the most vulnerable person in sight, or the first person in sight.

- The person may settle as soon as a pill is in his mouth, as soon as the police arrive on the doorstep or as soon as the ambulance arrives. In other words, he may be unable to exercise self-control until an external presence or event signals, "Things will be safe now." That imposes unmistakable boundaries around him to reassure him that he will not lose control.

- Self-control may be demonstrated in only one social setting. Behavior may be self-controlled when the person is in a community or work setting, but aggressive in the home setting. For other individuals, the reverse may be true. Typically, the violent behavior occurs in the less-structured setting. Individuals with violent behavior in certain settings will often show a different side of themselves to each of the people with whom they interact.

  - The individual may show more out-of-control behavior when a support person attempts to give him more freedom or independence than he can handle. An episode of out-of-control behavior may be the result when a basic restriction or structure is relaxed.

  - With protective supports and guidance, the person can be calm and productive. When he is confronted by situations beyond his emotional or cognitive ability to cope, there are a continuing series of violent episodes.

- When the person is secure–in a familiar setting or with a familiar person–he can remain self-controlled. When anxious, he may need every moment accounted for in order to remain calm enough to avoid escalating into threatening and violent behavior.

  - Between episodes of violence, the person is frequently described as pleasant, well behaved, happy-go-lucky, well liked and friendly.

INDIVIDUAL CHARACTERISTICS

- *Variability.* Often, a wide discrepancy exists between the things the person can sometimes do very well, and the things he cannot do at all. This is especially true of the individual who displays a lot of anger toward his world. Though skilled in some areas, he is still dependent on others to maintain that sense of order and continuity that is essential for anyone to guide his own behavior toward desired goals. On one day, he will work well at an independent level, and the next day he cannot attempt any work unless he sees the immediate promise of a reward.

- *Inability to sustain momentum at tasks.* This lack of ability is sometimes at the root of aggressive behavior. The person becomes frustrated with support persons giving him directions he can understand but cannot accomplish. He may assault the support person who gives him more than one thing to do at a time. This disability is discussed further in Chapter 4: Dependent and Functionally Dependent Behavior.

- *A one-track mind.* When not focused, the person may display impulsive or perseverative behavior. These disabilities are discussed further in Chapters 5: Persistent, Repetitive Behavior, and Chapter 6: Impulsive Behavior.

- *Inability to resolve conflict.* The person may be unaware of his own problem-solving, cognitive limitations. It is typically impossible to explain any other person's point of view to an individual with this disability. He usually attributes his own confusion to others having lied to, manipulated or somehow treated him unfairly.

■ *Acute need for clarity.* The person may be able to tolerate some changes and unexpected events. However, things may have to be carefully explained to him so he can interpret what is happening. Without such explanations, he may be highly dependent on a routine and ritualized daily program. When changes do have to occur, violent behavior can be the person's reaction to a lack of adequate preparation and explanation.

■ *Perception that others have all of the control.* The person may accurately perceive the control that others have over his life and react against it. Issues may include how much money he can have, where he can live, when he can visit home, and so on. He may have a history of physical, sexual, or emotional abuse at the hands of others in the past who have had complete control. (Individuals with these characteristics are discussed in more detail in Chapter 8: Emotionally Fragile and Reactive Behavior.)

Behaviors Reflecting "Developmentally Normal," Exaggerated Responses

■ *Oversensitivity and overreaction to other people.* The person may be too perceptive and too reactive to other people's emotions.

• One adolescent with autism would only hit his mother when she was experiencing and displaying physical distress associated with pre-menstrual syndrome. On the other hand, he could be quite empathic and function as an "emotional mirror." (See Chapter 5: Persistent, Repetitive Behavior for more discussion of this emotional state.) This behavior may present itself as crying when others are upset, becoming scared when others are feeling threatened, or becoming enraged when others are angry.

• According to her support person, one woman "takes her cues from people, not objects or tasks to be done or work required. If the people are fine, she is fine. If not, she is not. The more we can be who we are and respond less to her behaviors, the more stable she will be. For example, if I get worried or upset because she has come into a room with unsafe equipment, she will perceive this and will respond in a negative way. If I acknowledge her and carry on with the task that I'm doing, she will be fine."

■ *Oversensitivity and overreaction to unfamiliar environmental cues and unpredictable settings.* The person may have very little ability to generalize skills from setting to setting. He may be extremely dependent on, and highly sensitive to, specific environmental cues and routines for functioning. The person may be greatly distressed by any unpredictable features in his world. The slightest changes in routines and cues may create an extreme state of arousal.

• One man was well adapted in his home and workshop routine. His support persons took him on a camping trip, where he regressed in all areas. He would not leave the recreational vehicle to participate with others, and he became assaultive when forced to move from his chair.

- One woman assaulted her respite support person when she was not served breakfast at the expected time.

- One man was very dependent on structure and adjusted well in a stable day program emphasizing work skills and predictable, routine tasks. After many years, he was moved to a new program that emphasized unstructured socialization and variable community outings. After three months, he began to display forgetfulness, anger and aggression. He was unable to cope with the frequent changes and reduced structure.

■ *Oversensitivity and overreaction to other-than-expected outcomes.* Typically, unexpected activity can be explained to the person; that is, he can be prepared for events. However, the failure of an expected activity to occur can lead to a devastating outcome; the person may become enraged. This may erupt over something that appears to the support person to be relatively unimportant—a trip to the store that must be postponed or relief staff coming in to cover someone's absence.

- A man with moderate developmental disabilities was being driven home after a regular swimming outing was cancelled. The pool had been closed for repairs. Without warning, he tried to grab the steering wheel to make the car go back to the pool. When the driver stopped him, he assaulted her and would not let up until she gained physical control and removed him from the car. He walked back home.

- One man is a competitive sportsman who has a subtle motor disability. He expects to be successful at whatever he attempts. When he is intent on accomplishing an important skill and runs up against his motor disability, he can become so frustrated that he will attack the person who is attempting to assist him. Breaking tasks down into single steps that assure slow success can prevent some of this man's outbursts. Explaining in a reassuring manner that everyone makes mistakes and that it takes time to learn helps him remain calm.

■ *Violence modeled on the behavior of others, leading to over-arousal.* The person may be unable to judge the cause and effect relationship of behaviors that others display, both in real life and in fictional media.

- A boy was threatening to knife his support person. He was mimicking exactly a violent video game that had been used as reinforcement for on-task schoolwork. He handed over the knife immediately when someone said, "Give the knife to me." When violent video games were replaced with golf games, his threats of violent action diminished. Still, he would watch late-night horror movies and act out some of those scenes. He could not assess what was real and what was pretend.

- A man with severe developmental disabilities enjoyed floor hockey and roughhousing. He could rarely tell when the play stopped and the fight started. Carried away by the excitement of the activity, his play would turn into a rumble, with several people getting hurt. This diminished when all roughhousing was stopped and replaced with swimming and running—both more appropriate physical outlets. He simply became carried away by the physical activity.

Some individuals "absorb" and repeat the actions that they see or have seen others do.

- One man frequently observed two other men in his home being physically assaultive to other individuals. In an attempt to discipline those co-residents for minor infractions of house rules–such as putting out the salt shaker too early or helping at one of his jobs–he would physically assault them if they did not move fast enough.

- One man with a moderate developmental delay would threaten and physically assault his female support persons. He came from a home where his father had physically abused his mother frequently.

- A man with a severe developmental delay would attack male support persons when he was frustrated. He came from a home where his mother verbally and physically assaulted his father.

Learned, Functional Coping Responses

A number of life circumstances can provoke extreme over-arousal in a person with a developmental disability. Some of these are obvious, while some are quite subtle. Many individuals learn that they can reduce their state of arousal by engaging in violent behavior that will "make it stop." These are described as learned, functional, coping responses.

■ *Frustrated, expressive communication leading to over-arousal.* The person cannot get others to understand or respond to, what he is trying to communicate.

- One man with autism would become violent when pressured to do something before he was ready. He gave many subtle cues that indicated his readiness. When experienced support persons were able to "go with his flow," he did not become violent.

- One man did not want to go to a dance. When he was at the dance and indicated that he wanted to go home, he was told he had to wait. He attacked the support person who told him to wait. And, he calmed down as soon as the vehicle left the dance.

For further discussion of violence as a form of functional communication, see Chapter 3: Resistive Behavior. A wide range of literature dealing with augmentative and alternative communication provides more information on this topic. This is especially useful for working with individuals who are diagnosed with autism. For example, you can visit http://www.isaac-online.org, the Web site for the International Society for Augmentative and Alternative Communication.

As the noted behavior analyst Gary LaVigna advises, "Listen to the whispers of behavior and you may not have to hear the screams." Some of these communication attempts are simply a plea: "Listen to me!"

- *Over-arousal resulting from the threat of confrontation.* For some individuals, a direct conflict can provoke an extreme outburst.

- One young man is a hard worker with significant learning disabilities. He attends school in a fairly rough social environment. He tries to maintain self-control and will only become violent when he is teased or criticized beyond his level of endurance. Once he does become involved in a fight, it requires several people to restrain him.

- A large man with autism is a passive person whose behavior is mostly a reaction to events occurring around him. He may become agitated when people around him are upset. When an effort is made to restrain him, he displays a panic reaction and does harm to himself and others. His reaction is an attempt to escape a stressful, threatening situation, and since he cannot, he becomes so aroused that he attacks.

- *Impaired receptive communication (confusion leading to overarousal).* Many individuals who display violent loss of self-control have certain problem-solving and cognitive abilities that greatly exceed their receptive communication skills. The person may be very spontaneous and expressive in his use of language despite having a hearing or communication impairment. This gives support persons an unrealistic sense of how much language the person can take in. The individual becomes confused by his inability to understand what others want from him, or are trying to tell him. This confusion lowers his arousal threshold; small confrontations and conflicts that he would normally tolerate can escalate into a loss of self-control.

- Whenever he gets confused about his paycheck, one individual becomes anxious and angry. He then rejects or attacks anyone who attempts to help him and happens to use more language than he can decipher.

- One man attacked a person who was talking to him about becoming more independent. He had misunderstood the language being used. As he later explained, he thought the word independent meant "retarded."

- One woman with a developmental disability says, "People ask me a question, but I don't know what they mean." She adds, "If I cannot answer them, people will think I'm stupid." So, she aggressively protects herself by retaliating towards anyone who asks her a question she cannot answer.

- One adolescent woman screamed, "You're not helping me!" when her mother was trying to give her a lengthy explanation about a conflict they were having.

These individuals are not processing verbal input nearly as well as they express themselves. Their confusion could be due to a number of specific factors.

- *Diminished and/or variable auditory attention.* The person may be able to talk a blue streak, yet be unable to repeat more than three or four words. A person with this challenge may become confused by the number of words in a question as simple as, "Do you want eggs and toast, or cereal for breakfast?" The person may have no problem with, "Eggs or cereal?"

- *Diminished semantic processing ability.* The person may be able to repeat whole sentences, yet unable to comprehend the meaning of conditional words such as "if," "or," "when," "not until," "after" and "before." Or, the person may be able to process these words, but only in the context of familiar activity where personal experience allows him to understand what is being said. He may be unable to process such words accurately when being given novel information.

- *Diminished ability to process verb tense.* The person is unable to tell that events being referred to are either past or future. The person may perceive anything being discussed as current. So, he becomes frustrated and angry when an event–such as a new job, school or residential placement–does not immediately unfold as expected. It is difficult for an individual to understand the consequences of his actions if his mental disability involves inability to understand time-related concepts.

- *Failure to succeed at a task or social activity leading to over-arousal.* Individuals with a high drive to succeed and be independent may set themselves unachievable, impossibly high standards. Their drive allows them to overcome many–but not all–aspects of their disability. The person responds to each failure with extreme over-arousal. It is as though the person re-experiences all the old frustrations each time a new frustration arises.

 One man assaulted his grandmother when she called him to dinner. He was assembling his motorcycle carburetor and her dinner call distracted him, causing him to have to start over from the beginning.

Individuals who display frequent, violent loss of self-control often display a strong desire for social acceptance by others. Despite this desire, the person will typically have an unrecognized or unacknowledged learning impairment that seriously affects his ability to make social judgments. He may display significant task competencies, but be unable to read subtle social cues and verbal nuances. So, instead of engaging in important social interactions using these skills, he often behaves on the basis of his intense fear of social rejection.

 One adolescent boy can be friendly and well adjusted when things go well for him. He can happily toss a ball, play checkers or play tetherball with others on the playground. However, when there is no prop to help him interact, things do not go well. He has no idea what to say or do. If no one asks him to play, he will verbally abuse or assault others. This is his maladaptive attempt to retain some sense of control in this threatening situation.

Behaviors Reflecting a Disturbed Emotional State

The most difficult behaviors for support persons to understand and manage come from people with an emotional disorder who are prone to violence. The person can become threatened and over-aroused by an apparently benign situation that triggers a previous, overwhelming emotional experience. The support person may be unaware of this. Even if aware, the support person may still be unable to prevent the person from being triggered. (See the discussion of "emotional radar" in Chapter 8: Emotionally Fragile and Reactive Behavior.)

Behaviors Reflecting a Disturbed Emotional State

- Overreaction to emotional rejection ("crisis of belonging")
- Self-sabotage/fear of success ("failure identity")
- Fear of loss of control ("going out of control in search of control")
- Adjustment disorder
- Traumatic stress response
- Mental health crisis evoked by change in life circumstances.

These reactions are extremely aversive to the person who experiences them. In his drive to escape and avoid situations that trigger such reactions, he may learn some extremely maladaptive coping patterns. Following are a few of the more recognizable patterns of emotionally disturbed behavior.

Overreaction to Emotional Rejection

The individual tends to become violent any time he experiences a sense of personal rejection. This "crisis of belonging" is discussed in detail in Chapter 8: Emotionally Fragile and Reactive Behavior.

◼ The person may be experiencing grief, loss or abandonment that exaggerates his arousal responses.

◼ The individual may have great difficulty trusting others. He may be unable to believe anyone cares about him.

◼ The person may be demonstrating righteous indignation over being treated unfairly, being singled out. He may say, "No one else has these restrictions placed on them. Why me?" or "Everyone else in my family gets to stay at home. Why not me?"

- One woman was calm going to and returning from home visits when these took place on a consistent basis, with no irregularities. When one of her anticipated home visits had to be cancelled at the last minute, she ran out of her support person's home and began throwing rocks at the windows, screaming, "I hate living here!"

- One man with autism, and his siblings, went into foster care when his mother became too ill to look after her children. Some time after she died, the other children moved back home when the father remarried. When the man was told of this, he went into a violent rage. His focused aggression was intended to hurt the support person or break something of value to the support person. He eventually settled into that support person's home when regular phone contact was established with his siblings.

- One man could ordinarily accept corrective comments about his behavior. He tended to display aggression toward support persons only during the sad time immediately following a visit or outing with a special person.

Self-Sabotage / Fear of Failure

An individual's fear of failure, or "failure identity," may be so strong that he cannot give success a chance to occur.

■ This person knows that if he does not compete there is no chance he can lose. So, he sets himself up for failure. The rationale is that failure under one's own control is better than failure that is imposed. (See *Identity Society* by William Glasser [Harper-Collins, 1975].)

■ A person who has a fear of rejection may display behavior that deliberately evokes rejection from others. Following a violent, destructive or aggressive episode, he may experience great remorse.[1]

- One youth sets himself up for failure by wanting to own an impossibly expensive car, among other goals. This reinforces his concept of himself as helpless. He does not bother to put any effort into his dreams since he knows they will never come true. And, he is unwilling to accept a more reasonable goal. In an unstructured social setting, he will physically cling to other children. When they reject him, he violently seeks revenge.

- One man is competent when others organize his time for him. He loves approval and meeting the challenge of clear expectations. But, he cannot organize his own activities. On occasion, a support person who is unaware of this issue has left him alone, without specific instructions. He would experience anxiety, become destructive to his environment, then escalate to a state of high arousal in anticipation of a reprimand. Usually, he would physically attack support staff as they came in the door.

- Another man, who is dependent on support staff to assist him with money management, is angered by his dependency. His pattern is to protest in an attempt to provoke a fight, become aggressive if a conflict does ensue, run off to live on the street, and stay away until the department of human services finds another placement for him. He then has a brief "honeymoon" in that location until the first conflict arises over money management. This pattern was only resolved after he received a probation order that required him to remain living at one placement. Only then could he begin to work on better coping skills. Now when a conflict erupted, he would not leave but instead said to the support person, "You have to take me back!"

- One violent individual was moved to a new setting with little preparation. He was afraid of abandonment, yet abandonment is what he found predictable, thus safe, in a confusing and unpredictable world. His violence functioned to create the feared, yet expected, rejection. Predictably, his emotional conflict was extreme, and he experienced an agitated depression.

Fear of Loss of Control

This emotional state is sometimes called "going out of control in search of control." The person becomes over-aroused when experiencing an unpredictable situation. He may approach it with a great deal of learned helplessness due to his disabilities; that is, he quickly becomes overwhelmed because he has little ability to establish personal control.

- The person has an intense need for external structure to be consistently maintained around him. As soon as this is not done, he will display the functional—for him—behavior of going out of control, seeking the imposition of external control over his behavior.

- The person appears to be very rule oriented. He may rigidly adhere to his ideas of what is correct or expected behavior. This seems to function for him as a way of maintaining a sense of security and continuity. As long as rules and expectations are maintained by a significant person, he can be self-controlled.

- One youngster's teacher had a strict set of expectations for him to exercise self-control. On the first day the teacher was absent from school, he pulled the fire alarm. Following this, all substitutes would read the class rules to this boy at the beginning of each day, outlining the privileges to be earned for using good self-control. He was then able to be self-controlled for substitutes as well as for his teacher.

- One man tends to become violent when frustrated. He says, "I like punishment because it keeps me good." He said he wanted a person to live with who is "firm and strict, but won't get mad at me."

- One youth adjusted well to a rigorous classroom schedule. But, in an unstructured social situation, he would become frustrated and confused about what he was supposed to do to gain social acceptance. He displayed this confusion by rapidly cycling through a series of behaviors. First, he would fawn over others, then sulk and finally become aggressive. He would stop immediately if someone assigned him a familiar activity.

- Whenever she became disoriented, one young woman would act out with destructive or aggressive actions until someone would tell her, "Go to the corner," or "Go to your room." She always followed the direction to go be alone for a moment. Becoming aggressive was her coping strategy; going out of control ensured that someone else would establish external control over her behavior and tell her exactly what to do.

- Whenever he became threatened or disoriented, one man would instantly attack the person closest to him. If manhandled, he would become exceedingly violent. However, he would immediately stop and lie down on the floor when told, "Floor!"

Working with these individuals can be very confusing for a support person. They require explicit signals, learned over a long period of time, to use self-control. They need exact phrasing or actions from support persons to be able to make a "conditioned self-control response."

While it is not very hard to give the right cue to these individuals, the difficulty for support persons lies in believing that they have to give the exact cue a person requires.

Adjustment Disorder

Some individuals learn from experience that they can use their aggressive and threatening outbursts to control situations. This type of individual is not "out of control and looking for control," but rather in control by acting out of control. Like the person who fears a loss of control, this person requires an extreme degree of external structure.

Individuals with violent histories are frequently "lumped together" as a group, all believed to use threats and violence to "get their own way." However, the majority of people discussed in this chapter become violent while trying to defend themselves from a perception of danger or loss of control. The few people mentioned here who do act out of control in order to take control do so because of a disturbed personality pattern. For them, these behaviors are among their regular social interactions, appearing even when the person is not experiencing physiological arousal and a fight-or-flight reaction. Simply put, this person is projecting his anger and pain outward onto the world.

■ When frustrated in any manner, an angry outburst is the person's first reaction. He will make demands of others and control them as much as he is permitted to do so.
  - His destructive actions are purposeful (clearly intended to break something), and his aggression is deliberate (clearly intended to hurt someone).
  - His angry behavior looks like retaliation or revenge toward the person or thing that is immediately thwarting his goals. He acts like an emotional bully, throwing his weight around.

■ The person is more than just emotionally fragile. He will become dangerous to others when he senses rejection. His reactions may mimic those of a person experiencing traumatic stress response.

■ When not angry, the person may be eager to please and eager for approval. He may also be responsive to praise.

■ The person typically has an extremely poor self-concept. He has little sense of involvement with his world or of belonging. It is almost as though nothing anyone can do will ever be right or good enough for him.

■ The person may need to perceive himself as an equal and in authority. He may highly identify with the support person whom he perceives as being in a position of power, and may treat anyone else with indifference, neglect, threats or aggression, as if to say, "Get out of my way," or "Get out of my world."

 These actions are guaranteed to trigger a violent outburst!
  - Reprimanding or nagging
  - Arguing with him or engaging his arguments

- Imposing any type of artificial penalty
- Treating him in a way that makes him feel unjustly singled out.

■ The individual's violence may be premeditated, aimed at seeking revenge against the person he believes has crossed him. One woman was angry at a support person for trying to give her advice about being more responsible for her actions. She hit the support person, then went outside and broke the antenna off the support person's car and threw a rock at the windshield.

■ The person's behavior seems to be expressing one of the following.
"I'm looking for and expecting special treatment."
"I have the right to beat the heck out of whoever crosses me."
"Give in to me or I'll tear you apart–verbally or physically."
"Once I get mad, I don't have to be responsible anymore. It's someone else's fault!"

 One man copes with his frustrations and anger by blaming others and using insulting, demanding and threatening comments. However, he becomes explosive if he is not handled with kid gloves in return.

Traumatic Stress Response

Some individuals have an unfortunate early childhood history of emotional or physical neglect, or physical or sexual abuse where they learned that the world is an out-of-control, rejecting, confusing, unsafe and threatening place. As a result, circumstances in adulthood that cause a person to experience a loss of control, rejection or disorientation, which may also trigger extreme arousal states. The person involuntarily connects the distressing emotion to the earlier trauma, when he experienced the same feelings. In fact, he appears to re-experience the emotions associated with the earlier trauma, not just remember them.

The individual may attack the support person to take revenge for previous experiences of perceived insults or rejection.

- One young woman had been sexually assaulted several times as child. She would display increased agitation and aggression during her menses.

- Another woman was physically abused as a child when she would make mistakes. She had an "anger pot" that was full, but felt she had no right to express her anger. However, whenever her support persons made mistakes, she violently exploded at them. She was overcome by the suppressed rage from injustices she suffered in the past. She met any socially acceptable outlet for "objection" with extreme over-arousal.

- One man would sometimes begin to talk about a Mr. X who was going to tear his head off. He would then insist, "I gotta get out of here." If he was prevented from running away, he would become aggressive. It was later determined that Mr. X was an extremely violent co-resident from an old institutional setting, who used to threaten others by saying, "I'm going to tear off your head." The over-aroused man was reliving the memory of those episodes.

Mental Health Crisis Evoked by Major Change

■ Some individuals who become violent are experiencing a mental health crisis. They become overwhelmed and confused by experiences they cannot understand or anticipate. The crisis may originate with changes in their internal state due to a psychiatric condition. Or, it may occur when their living or working placement changes.

■ Changes in the pace of life can evoke a mental health crisis in a person who is easily threatened or stressed. The person may be involved with school, job or placement changes, causing separation from familiar faces and familiar physical surroundings.

■ Changes in socialization patterns, an adjustment to new medications or upsetting family issues can also lead to major distress. The person may be able to cope with one of these changes, but not two or more occurring at the same time. He loses his precarious mental health balance, and becomes distressed, angry and explosive. He may also experience separation anxiety and abandonment, or the group of reactions that are typical of Post-Traumatic Stress Disorder (PTSD).

Symptoms of an Extreme Mental Health Crisis

The person:
- Becomes unresponsive to verbal intervention
- Cannot rationalize
- Cannot process verbal directions
- Is overwhelmed by any sensory input
- Cannot understand or resolve any conflict or contradiction
- Cannot properly process any emotional messages
- Feels overwhelmed and confused by all of the above.

■ The person might benefit from a degree of sensory isolation to protect him from having to process confusing sensations. However, it should be limited since he also feels abandoned, angry, confused, disoriented, lost, anxious, overwhelmed and threatened by anything he is unable to understand. He experiences a loss of control and, therefore, helplessness. He may become depressed.

■ The person becomes desperate to make contact to anchor himself to some reality that he can understand. Yet, he is unable to sustain these contacts. In this state, he may be described as "appearing to be a different person."

To learn more about traumatic stress responses, extensive literature is available on PTSD, psychological trauma and sexual abuse.

Opportunistic, Aggressive Behavior

Some individuals are more clearly opportunistic. In fact, the opportunity to go into high arousal essentially seems to reinforce their behavior. They thrive on the emotional conflict that they can create around them. For instance, an individual may create situations where he can induce support staff to come close (for example, "Tie my shoes," or "Give me a hug"), giving him the opportunity to strike out. Or, he may indicate that he is calm and ready to carry on with an activity, and when a support person is once again within close range, he will immediately act aggressively. It is the close contact, in itself, that provides the trigger to engage in physical assault.

 These situations may not be so dangerous when the person strikes out only once. However, it is extremely dangerous when the person escalates into extreme arousal after the initial attack and continues the assault. In such cases, support personnel must remain constantly vigilant about their personal distance from the person for their own safety.

Behaviors Reflecting a Physical or Psychiatric Condition

- A large number of physical conditions can be associated with a lowered threshold for arousal. Individuals with these conditions may experience over-arousal and fight-or-flight reactions in response to what appear to be relatively minor triggers.

- Any of the generative factors described above can coexist in a person who also has a physical condition. A significant feature of violent loss of self-control associated with a physical condition is that the behavior is not functional for the person. It is an "automatic," biologically defensive reaction to the experience of over-arousal.

- A person who displays violent loss of self-control may have an identified organic brain dysfunction, such as temporal lobe epilepsy; pressure on the brain from arrested hydrocephaly or a blocked shunt; childhood meningitis; cerebral palsy; fetal alcohol syndrome; and so on.

- Often a person with an organic brain disorder will display disinhibition of response when emotionally aroused. The response is much larger than we would expect in a person without such brain damage. This behavior may include both *emotional* disinhibition and *behavioral* disinhibition.

 One girl with a physical disability depends on others for her physical care, but constantly tries to do it all by herself. Working one piece at a time, and using all the time in the world, she is able to accomplish tasks such as dressing. On days when she is still recovering from nighttime seizures, she is unable to do this by herself. She may explode with a violent temper tantrum that lasts until she falls asleep, exhausted.

- Individuals without an identified organic disorder may have a developmental history of having panic reactions to unexpected noises and situations that are confusing, disorienting or unfamiliar. As an infant, the person may have been described as "tactile defensive" or "oral defensive." These responses indicate that he has had a low arousal threshold as an aspect of a congenital condition.

A woman with autism who tends to become overwhelmed by sensory experiences may display violent loss of self-control during a party. She can maintain control for a short period of time, but not if she is asked to remain for twenty minutes in a room with a dozen people talking and laughing.

■ The person may have an identified genetic or hormonal syndrome that is sometimes associated with low arousal threshold, or over-arousal and disinhibition. Two such conditions are Prader-Willi syndrome and Marker-X syndrome.

■ Any physical dysfunction or discomfort increases the likelihood of over-arousal. The person may be experiencing chronic or acute pain, or simple discomfort due to temporary illness or injury. For some women, explosive episodes are more likely in the days prior to, or during, their time of menstruation.

One nonverbal woman had advanced osteoarthritis throughout her body. Her bones were described as paper thin. She would unpredictably strike out at her support persons while they were wheeling her in her chair. The shifting of her weight would occasionally cause her excruciating pain.

■ The person may be experiencing a significant psychiatric disorder that is producing changes in his internal state, arousal levels and sense of security.
 - A disturbance in eating and sleeping patterns may indicate a mood disorder such as depression.
 - The person may be experiencing morbid thoughts and nightmares associated with either real life or imagined experiences. In addition, he may have little ability to distinguish between the two.
 - A person with a psychiatric disorder may be unable to tolerate any unstructured time or time that is not positively oriented by a support person. His mental health disorder may be such that, without external focus to fill in the down time, he hears voices, or has paranoid or obsessive thoughts or fears. Coupled with escalating anxiety and arousal, this leads to an explosive loss of self-control. It may be extremely difficult for such a person to become more independent. In fact, "independence" and lack of structure may be the trigger for the person's mental health disorder.[3]

Interventions
Violent, Aggressive and Destructive Behavior

PREVENTION

It is essential to protect this person from uncertainty and from negative emotions. He may have experienced intense fear and negative reactions from those who have cared for, supported or provided services to him. Thus, his violent behavior may simply reflect his support person's current mood. Often, if the support person is angry with him, he will react with anger. Conversely, if the support person is mature, confident and certain about what needs to be done next, the individual can reflect this demeanor.

Firmness vs. certainty. The person with a disability is sometimes introduced with a comment such as, "You must be firm with her." What the individual may actually require is for the support person to be absolutely certain about expectations.

Testing behavior vs. threatening behavior. The child or adult who requires external guidance for his actions will often engage in testing behavior. Through his behavior, he may be asking, "Who's in charge here?" or "How far can I go?"

His testing may take the form of threatening actions like poking at the support person, raising his voice, and so on. The person may actually ask, "What will you do if I do this?" The support person may perceive this statement as a threat; however, it is not unusual for the person to relax and cease the testing of limits once he has a secure answer to his question.

All support persons should keep a list of every testing behavior ever used by the person, as well as a predetermined response for each. Do not be caught by surprise! Be confident, and "pass the test" quickly by having the right answer beforehand.

■ When the person is in an aroused state, decrease your expectations. De-escalate the situation before the person decompensates. Never pressure the person, act confrontational or "back him into a corner."

To decompensate involves loss of mental and emotional control. The condition may occur during the onset of a psychotic episode. In a person who does not have a psychotic disorder, it may occur when stressors he faces are so great he cannot cope.

■ Always be prepared to use calming activities, and change your day plan to include these activities. Initiate with the person only activities that are personally meaningful; cooperative and self-controlled; and ones he chooses to do.

■ Provide extreme structure for a person who reacts extremely to lack of structure. Rather than living on the edge with him, your goal should be to constantly set the person up to succeed! This means always being two or three steps ahead of him.

■ Try to provide the person with a reason for wanting to be where he is. The best reason is always positive involvement with people who care about him.
  - Set up nice-day activities throughout the day. If the person is focused on feeling that "people care for me," he will often be able to maintain self-control.
  - Arrange to have regularly scheduled positive experiences. For example, provide a choice of blueberry or regular-flavored syrup for pancakes at breakfast; an option to play cards at noon; or an outing for the end of every week. When the person is in a stormy mood, encourage him to focus on the next pleasant activity that is scheduled.

Never take scheduled nice things away. Consider them incentives like the two hundred dollars that is collected for making it around the board in a game of Monopoly. The scheduled activity is not a reward for positive behavior; it is a predictable and positive life structure that is achieved simply for "being in the game" and surviving another round. It is in there to give life some meaning that is not tied to specific behavioral expectations.

Key to Prevention

Use intervention with the environment and people providing support. Remember the six A's: Acknowledge, Anticipate and Avoid problem behavior. Have an Accepting Attitude; Accommodate the person's needs and deficiencies.

- Prior to any activity or outing, remind the person of the rules for self-control.

- Assist the person to maintain a sense of continuity. Give him a prop and a role for entering each phase of his day. The prop and the role both assist him in mediating his experience in any predictably noisy and disorienting situation. For example, let him carry a tray and serve refreshments at a party. Let him carry attendance sheets to the office to mediate the traffic in a noisy hallway. Keep him positively focused.

- Prearrange social events to provide the person with explicit direction about what he could be doing to gain an accepting response from peers.

Communicate at a level most comfortable to the individual. The person is very sensitive to emotional messages, and is easily confused by conflict. The support person should never send a double message such as, "I like you, but…"
  - The worst way: "Don't do it that way!"
  - The better way: "The right thing to do is this _____!"
  - The best way: (with a smile) "This is the way we do that here!"

- Avoid any sense of criticism. Other alternatives to saying, "No," "Don't" or "Stop" are discussed in Chapter 6: Impulsive Behavior.

- Give information to the person in the here and now. Instead of just explaining things, show him. Do not expect a volatile person to "imagine" what you are talking about. Be concrete and explicit.
  - If the person will be attending a new school or workshop, or moving to a new group home, take him there. When you walk in the door, tell him, "This is the home!" "This is the classroom!" "These are the students!" and "Here is what you will be doing!"

- Enroll the person in highly structured social activities such as tai chi, aikido, checkers, Monopoly, computer games, and so on. Make all the rules for interaction explicit, and provide the person with external guidance and prompting for each sequential action.

- Provide the person with organized outlets to burn off pent-up energy. Scheduled exercise can be very beneficial.

■ Individuals who display violent behavior may be mimicking the macho images they have seen in the entertainment and news media. Law enforcement shows, exhibition wrestling and other extreme sports, and action-based video games all provide images that individuals may be unable to keep separate from their daily thoughts and actions.

To prevent one person from viewing violent, late-night movies at bedtime, one support person turned off the electricity to the section of the house that had a television. Another support person unhooked the cable connection at the wall. Yet another support person would provide sports video games to replace those with violent action. The whole staff was advised to provide nonviolent videotapes to satisfy the person's viewing desires.

■ For the person with fear of failure who will sabotage every planned, positive activity, stop planning. Make the pleasurable activities and events become unpredictable. Keep them contingent on periods of self-control, but do not pressure the person with the expectation that the positive event is contingent on his self-control.

  - Determine when a "good" period has lasted long enough. Then, wait for a "teachable moment," and ask the person to come along for the ride. Be prepared for him to refuse to come at the last moment. This means accepting his decision and having an alternative activity ready so he will not resent being left out after others have gone.

GUIDANCE

Guide the person using four specific steps: offer a sense of safety and security; use perfect communication; help the person think; and help the person make good choices.

■ **Offer a sense of safety and security.** The key to management of an explosive person starts with providing him a sense of security and safety, including familiar, comfortable boundaries. It also requires protecting him from any form of conflict or confusion. Assume that the person is unable to learn from mistakes or correction. Provide support and positive direction. Remove all sense of pressure. Keep a smile on your face, and offer tender loving care and encouragement.

A support person may prefer to avoid contact with people who are threatening, but that is not realistic or practical. The best approach is always to be prepared to provide increased positive interaction on a ratio of at least four positive to one negative interaction. This minimizes the individual's feeling of being at risk, and his perceived need to use threats. (For more information on dealing with a high frequency of oppositional behavior, see Chapter 3: Resistive Behavior.)

■ To diminish the potential for the person to perceive a support person as a threat, let him observe you using nonverbal, non-threatening physical communication. For example:

  - Sit or stand in a comfortable, open posture.
  - When in motion, move without tension or hurry.

- Nod your head "yes."
- Have a ready wink and a grin on your face.
- Let the person with challenging behavior overhear the support person making positive comments about him to another person.

■ The person may be experiencing momentary dissociation between his emotions and his immediate experience. He may be reliving a past experience that created a similarly anxious and disorienting state. The key can sometimes be to reorient the person to a familiar place. Look for verbal slogans that trigger the person to use self-control.

 Create a manual of self-control cues to which the person will sometimes respond. Get together everyone who provides support, and summarize what works some of the time. For example:

"What's next?"	"Be a lady. "/ "Act like a man."
"Show me, cool dude."	"Show me the queen."
"Can you handle it?"	"Show me good hands."
"Tell me when you're ready."	"Chill out, dude."

At a moment when the person is dissociated and disoriented, such familiar phrases can lead him to reassociate and reorient to the moment.

 Find out if there are any "wrong words." It may be equally important to list these and avoid using them since they are associated with very bad prior experiences. Some individuals react with an aggressive attack when told one of these things in a disciplinary manner. For example:

"Try again."	"Stop and think."
"Look at me."	"Hands down."
"Go to your room and calm down."	"Control yourself!"

■ **Use "perfect" communication.** Be aware of the person's receptive language deficiencies, and provide information in a way that he is able to process. Identify his needs before you speak.

Key to Guidance

Use positive intervention with the person. Use human relations techniques to engage him in other behavior without confronting him about problem behavior. Use suggestion, positive motivation and humor along with the three D's: Displace, Divert and re-Direct the person's behavior.

- How many words can you use at one time?
- How fast can you speak?
- How long do you need to pause between sentences?
- Can the person understand verb tenses?
- Does the person need visual references?
- Do things need to be written for the person?
- Do you need to wait for the person's response to your first comment before making your next comment?

- For a person who is escalating, try the use of friendly humor and gentle distraction. Watch for his signals about when it is okay to be humorous. Sometimes, when the person seems wary, irritated or unresponsive, it is time to be official and serious about his need to vent emotion. For example, ask, "I hear you are very upset right now. Can I help? Would you like to hold my hand? Would you like to talk?"

- Sometimes, changing faces of support persons can de-escalate a person's state of extreme arousal. Just having a fresh, familiar support person come in—someone who is not associated with the current source of frustration—can bring relief.
  - Appeal to the person's sense of relationship. Often, it is not the "program" that works with an individual, but the "personality match" that meets his emotional need for acceptance during times of greatest distress. Some individuals can be diverted with a gentle reminder like, "Do you realize you're trying to hurt someone who loves you? Let me help you."

 A person who is involved with his support person may be pushing the support person's negative buttons as a covert request for reassurance. The message is: "Prove to me that you can keep me safe no matter how out of control I become."

  - Offer the person immediate, step-by-step direction and answers to all of his questions, concerns and confusion.

- **Help the person think.** The child or adult is likely to have great difficulty in logically thinking situations through for himself. Help him to "line up his thoughts" by slowing these down to just one at a time. Write down statements with him or for him in a "bullet point" format.
  - By writing, you can slow the pace of the person's thinking and assist him in focusing. This way, the support person is being there for the individual, not reacting to the individual's emotional distress.
  - Rehearse written statements with the person. Remove any conflict or complexity from the discussion, including ambiguities about time. Be concrete and visual about who, what, when, where, why and how. For example, show the person on a calendar when important activities will be taking place.

- Explain clear expectations for self-control. For example, one person said, "It's all right for retarded people to hit." When it was explained to him that this was not right, he greatly decreased his aggression.
  - It can sometimes help to "tell" the person exactly what to do. Give him the answer! For example, tell him, "Come tell me when you get upset," or "Ask me for help."
  - It can sometimes help to "tell the person what he is thinking." Validate what you can tell he is feeling. For example: "You look upset and need help. I know you don't want to blow."
  - It can sometimes help to reach for the person who is overwhelmed. For example, ask, "Will you let me help you?" or "Want to be left alone for a while?"

■ **Help the person make good choices.**

- Reinforce any degree of cooperation and voluntary participation. Support the person in using any degree of self-control while the support person gives direct guidance for his overall behavior. Prompt him to think for himself.

- Despite some individuals' extreme emotional sensitivity, it is still occasionally necessary to confront inappropriate behavior. It is essential to do this without emotionally confronting the person. The Hierarchy for Communicating External Control tells the person that external control is here, and that expectations for self-control are being maintained and assisted.

Hierarchy for Communicating External Control

- Start with > "What are you doing?" or "What should you be doing?"
- No self-correction of behavior? > "It's time to do _____."
- Still no self-correction of behavior? > "I'll help you do _____ now."
- Self-correction of behavior at any time > "Good job doing _____!" or "Thank you for doing _____." or "Thank you for letting me help you do _____."

- Coach the person to make a "good choice." Set him up to make successful choices. Present life as a multiple-choice test where the person is provided with the answer key before being asked questions that may confuse him.

- The person may be unable to answer open-ended questions, such as, "What do you need?" or "What do you want to do?" This could escalate the person's confusion. (See section titled Acknowledge Responses to the Presentation of Choices, pages 94-95.)

- Offer choices in a hierarchy. Allow the person to "recognize" the choices being presented to him. For example, ask him, "Do you need quiet?" or "Do you need to go back to bed?" The question is always: "Do you want this?"

- Offer a "forced choice." It may help some individuals to be given a "forced choice" between two options offered by someone else. Then, direct the person to "sit and think about it." And, clearly state the expectation: "Let me know when you are ready to make the right choice."

For the person who tends to be oppositional, it can help to offer the least desired choice first. This allows him to be in control, and still make what is probably going to be the best choice for him. He gets to say, "No, not that. I want this!"

■ Allow extra time. It may help to give individuals five minutes' notice that they will be asked to make a choice. For some, this supplies the time needed to digest the idea and remove any sense of pressure or loss of control.

Training

The goal with individuals who tend to become violent is to teach them, over time, to internalize self-control over behavior that currently requires constant, external control. The person needs to learn the skills necessary to gain control in a socially acceptable manner. We teach him that it is normal for people to become anxious and threatened, but it is not okay to cope with these feelings by hurting or frightening other people. Teach individuals how to maintain control in a manner that others are able to live with.

■ Teach self-advocacy and self-assertion skills. Assertiveness, which replaces both the feeling of being threatened and the desire to threaten or harm others, should be taught and reinforced regularly. And, learning to advocate for oneself must be a part of assertiveness training.

- Teach the person to recognize sources of confusion and distress, and how to reduce them. This sometimes involves asking the person how he felt about past situations. It always involves helping him plan, whenever possible, for both an assertive reaction and a positive change in his feelings when a known stressor is pending.

A woman was facing an upcoming change in her routine that was sure to cause her distress. The support person discussed the change with her several times. Then, they practiced asking specific, relevant questions and stating or signaling her needs, such as, "Where are we going next?" or "Will John be there, too?" or "I don't eat salty stuff."

- Teach the person to explain his disability to others. Often, it helps to give him a printed description that he can hand to others. For example:
  - "I'm trying my best. Talk to me slowly."
  - "Please show me just one thing at a time."
  - "Please let me finish what I'm doing before giving me something else to do."
  - "I get confused and can't remember sometimes. You have to write it down and show me."

- Anger management, taught in group or individual counseling sessions, can be useful for some people. This training usually involves learning personal problem-solving skills and relaxation training. Acquiring these skills can provide individuals with some alternative coping strategies. Many individuals with disabilities will benefit most if they repeat the sessions several times.

Some individuals can be taught to experience and safely release their pent-up anger and other threatening feelings through the media of art therapy, play therapy or music therapy.

■ Motivate the person to learn self-control. Every support person should be familiar with a number of learning principles. It is beyond the scope of this chapter to summarize them all. (One relevant source is *Alternatives to Punishment: Solving Behavior*

Problems with Nonaversive Strategies, by Gary LaVigna and Anne Donnellan [Irvington Publishers, 1986]. See also "General Tips for Teaching a Dependent Individual" in Chapter 4: Dependent Behavior.)

Key to Training

Use positive intervention with the person. Employ motivation and skill development programs, and teach alternative coping skills over time.

- An essential factor in learning self-control is motivation. Try to give the person a concrete reason for performing actions that he can see are in his own best interest. Make the connection for him. When he wonders why he should bother to use self-control, offer explanations he can relate to on a concrete level.

The best motivation for self-control occurs when the person comes to value and have pride in being self-controlled. This can be taught. Pride and positive self-image are based on receiving positive feedback for maintaining self-control. Pride is destroyed by punishment for lack of self-control.

- Communication books and journals are often used to improve communication between the residence, school day program and/or workplace. When books document episodes of violence, the individual with challenging behavior will frequently trash them or the person attempting to write in them. So, episodes of loss of control may be better communicated by telephone.
- It can be helpful to turn a negative communication book into a "Proud of Myself" book. The person could give himself a sticker after each thirty-minute period of using good self-control. Debrief him and give emotional support at the end of each time period. The person will be pleased to bring such self-pride books back and forth.

■ Motivate the person with opportunities to gain increased status. Give him opportunities that allow him to step into an important role, such as:
  - Greeting people at the door or handing out library books
  - Making important choices more frequently
  - Exercising special privileges such as computer games or videotapes.

Offer these options in direct connection to periods of self-control and appropriate decision-making.

■ "Avoid the use of punishment" is one of the most difficult instructions for a support person to follow when working with a volatile individual. However, it is usually necessary to protect the volatile person from any sense of loss or the feeling that something is being taken away. Either of those feelings will typically evoke a loss of control.

One student was receiving stars on a calendar at the end of each day of good self-control. She was highly motivated to win all her stars for an outing at the end of the week. The first day a star was not earned, she ripped up the calendar. She could not tolerate the empty space that reminded her of her failure.

To improve on this method, use an unlined sheet of paper. Provide the stars for self-control, but do not include any blank spaces that would draw attention to failure. This protects the person from perceiving the loss of a star.

- Using artificial time limits can be a setup for failure and self-sabotage. It is essential to allow the individual as much time as it takes to get the number of stars needed for the special activity. And, the person should never lose the day he used good self-control. It may just take a while to have a lot of good days.
- Another method is to give each participant three gold stars for using self-control. Then, on a day when a person "loses it," he can give himself only two or just one. After all, a person usually does not lose it for the entire day. This allows the person to remain proud of himself for the degree of self-control he did maintain. It also encourages him to accept some responsibility for needing to try harder, without feeling like a failure.

One woman chose to give herself an A on a good day and a C on a bad day. She was honest. On a day when she tested hard but did not actually break the limits, she would only give herself a B.

- If possible, make the person's progress toward reward very visible. For example, glue a picture of a computer disk onto cardboard, and cut it into ten pieces. Place an exact copy of the picture–one that is not cut–into a frame. Hang the picture in a prominent location. For each period that the person demonstrates self-control, give him a piece of the puzzle to add to the picture. The computer privilege is earned once the person has acquired all the puzzle pieces.

This powerful motivational method can be applied to various rewards, such as earning money, obtaining a desired video, attending an activity at a particular place (the swimming pool, rec center, and so on), or visiting with a favorite person.

■ Teach the "safe relationship habit." For individuals who self-injure, support staff should always find an alternative behavior that could be modeled and prompted to help the individual express his frustration or inner turmoil. The alternative behavior should be one to which a support person can say, "Yes, do this."
  - What behavior could replace using one's hands and arms to hit, pinch and head butt himself and/or others? Find a ritualistic hand-arm action that could be modeled, coached and rehearsed as a momentary interruption in the chain of arousal. The idea is to choose the most natural alternative movement for the

individual. This could become his "serene posture."

- Try to find an "opposite" behavior. Options include:
    - Place both the individual's hands under his armpits and squeeze down with his arms.
    - Take both his hands and press them together.
    - Place his hands in his lap.
    - Have him press his hands onto the table directly in front of him.

■ The next step is to have the individual practice the behavior sequence frequently, especially when it is not associated with any requirement to assume control over the his disruptive behaviors. Coach the person to pause, assume his "serene posture" and wait for a moment between every event, action or transition. Doing so many times throughout the day establishes the behavior as part of a predictable structure, a "punctuation mark" between each "paragraph" in the individual's day.

■ Prompt the quiet moment exactly the same way each time, so the individual becomes accustomed the slowing of life, a still point that signals that he is ready to respond peacefully to whatever is coming next. This can also serve as a method of systematically interrupting an escalating chain of arousal. After each pause, the support person should give the individual a visual and/or verbal choice to engage in some aspect of his familiar, daily schedule of activity. And, try to make an alternative behavior "portable" with the potential to generalize to multiple environments.

CRISIS MANAGEMENT

Methods described here are a compilation of crisis management techniques that work with a large number of individuals who display violent loss of self-control. It is a good idea to consider in advance which methods might be effective with each individual you serve or support, and to re-evaluate regularly what is working and what is not.

■ Decrease the escalating state of arousal by using two techniques: external controls and exceptional human relations.

- *Using external controls.* For most people, a variety of prevention and guidance approaches will work to dissipate their escalating state of arousal. When such approaches fail, the person has likely entered into an arousal state beyond his ability to control.

Key to Crisis Management

Use direct intervention with the problem behavior. Remain calm and always use guidance techniques first. Accommodate the person's special needs and disabilities. Respond to chaotic behavior with a prearranged plan for surviving the crisis while bringing challenging behavior to a stop! Interact positively with the person as soon as she exercises a degree of self-control. Have a plan for how to re-enter normal life.

 Some people who become frustrated or disoriented appear to experience a state of hyper-arousal, or hyper-excitability that evokes a near-panic response. At this point, the arousal-anger may take on "a life of its own." The person may be inconsolable until he has physically exhausted himself. He may have no other choice than to act out his emotional arousal.

- The moment it becomes apparent that the person is in an escalating cycle, bring in extra, external controls. Five to ten minutes of agitated behavior is long enough. At that point, life is getting to be more than the person can handle. If there is an established "crisis medication" in the person's program, offer it sooner rather than later in the cycle.

- Try to provide the person with an opportunity to use any degree of self-control. For example, try offering medication by setting it on a counter and asking him to take it when he is ready.

- *Using exceptional human relations.* Treat any person who is caught up in an escalating state of arousal as though he is experiencing a mental health crisis. Respect his extreme emotional sensitivity and vulnerability. Protect this susceptible, explosive person from having to deal with too much at once. Be non-threatening. Do not show tenseness or anger in your face, voice or posture. Any attempt to engage or confront the person will lead to argument and escalation.

Sometimes reverse psychology can be effective. "Excuse me, this is not something you are supposed to do. I should have done that myself." The person may say, "Go ahead, do it yourself." Now at least the person is not hitting! The person may say, "That's okay, I'll do it for you." This is an example of letting the person off the hook so he can take the hook.

Keep your approach easy, low-key, simple and accepting. At the same time, give the direct, explicit guidance the person requires.

■ De-escalate by allowing task completion.
   - For many people, coping with anxiety is accomplished by retreating into compulsive, ritualistic behavior. Allow the person to complete what he is doing; attempting to stop him could easily provoke a violent episode.
   - Help the person complete what he is attempting to do. When walking past a barbershop, the person may suddenly want to have a haircut–immediately! The support person may recognize that he is becoming more and more aroused, agitated and unwilling to be diverted. It is probably best to allow the haircut to protect him from escalated arousal and disinhibition.
   - When a person enters a crisis level of arousal, he may perceive every issue as life-threatening. He may become angry about not knowing the answer to a question that he perceives as critical to his survival. Hearing "I don't know" from a person he relies on for guidance will usually make things worse for him.
   - It is essential to provide the person with a resolution for each issue of the moment. Deal with questions as soon as they are raised. Address them in a definite manner. If possible, write down facts that are known and certain. Contact those who can resolve issues on a factual basis.

■ Use exceptionally clear communication.

- When trying to help the person "come down" from a crisis state, a quiet environment can be extremely important. Unfocused background noise can severely impair a person's ability to concentrate, sort out his perceptions, and process verbal information. Be less verbal, rather than more verbal.

 One woman would attack the support staff when she was in an aroused state if told, "Get your coat for a walk." However, she was able to accept the invitation when her coat was held out in front of her, with nothing else said.

- When talking with a person who is in an aroused state, vocal tone is very important. Use a level and low tone of voice. Use short, direct sentences. Be clear, explicit and concrete in your choice of words.
- Model the correct emotional tone to the person, being confident and certain of yourself. Body language can also communicate confidence. "Stand tall." Be friendly and accepting while communicating a secure, mature, confident manner.
- Some individuals cannot feel safe unless they know their support person is in charge. The person needs to perceive that the support person will protect him from a world he experiences as threatening. He may "test" the support person to verify that she is actually in control of the situation.

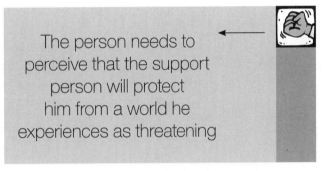

The person needs to perceive that the support person will protect him from a world he experiences as threatening

 A support person who is threatened by an individual's testing behavior may unintentionally escalate the threatening behavior. This is most likely to happen with an individual who is oversensitive and overreactive. His highly tuned "emotional radar" reflects back and exaggerates the emotions presented to him in his immediate environment.

- To work successfully with a person who can be very threatening requires confidence and emotional maturity.
- Keep cool. For many individuals, saying "Give me a break" may be enough to end an arousal cycle, while acting timid would escalate it.

■ The support person needs to give both the appearance of being fair and actual fairness!
  - The person who is over-aroused may also be unresponsive. In these moments, it may be necessary to demonstrate to him that the expectation for self-control remains unchanged.
  - It will help some individuals to be asked to remember the rules. The person may be able to respond to an impersonal comment such as, "It's policy. I have to help you be safe."

- For some individuals, it helps if the support person simply restates the rule for what is expected then walks away. It is important to wait for the person to be ready for this reminder. Wait for the teachable (or reachable) moment.

■ Offer a "way out" of the crisis. One of the most important supports we can offer the person who is out of control is a way out of the crisis. We function as a lifeline for him when we allow him to connect with the support person in a supportive manner.
- It may be sufficient to say, "Come with me. Sit down here…calm down."
- You might suggest that the person sit down while you get him a cup of water or a cold washcloth.
- The support person can sometimes help the person to feel competent by asking him a question that he always knows how to answer. For example, ask the person about the picture on his desk, who is in it, and what was happening that day. Ask him about a very recent event or period of time when he felt successful and proud. Use few words; the goal is to help the person focus on the familiar.
- The person who is escalating due to a sense of pressure can frequently be calmed by bringing in a new face.

• One woman was able to stop herself in the midst of her worst rage as soon as the support person who best knew how to talk to her walked in the room.

• One man could de-escalate when given the option of making a phone call to an authority figure who could assist him to regain control. When asked, "Would you like to call your social worker?" the person usually accepted the offer, and the crisis was over.

■ Help the person avoid emotional escalation by taking dictation. Have paper and pencil ready, and ask the person to tell you what happened. If the support person listens carefully while he is talking, the individual may be able to vent his feelings without escalating into loss of control.

One person was willing to make a tape recording about what had caused him to feel threatened and angry. While making the tape, he was too busy to trash his room!

■ Use a pre-established avenue for escape. Prepare for the crisis so the individual with challenging behavior can remove himself from the perceived threat. He must not feel that someone has "cornered" him.
- Have a pre-established avenue of escape from crisis situations. When individuals know how to exit with permission, they will often choose this option rather than become violent.
- To encourage the person to participate, ask him before going into any situation, "Where will we go if we need to find a spot to relax in a hurry?" Make finding this spot into a game you both play. This pre-establishes in the person's mind that the procedure might have to happen, and that things will work out if it does. You both are ready for it.

- The person may run away from the support person as a means of controlling himself or avoiding a perceived threat. In certain situations, this leave-taking is the most appropriate and self-controlled thing the person could possibly do. If it can be safely done, allow the person to run while you shadow him at a distance.

> Do not expect recovery of self-control in any distracting...environment where the person has not been explicitly taught a safe procedure for calming down.

■ Use a pre-established "return to normal" plan. When the person has calmed down and has exercised self-control, the crisis is over. Attempting to have him make restitution can often evoke another confrontation and crisis.

But, how can the support person and the volatile individual re-enter a daily routine without terrible hard feelings and reliving the bad behavior over and over again? This is accomplished by sticking to a pre-established plan that accommodates the needs of all parties concerned.

- Use a ritual for re-entry. The more familiar, emotionally neutral and uncomplicated the ritual, the easier it will be for the individual to put the crisis behind him.
- Be objective. When interacting with the person following a violent episode, keep the focus on behavioral expectations, not "right vs. wrong" or personality differences.

One man often tried to discipline his housemates. If personally corrected or told, "Stop that," he would attack the support person. On the other hand, if the support person said, "Discipline is my job," he would back away without a violent loss of self-control.

- Resume familiar activities. Following a violent episode, start or return to an activity that is personally involved, cooperative and routine. For example, look at the daily schedule for what is next, and tell the person, "You belong here."
- Show the person how to move on. Invite the person to become re-involved on a positive note. Coach the person to remain in control and to self-pace his re-entry. For example, ask the person to look at a book for a while and say, "Come and help me with dishes when you're ready."

■ Provide environmental supports. Do not expect recovery of self-control in any distracting, disorienting environment where the person has not been explicitly taught a safe procedure for calming down.

- Make use of any familiar, comforting object that draws from the person's repertoire of skills. For example, offer him a chance to play a favorite instrument, watch a favorite movie that calms him or listen to music.
- Some individuals need to be allowed to "sleep it off" following an explosive

episode. This gives them time to "decompress" and escape from experiences that have overwhelmed them.

- Some individuals find it helpful, when the violent episode is over, to be directed to a room to sit down, calm down and go over the rules. For this reason, it is helpful to write down all rules for the house, school, day program or workplace in advance. The list should be simple and explicit. For example:
    - Create a poster with two columns or boxes that state, "DO: ask for help, keep calm, look nice, do chores" and "DON'T: yell, break or hit."
    - Create a book with pictures that demonstrate the appropriate behaviors, with Xs drawn through inappropriate behaviors.

 One man was brought back into a state of self-control and belonging by being offered a meaningful role to play. Support staff asked him to plan an invitation list and menu for a dinner party.

■ Debrief but do not criticize. Later on, the person may wish to talk about the violent episode. Allow him to talk, but be cautious about any attempt to correct his recollection of the episode. This could trigger an additional confrontation.

■ Protect the support person and other individuals. It may be impossible to protect a person from all the circumstances that arouse him to the level of displaying violent, aggressive and destructive actions. Even with the best planning and programming, "life" will always intrude and provoke some recurring violent behavior.

In summary, a predetermined, coordinated plan should always be in place for protecting those who come into contact with the person who is frequently aggressive and violent. It should be based on consensus between the organization that provides services or supports, any individual (such as a family member or friend) who provides support, the government agency that provides oversight, and all staff. This ensures a supportive environment for the person with a disability.

1. **Be prepared in order to remain calm**. Do not work with the person who has the potential for violence until you have closely observed other support persons working successfully with him. Become familiar with procedures that work well with him when he is in a noncrisis state.

2. **Remove the target.** Keep in mind that the person in an aroused state may become vigorously focused on one person as a target for his aggression.
    - *Aggression directed at the person who is trying to help*: When the person is becoming tense, it may be most helpful to ask him if he would like a particular person to leave him alone. For example, "Want me to go away?"
    - *Aggression directed at no one in particular*: Sometimes, a person who has no awareness of how to reduce the arousal-panic state will strike out in a directed manner at whoever happens to be nearby. Remain calm and protect yourself while attempting to calm the person.

3. **Stick to procedure.** Be certain that you are familiar with crisis management procedures that have been established for bringing crisis episodes to a close ritualistically. Be prepared with a backup plan, and use it when nothing else works.

4. **Maintain safe physical and psychological boundaries.** With individuals who have a potential for violent, aggressive behavior, remain vigilant and aware of their location and mood state. Remain aware of your body distance from the person and confident about the presence or location of backup.

   - Some violent crisis situations will only be manageable with the physical presence of backup. Some individuals will have warning signs that indicate the necessity for having an extra "body" around. Listen to experience and these warning signs. Provide for the extra "body" to reinforce the fact that external control is available.

   - Some violent individuals will only go out of control when there is just one support person around. This represents an "opportunity" for them to go out of control. Such a person represents a danger to support persons. When in an aroused state, these individuals should always have at least two support persons present at all times to provide visible and physical backup.

5. **Protect everyone present from out-of-control behavior.** Gather two or more support persons who are trained to defend themselves while protecting the volatile person.

   - Offer the person a "way out" rather than "cornering" him.

   - Intervene to protect the person and others. If restraint is required, rely on professionally trained personnel, such as emergency medical technicians, police officers and intensive care support staff.

   - Remain aware that restraint is not a solution. It is a momentary method of protecting others from serious harm when all other prevention, guidance, training and crisis management procedures have failed.

   - Assess the need to refer the person for a psychiatric evaluation. It may be necessary to consider medication for use in emergencies.

6. **Recognize the reality for the support person.** At times, an individual has been so threatening and destructive that a support person is too intimidated to work with him. Offer the support person "critical incident debriefing" and agency support.

Relocate the Individual: The Last Resort

It may be necessary for the person to move to another home, school, day program, or other significant place where no support person has been conditioned to be frightened of him. If this occurs, make this plan with the person's participation.

   - "Set up" the person to perceive any residential move as positive and made by cooperative choice. Diminish the possibility that he will perceive a move as yet another rejection. Also, diminish the possibility that he will see the move as evidence that he got his way by being aggressive.

Techniques for Special Cases

Special Case 1: Predictable Cycles of Individual Behavior

Some people show a predictable pattern, or cycle, in the buildup of emotions leading to a loss of control. These individuals seem to be riding an escalator that they cannot get off until they reach the top. They may be quite flexible at other times, but become inflexible and rigid when emotionally aroused. Many of these individuals can inhibit their violent outbursts if properly interrupted early enough in the cycle. (Remember: "If you listen to the whispers of behavior you may not have to hear the screams.")

Individuals who respond to cues to use self-control do not need behavior modification, warnings or discipline. The person does not know how to get off the escalator and calm himself down. But, he is quite able and willing to respond to someone who will show him a way off in a friendly and non-threatening manner.

■ Pay attention to early signals, and intervene quickly. Otherwise, destructive and violent behavior (the escalator) becomes the "only way out" for the person who has no other way of overcoming feelings of frustration and confusion. A person cannot get off the escalator and use an alternate route if it is not readily available.

■ Carefully observe the person to identify his early warning signs. Every person's behavior is unique, but many individuals follow a predictable pattern in a discrete series of escalating steps. The key to successful intervention begins with this careful observation. Following are some examples.

- One person frowns, sucks her lip, mutters negative feelings, then violently attacks.

- One person is irritable in the morning, scolding his cats. He assumes increasingly threatening postures with those he meets as the day goes on, and then he attacks.

- One person changes his vocal tone, tenses up, uses different body language, then hits someone.

- One person takes physical control of objects to use them as playthings, stops paying attention, says no, gives objects back to the support person, then hits someone.

- One person will say, "I'm in a bad mood" then "I'm not going." Next, he fidgets, starts to pace, annoys others, becomes needy, displays forced laughter, then becomes violent.

- One person teases for a moment then explodes violently.

■ Create a standard approach. Once you have identified the sequence of buildup behaviors, create consistent guidelines for every support person to follow at each step in the person's cycle. Guidelines must identify which behaviors will be redirected, and which ones require the support person to respond by removing pressure.

■ The very beginning of a cycle is not always obvious. The behavior may just be frustrated venting of emotion or inappropriate attention seeking, with no potential for escalation. Guidelines must identify which behaviors will be redirected, and which ones require the support person to respond by removing pressure.

 In the earliest part of a person's cycle, it may be all right to ask him if he needs help because he may still be "thinking" and responding to language at that point. At the next stage of escalation, he may not be able to answer a question, and it may be necessary to remind him of the right thing to do. The rule of thumb is to start off by expecting self-control, but be prepared to step right in to provide necessary external support and direction.

■ Timing can be critical. Do not hesitate if the signals are there! Respond to the very first indication of distress, frustration or arousal.

 One person says no, shakes his head, bites his hand, pinches, tries to escape, falls on the ground, then becomes violent.

■ Remove pressure. With the first indication of distress, avoid or remove any form of pressure or emotional challenge. This will help the person de-escalate. For example, momentarily withdraw and "ignore" an initial outburst. While this gives the individual an opportunity to engage in a self-calming activity, it does not directly model, coach, prompt or rehearse self-calming behaviors to ensure successful practice.

■ Offer to assist and reconnect with the person. The next part of the cycle indicates the person may be in need of assistance. Identify when to give him cues to calm down, and when to engage with him in a structured practice to help him calm down.

 When one man is responsive, he will sometimes accept clear and certain redirection from support staff to remove himself from the immediate area. Or, he may accept coaching to practice alternative self-calming skills such as breathing, stretching, or use of a warm blanket or weighted vest.

■ Use a diversion. After it becomes obvious the person needs assistance, the next part of the cycle will indicate a need for something to take the person "off the hook." For some individuals, diversion may be introduced as an idea to consider. For others, the situation may require a prop and direct instruction to do another activity. Bring in diversion and redirection as though you are "administering a treatment."

 One child would tease then explode. The cycle stopped if the support person said to him, immediately after the first tease, "Here is your chair and a book."

Following a brief episode of aggression or self-injury, verbally and physically coach the individual to demonstrate "nice hands" or "be gentle."

Responding Calmly to a Cycle of Escalating Behavior

Do:

- Keep yourself calm.
- Ground the person in reality.
- Stay one step ahead of the person.
- Focus the person on an activity he knows well and can competently perform.
- Anticipate what might agitate the person, and protect him from exposure to agitating circumstances.
- Avoid giving in to fear.

Don't:

- Get caught up in the emotion the person is displaying.
- Criticize the person or pressure him in any way.
- Engage the emotionally distressed content of the person's communication.
- Try to restrain the person physically once he has gone out of control.

■ Practice the skills needed for fearlessness.

Of course, it is very difficult and "unnatural" to have no fear in the presence of someone who unpredictably hurts support persons. Yet, being fearless is necessary to being able to project calm into the person's escalating emotional space.

- To achieve fearlessness, a support person must develop a disciplined focus through mindfulness. The goal is to provide "antidote" thoughts that can displace your sense of threat. (See http://mahavat.blogspot.com for a bibliography of sources on the practice of mindfulness.)
- Another way to overcome fear is to "give fearlessness" to another person by making a daily practice of protecting other living beings from fear or danger. This might involve actually rescuing someone from harm or offering prayers for the deliverance of the vulnerable. (See http://www.tharpa.com/background/fearless.htm for further discussion of meditation and Buddhist practice.)

Special Case 2: The Person Who Is Out of Control but Searching for Control

Some people displaying violent behavior are unable to demonstrate self-control until they are placed under "court order." This order, or rule, must prescribe that the person is not to lose control. Usually, it is reinforced on a daily basis through extra supports and frequent visits from an important authority figure. This can be very comforting to some individuals; they feel reassured by an absolute, external authority that exists to impose rules for their behavior when they are otherwise unable to do so.

- Recognizing the person who is out of control but searching for control
    - This person can recognize his own cycle of arousal and is frightened by the experience of losing control. He finds it so aversive that he would do anything to prevent it or make it stop. So, even as he is losing control, he is seeking control.
    - For this person, it is quite functional to display violent behavior because it immediately brings him attention, control and structure! Intense, disruptive activity is often a desperate attempt to exercise some degree of control, regardless of the cost to himself.
    - The person displays self-control in the immediate presence of a strong authority figure and when constantly reminded of that expectation. As soon as boundaries are present, he feels safe and able to remain calm.

- When allowed three chances, the woman never takes more than two.

- When the second the pill goes in his mouth, the child settles down.

- As soon as the ambulance arrives at the door, the man stops threatening people.

- As soon as the police arrive, the woman stops throwing things.

In cases like these, out-of-control behavior is "testing the limits" to find out if someone will assume control. The crisis ends abruptly. .

- Maintaining the necessary structure

At some point, support persons may perceive that the individual's behavior has gotten "better." They may relax the consistently maintained structure, including the reinforced, high expectations for self-control. They may also reduce medications. As a result, the individual may experience a lack of external boundaries and difficulty predicting reactions from support persons. Therefore, he may revert to out-of-control, violent behavior as he searches for control.

> Reminding some individuals after they have broken the rules can lead to arousal, disinhibition and defensive retaliation, rather like a high-speed chase.

Some individuals require structure in order to function. Withdrawing that structure automatically causes the person to struggle, and may cause him to lose trust in the support person. He may "get even" with the support person who is unable to protect him from this distress. Furthermore, the person takes even longer to respond to expectations for self-control following an outburst due to a relaxation of structure. Most likely, he will start off with more testing behavior. Obviously, this sequence of events does not help anyone.

- ■ Using reminders and cues

Some individuals always need a reminder to be able to follow the rules. The reminder can take the form of a specific person or a specific cue that is verbal, visual or physical.

- The support person as the reminder. For the support person who must keep constant structure in place for the volatile person, it may help to regularly visualize the "officer on the corner." For example, if you see a police officer in the area, you will watch your speed and obey all the traffic signs. You have little inclination to test the limits. You know you will get caught but–more importantly–you have just been given a visible reminder to follow the rules of the road.

- Reminding some individuals after they have broken the rules can lead to arousal, disinhibition and defensive retaliation, rather like a high-speed chase.

- Many individuals with a mental disability have difficulty stopping and starting behavior on cue. This is discussed in more detail in Chapter 5: Persistent, Repetitive Behavior: Perseverative Responding.

- ■ Maintaining structure with different support persons
Each new support person who interacts with the individual has to re-establish control.
- Remember, a person with intellectual disabilities is likely to find it very difficult to generalize learning. So, if he can show self-control in response to one support person, but not others, it is probably best to develop his positive response to the new support person in the presence of the old one. Do this using identical prompting procedures. For example:
- Verbal cues: "Corner" or "Hands down" or "Chair" or "Room!"
- Visual cues: "okay" hand gesture, tapping the heart, pointing to the rules
- Physical cues: a tap on the person's hand, three knocks on a wall or table.

If the person responds differently to different people, it can be dangerous to experiment with new approaches. Use what works best. Most likely, the person must rely heavily on cues that were established over a long, difficult period.
- If the goal is to fade specific verbal cues, always be prepared to revert immediately to the conditioned ones. When the support person observes a sequence of arousal building up, she should use the most direct, successful method for prompting the person to self-control as early in the sequence as possible.

- ■ Minimizing confusion in activities
These individuals tend to be most happy when they know exactly what is going to

happen and when. Vigilantly regulate the flow of activities for the person who will go out of control in search of control.

- Avoid letting problems develop in down time when there is less structure and direction for the person's behavior. Successful programs usually include a daily calendar and an hourly schedule of activity.

- Provide the list of the black-and-white rules required for each individual. If possible, list them in point form under the headings, DO THIS, and DON'T DO THIS.

- Consider making a special list that states: FOR SUPPORT PERSONS: BELIEVE IT OR NOT, DO THIS. Ensure that every support person who is new to the volatile individual knows in advance which expectations the person is used to following and how they are communicated to him.

■ Time to change the structure?
Be prepared to provide this level of support for the person's entire life. Despite how we may see it, some people actually function best in a daily routine that looks like "probation for life."

- What time might be the right time to lower the degree of structure? This "test" should only be performed with support persons who are highly familiar with the volatile person. They may be capable of relaxing a degree of structure and immediately re-imposing it, if necessary.

 In real life, the "test" of the person's ability to tolerate reduced structure tends to happen with new or relief support persons who are not totally familiar with the person's extreme need for structure.

Special Case 3: The Person with a Personality Disorder

Individuals with personality disorders can be dangerous to an uninformed support person because of the complexity of their emotional, behavioral and psychological issues. In some instances, their violent behavior is not an arousal reaction that can be systematically prevented. Therefore, a support person who works with a child or adult displaying a personality disorder should always receive professional guidance that provides approaches tailored specifically to the individual.

While the following guidelines offer some direction, it is beyond the scope of this chapter to deal in depth with the management of borderline personality disorder and criminal behavior.

The person with a personality disorder appears similar to one who goes out of control in search of control, but he is actually in control by acting out of control. He may be described as:

- An emotional bully who requires constant reminders of external structure, as well as rules, expectations and payoffs for self-control.

- A person with many good reasons for having bottled-up anger, often behaving like "a hurricane looking for a sail."

- A person who feels greatly mistreated, and is looking for an excuse to "tear your head off."
- A person who can turn every request or direction into a nit-picking confrontation.
- A person who will push the limits or take extra advantage of any situation in an attempt to assert his rights.

■ These individuals can be extremely challenging since most people have a natural tendency to be frightened of a bully–to back off and leave him alone. This is not an adequate response. The person needs to be kept under a constant, tight rein with few behavioral alternatives.

 Provide the person with a "box of expectations" for self-control. The approval and other rewards for self-control that are attached to these expectations must be very powerful.

> Goal 1: Have him peacefully enter the box of positive expectations.
> Goal 2: Have him come out walking and looking for positive direction and cooperation, not a fight.

■ In an unfamiliar situation, some individuals must find out who is in control. If they do not discover a confident person in charge, they may attempt to assume control with a display of threatening or aggressive behavior. This, in effect, fills the power vacuum with disruptive behavior. To avoid this, support staff must maintain authority and control.

■ The person is often obsessed with fairness and justice. Avoid stimulating the person's sense of persecution. Do not become confrontational; instead, provide fair ground rules that set behavioral limits that apply to everyone.

- Have a rule worked out in advance for every challenge. (Meet the person at every turn.)
- Present the rules as written lists of expectations and privileges.
- Operate the rules with the precision of a computer.
- Appeal to the person's sense of justice when recalling a rule or expectation.

■ Allow this type of individual to indulge his ritual and compulsions. Set consistent boundaries and clear expectations for how the support person should respond to these behaviors.

■ Whenever possible, allow the person to have control in the context of a framework provided by the support person.

- Allow him to have a choice between two options that the support person provides. If possible, use the object of the person's compulsion as a payoff for self-control.
- Be extremely, behaviorally specific. Once a rule is established for a setting, do not modify it.
- Offer clear boundaries for the person who tends to be impulsive, and becomes angry when thwarted. "You can do X as soon as we finish Y."

- State the rule and walk away. Do not threaten! Remove any emotion from the reminder of the rule. Remind the person of what he gains for remaining self-controlled, not of what he will lose for losing self-control.

■ If the person starts an argument to prove you are persecuting him, do not become defensive. Do not engage the argument. Stay calm, and make a statement about the reality of the immediate situation. For example: "We will be leaving in ten minutes. Make up your mind if you want to come or not." Give the person room to express himself–emotionally vent–but make it clear that no privileges or further choices are available until he accepts one of your options.

■ When the person becomes used to following the rules, allow more choices and more self-control. Always keep the choices behaviorally explicit, and present them in the form of contracts. Increasing the person's "freedom" without continuing to clarify his boundaries tends to re-ignite emotional bullying.

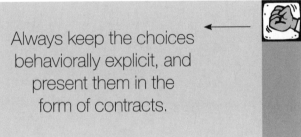

Always keep the choices behaviorally explicit, and present them in the form of contracts.

■ Before structured programming is successful, the person will often try to provoke a confrontation as an excuse to go out of control. For example, he may refuse medications. Or, he may verbally abuse the support person to provoke a controlling response. He seems to be saying, "Let's see if I can make you look like a sail, so I can blow you away with my hurricane!" However, do not fall into this trap. Enforce the rules, and let the consequences follow naturally. Remove other people from the room. This type of person will rarely hurt himself. But, if you try to physically control the person, it often stimulates a catastrophic reaction.

■ Be prepared with a pre-arranged plan for times when the person does become explosive. Always follow through with it.
- Prevent the person from gaining control by "upping the ante." When a person who has been using violence to control situations finds that his behavior no longer works, he may escalate to a greater level of violence. Be prepared with an extremely structured and physically protected environment so that when escalation occurs, it does not become a successful method for the person to achieve his goals.
- Use containment to protect others only if necessary for safety. Do this in accordance with agency guidelines and only with personnel who are well trained and certified in providing safe containment practices. (Also, be sure to work within any federal and state guidelines that apply in these situations.)

In This Chapter

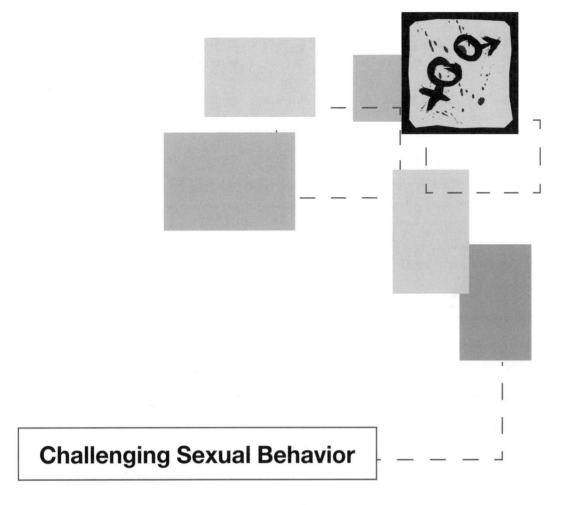

Challenging Sexual Behavior

Editor's Note: A substantial portion of the information in this chapter was provided by Dave Hingsburger. For details, see the Notes section.

Challenging sexual behavior appears in a number of forms, all of which fall into four general categories.

Public, intrusive, impulsive or excessive, sexual behavior. Certain sexual behaviors will always present a challenge to those who support a person with disabilities. These include public or excessive masturbation, impulsive sexual touching, public self-exposure, and publicly engaging in sexual relations.

Sexual behavior directed toward inappropriate persons. This behavior may be acceptable with an age appropriate peer but happens to be expressed toward inappropriate persons–support staff, teachers, and so on.

Behavior that compromises the safety of the sexually vulnerable person. Some challenging sexual behavior is directed toward extremely vulnerable individuals. Their susceptibility arises because they are too trusting and unable to judge another's motives. They may also show a lack of resistance to receiving affection and/or cannot report sexual abuse by others. Support personnel are responsible for the protecting these highly vulnerable people.

Noxious and/or dangerous sexual behavior. This most difficult behavior may include voyeurism, fetishes for non-dangerous or dangerous objects, and talking about or threatening others with one's sexual fantasies. The most dangerous forms of behavior include exploitation of children or less functional adults with disabilities; sexual coercion or violence; and rape.

Some challenging sexual behaviors are disruptive actions that just happen to be sexual in nature. These generally fall into two categories:

Behaviors resulting from cognitive deficits (deficits in sexual knowledge, social skills and/or assertiveness)

Noxious or deviant behaviors that represent excessive arousal in response to an inappropriate sex object or method of sexual expression.

There is no single best method for managing individuals with challenging sexual behavior. It is essential to look at the *manner* in which a person expresses a behavior. The nature of her disability should dictate the methods used. The following discussion includes a description of each category, several typical examples and suggestions for intervention.

Public, Intrusive, Impulsive or Excessive Sexual Behavior

When expressed publicly, impulsively, excessively or intrusively, disruptive behaviors that are sexual in nature always present a challenge to the person providing support. These include public masturbation; excessive masturbation; impulsive sexual touching; public self-exposure (taking off clothes); and public heterosexual or homosexual behavior.

Public Masturbation

Definition: In a non-private context, the person repeatedly touches herself in the genital area, either on the outside or inside of clothing. The person exposes herself in the process of self-stimulation.

- At school, a fifteen-year-old student masturbates whenever he is not given continuous step-by-step direction during an activity. He also has an early history of pushing over physically disabled peers when not given direct, continuous supervision. Teachers and support persons react immediately to his masturbation, but everyone uses a different approach.

   The student can accomplish many things when shown and directed on a movement-by-movement basis; however, he is unable to initiate any sequence of behavior. Staff resolved the problem by constantly directing his activity non-emotionally and providing him with a selected time of day to engage in private masturbation.

- At a workshop, a man who tends to be extremely nervous would frequently adjust his underclothing and tuck in his shirt, rubbing at his groin. The support person would send him to the bathroom to do this in private. He would stay in the bathroom until someone else needed to get in–sometimes for several hours. This behavior jeopardized his placement in the workshop. However, when told, "Go fix your shirt and come right back," he would do exactly as he was told. To resolve this, the staff taught him to fiddle with his Medic-Alert bracelet when he was nervous and leave his shirt alone.

- In a residence for individuals with profound intellectual disabilities, one woman was constantly injuring her skin by pulling at her breasts. Wearing a padded brassiere reduced her breast irritation. Another woman continually pulled at her groin with her hands under her clothes. Wearing an apron with pockets reduced her behavior. For a third woman, it was necessary to design special jumpsuits to prevent continual self-stimulation of her groin. (See Chapter 5: Persistent, Repetitive Behavior.)

Behavior Characteristics

- A support person will usually respond to public masturbation with an emotional and controlling reaction. Thus, the person with a disability may use the behavior as a functional means of gaining attention or external control over her behavior.

- Masturbation may be a response to boredom. It may simply be time-filler behavior that only occurs during down time, similar to rocking or spinning, because she has nothing better to do.

- The person may be cue-dependent and, unless directed, may not know what else to do. She may be unable to initiate or organize her own behavior, and may not know any other way to "ask" for external direction.

- The behavior may serve to reduce anxiety.

- The behavior may be pleasurable self-stimulation, and the person simply has no awareness of the meaning of "public" versus "private" behavior.

Interventions
Public Masturbation

Prevention

- Keep the person's hands occupied with activities that she finds interesting. Eliminate down time as much as possible, and provide frequent, physical outlets like exercise, sports and walking.

- Alter clothing to prevent the person's hands from gaining access to erotic areas. Consider the use of aprons with pockets, or jumpsuits without pockets.

Key to Prevention

Use intervention with the environment and people providing support. Remember the six A's: Acknowledge, Anticipate and Avoid problem behavior. Have an Accepting Attitude; Accommodate the person's needs and deficiencies.

GUIDANCE
- Direct the person to a private place, and allow time for engaging in self-stimulation.
- Divert the person with an alternative activity.

 Consider that a support person's personal beliefs and attitudes will affect her responses to people who engage in self-stimulation. Ensure that the person receiving supports is not being given any negative emotional messages that cause her to feel she is bad or wrong for engaging in this activity.

TRAINING
- Teach the person the meaning of "private" versus "public."
- Teach relaxation and socially acceptable options for reducing anxiety.

CRISIS MANAGEMENT
Establish a standard, non-emotional response that can be used by all support persons. Interrupt the public masturbation, and redirect the person using the pre-established method. Make sure every support person's response is constant, boring and predictable.

Excessive Masturbation

Definition: People providing support may differ considerably in defining "excessive" masturbation. Without question, masturbation to the degree of self-injury is excessive. Also, because it is a solitary activity, masturbation is excessive if it is frequent enough to make the person unavailable for other activities.

BEHAVIOR CHARACTERISTICS
No specific behavioral or individual characteristics are typically associated with excessive masturbation; however, several factors may contribute to the activity. David Hingsburger, an author and expert in the field of disabilities, cites the following factors: inaccurate sexual education, lack of social awareness, lack of alternative activities, lack of adequate lubrication, medical problems, or the side effects of certain medications.[1]

- *Inaccurate sexual education.* One man who spent excessive time masturbating was asked if he did so until the "white stuff" came out. He said no. Asked why not, he said, "It will make you sick," a "fact" his mother had told him. Furthermore, he believed that only "handicapped people do that," and he did not want to be seen as handicapped. As a result, he was in a state of perpetual arousal. This was resolved by providing him with accurate sexual education and training him to masturbate until he ejaculated.[2]

- *Lack of social awareness and/or lack of alternative activation.* One blind man would come home from his workshop, go directly to his bathroom, and stay there masturbating until he was called for dinner. Calling him to join the group for tea and cookies within twenty minutes of arriving home eliminated the problem.

- *Accidental learning due to lack of lubrication.* A man was referred to the sexual counseling clinic with the complaint that he was masturbating excessively and with feces. His excessive masturbation had caused the skin of his penis to become scarred and bleeding. Somehow, he had discovered that using feces made it hurt less. This was resolved by providing him with a lubricant and training him to use it. What originally appeared to be deviant behavior was an example of accidental, deviant learning.[3]

- *Medical problems.* A man who had never displayed problems with masturbation began to injure the skin of his penis through excessive masturbation. On medical investigation, he was found to have prostate problems and difficulty ejaculating. Medical approaches were initiated to solve the prostate problem.[4]

- *Medical problems.* A woman was reported to be aggressively masturbating by ripping at her vagina. Medical investigation revealed an advanced yeast infection. Appropriate medication eliminated the scratching behavior.[5]

- *Side effects of medication.* One man was accustomed to masturbating several times a week. He suddenly began to display bizarre behavior. He was observed slapping his penis against the wall and attempting to stimulate his penis with a knife. Medical investigation revealed that a recent change in his medication had caused him to lose the ability to gain an erection. Appropriate adjustment to his medication eliminated this difficulty.[6]

Interventions
Excessive Masturbation

PREVENTION AND GUIDANCE
- Provide the person with access to lubrication.

- Ensure that the person has sufficient opportunities to engage in alternative activities she finds interesting.

- Ensure that the person receives regular medical attention, and guidance about medication side effects.

TRAINING
- Provide the person with accurate sexual education, and facilitate her acceptance of her own sexuality.

- Where required, train the person to use lubrication to gain sexual release.

Key to Guidance

Use positive intervention with the person. Use human relations techniques to engage her in other behavior without confronting her about problem behavior. Use suggestion, positive motivation and humor along with the three D's: Displace, Divert and re-Direct the person's behavior.

CRISIS MANAGEMENT
Always seek a medical evaluation when there is an unusual change in a person's degree of masturbation or self-stimulation.

Impulsive Sexual Touching

Definition: Impulsive sexual touching generally constitutes isolated, single displays of behavior that are sexual in nature. If allowed to progress without interruption, these behaviors do not lead or escalate to other more dangerous behaviors.

These behaviors are characterized by a lack of self-control. Impulsive sexual touching means invading another person's space by hugging indiscriminately; putting one's face up against another's; or touching another person's hair, clothes, and so on. This also includes aggressively or suggestively grabbing at another person's groin, buttocks or breasts, and intrusively rubbing one's body against another person's.

- One woman would tickle men who lived in her house until the support person told her to stop. At this point, she would grab her victim in the groin, creating a great struggle as the support person tried to make her remove her hands. The more effort put into removing her hands, the harder she struggled.

  For this woman, hearing any instruction to stop what she was doing would usually lead to intensely disruptive behavior. Involving her in several small, helpful work projects, increasing her scheduled social outings, and moving her to a space where she could freely roam when not otherwise occupied resolved this behavior. (See Chapter 7: Socially Disruptive, Attention-Seeking Behavior.)

- At social dances, one man would grab at the breasts of women he found attractive. When confronted, he would always say, "Wilma tickled me." It turns out that Wilma had been his girlfriend for many years until she unexpectedly moved away. This man was practicing his well-established courtship habit of tickling the woman he liked. Giving him training in more socially appropriate forms of courtship, such as holding hands and hugging, displaced his breast-grabbing behavior.[7]

- When approaching to ask something, one woman would always push her body directly against the support person's body, and put her face very close. This was resolved by verbally and physically prompting her to "stand at arm's length."

- A young man with similar behavior that invaded other people's personal space would become agitated and violent if told to step back. This was resolved by asking him, "What's the rule?" He would repeat the rule, then step back by himself. (See Chapter 6: Impulsive Behavior.)

- One young man constantly approached the support person and touched his hair, arm and/or face. He was like a moth around a flame, in constant motion. He was only able to remain still and quiet when held closely and gently massaged by the support person. Otherwise, it was necessary to keep him continuously occupied in simple activities. (For suggestions on working with this behavior, see Chapter 5: Persistent, Repetitive Behavior: Perseverative Responding.)

- One man would threaten female staff by touching them on the buttocks whenever they passed by. This was resolved by providing only male support staff and closely supervising him to prevent the opportunity for inappropriate physical contact with any woman. In closely supervised social settings, the man was able to behave appropriately after he completed self-control training that rewarded him for keeping his "hands down."

BEHAVIOR CHARACTERISTICS

■ Often, when given a reminder about touching, the person will immediately put her hands down or step back, then repeat the behavior within minutes of being corrected.

■ Excessively close physical contact is often associated with repeated questioning. It seems as though the person cannot feel reassured, no matter how many times she is told something.

■ Individuals may have difficulty picking up on social cues that are not direct and explicit. They may not be aware of the social rules for personal space and acceptable social distance. Or, they may have difficulty remembering them.

 Think about how we violate social and sexual rules in group homes. With inevitable changes in staff, strangers are constantly intruding on the personal space of individuals we serve and support. We intrude on a person's privacy in the bathroom. We inadvertently model a double standard that says public nudity and a lack of personal space are okay for her, but not for us. The person with intellectual disabilities is already struggling to discriminate which settings call for which behaviors. This double standard makes it even more difficult.[8]

■ The person often has impairments in the areas of language processing, distractibility and attention span.

■ The person may appear to be trying very hard to gain attention, affection or acknowledgment, but possess very few appropriate social skills, so has difficulty meeting these needs.

■ These individuals often have difficulty organizing their own behavior. Touching or getting close seems to provide them with a degree of continuity.

■ The person may have a dysfunctional sexual learning history, and may be using an impulsive, learned social response to the support person's presence. The person may be neurologically impaired to the degree that she is unable to exercise voluntary self-control over her impulsive behavior.

Interventions
Impulsive Sexual Touching

PREVENTION

■ To avoid accidentally reinforcing what may be attention-seeking behavior, never react instantly.

We will always experience the strongest emotions in response to another person's most intrusive behaviors. Unfortunately, individuals who find it extremely difficult to learn the connection between cause and effect may find it easy to learn that intense social reactions are provoked by physical contacts of a sexual nature.

- Provide verbal prompting and rehearsal of the rules prior to any event where impulsive sexual touching may be attempted. For example, ask the person, "What are the rules about touching?"

- Provide opportunities for appropriate physical expression to meet the need for contact, such as dances, floor hockey and other forms of physical play. Set time aside to give socially appropriate affection by holding and comforting the person.

- Provide adequate supervision to divert and prevent impulsive sexual touching for individuals who are unable to respond to guidance and training. (See "Special Case: Attention Seeking for Nurturing and Affection" in Chapter 7: Socially Disruptive, Attention-Seeking Behavior.)

GUIDANCE
- Help the person pay attention to social expectations for controlling impulsive sexual touching. For instance:
    - Ask, "What are the rules for touching?" and "What are you doing?" and "How are you supposed to touch?"
    - Use positive reminders such as, "You are supposed to touch like this."
    - Draw the person's attention to a positive model who is displaying socially appropriate physical contact.

TRAINING
- Use instructive and directive feedback to motivate self-control over impulsive sexual touching. For example, tell the individual, "Stand at arm's length and shake my hand," or "Stand beside me and hold my hand."

- Teach social distance. Teach the person to respond to the verbal cue, "Hands down." Teach the person appropriate nonsexual touching. Teach and identify locations where nonsexual touching is acceptable.

- Use verbal and tangible rewards to give explicit, positive feedback to the person maintaining self-control and following the rules. For example, "Good for you. You remembered the rules all by yourself."

- Teach appropriate, social courtship skills.

CRISIS MANAGEMENT
- For people who are unable to respond to prevention, guidance and training, give brief social feedback, such as, "That makes me feel bad." Guide the person to a brief time away from social contact, while providing preventive and protective supervision. Then, engage the person in a directed activity.

- For some individuals, supervision may be required twenty-four hours a day to prevent constant crises. Some individuals can self-inhibit when they are directly supervised, but not when they are out of sight of a responsible support person.

Public Self-Exposure

Several causes can contribute to public self-exposure. Among them are confusion, disoriented agitation, self-activation, accidental learning, anger and hostility.

- *Confusion.* One man occasionally comes out of the bathroom when he is not wearing any clothes. He displays many of the characteristics of early onset Alzheimer's disease. He becomes forgetful about why he is in the bathroom. When he takes his clothes partway off, he thinks it must be time to take them all off. Then he wanders out with a confused look on his face. To resolve this, the support person becomes gently directive. She simply says, "Time to get dressed."

- *Disoriented agitation.* One large man has a chronic psychiatric condition that becomes intensely acute about three times a year. When he is in an agitated state, he engages in a number of bizarre behaviors, including taking off his clothes. To prevent these behaviors, one or two support persons would stay directly beside him to comfort him and give gentle reminders of appropriate behavior. This careful support is maintained until he is settled, or until medication is able to calm him.

Draw the person's attention to a positive model who is displaying socially appropriate physical contact.

- *Self-activation.* One woman would continuously keep herself busy by taking her clothes off and putting them back on. To resolve this, support staff made sure she always had a light cardigan sweater at her disposal to remove and put back on at will. (See Chapter 5: Persistent, Repetitive Behavior: Perseverative Responding.)

- *Accidental learning.* One man who lived in a group home would occasionally drop his pants when support staff showed their anger toward him. As it turned out, he always did it on a Monday following a visit with his parents. His parents reported that when he was a young child, they would punish him by having him take down his pants for a spank with a plastic paddle. Obviously, his behavior was not exhibitionism. It was an "obedient" reaction–a learned response to a generalized social cue.[9]

- *Anger.* One woman would became very angry and tear everything off when denied the clothes she wanted. She would refuse to wear the outfit, demand another, and sometimes go on to refuse every single item in her wardrobe.

This was resolved by always offering her an opportunity to dress herself with a choice of two outfits from her wardrobe. If she refused both, the support person would persuade her to dress in a jumpsuit with the offer of a favorite sweater. Following a period of voluntary cooperation with the jumpsuit agreement, she would again be offered the original choice of two items from her wardrobe.

- *Anger.* One woman would strip and shred her clothes if there were any imperfections in the ones she was offered. She would also do this if she was offered anything other than a blue shirt and pants. To resolve this, support staff carefully went over her clothes the night before looking for imperfections. And, enough duplicates of the blue shirt and pants were kept on hand to satisfy her preferences.

- *Hostility.* One man would occasionally expose his penis to female support staff while making sexually threatening comments to them. This was resolved by providing a male support person to continuously maintain protective and preventive supervision.

■ Public self-exposure will almost always "force" a support person to respond to the behavior. It is possible for the behavior to inadvertently become a functional means by which the person achieves a resolution of tension or expression of emotion.

■ Individuals who expose themselves usually have limited means of appropriate self-expression and are quite deficient in social coping skills.

■ The person may be experiencing a strong sense of helplessness due to her lack of ability to predict or control what is happening in her world. She may expose herself due to emotional regression in response to current circumstances.

Interventions
Public Self-Exposure

PREVENTION AND GUIDANCE

■ First, attempt to respond to public self-exposure as though it is an accident. Try to prevent it from inadvertently becoming the person's means of obtaining attention or emotional control over others.

■ The key is to be non-emotional in all interactions with the person during periods of public self-exposure. Calmly direct her to the bathroom or the bedroom to put on her clothes. Then, stay with the person to help her become oriented and engaged in a familiar activity.

■ Try to provide the person as much choice as possible, even if this is in the form of forced choice between two clothing alternatives you are providing.

■ Try to give the person as much control as possible. Provide structure by following routines and schedules in the same manner on a day-to-day and week-to-week basis to make her world more predictable. Provide for idiosyncratic clothing preferences.

TRAINING

■ Provide positive consequences to give reinforcing feedback for accepting clothing and for staying in the clothes that are provided.

■ Provide skills training to develop and rehearse alternative, prosocial methods of emotional expression.

CRISIS MANAGEMENT

Provide close protective and preventive supervision of the person as required to ensure that she, and others in her environment, are safe.

Public Sexual Behavior

Individuals with intellectual disabilities who find partners and form consensual, sexual relationships often have no socially sanctioned, private place to engage in sexual behavior. When there is no opportunity for private sexual expression in a bedroom, car or front porch, the only options may be a public park, a secluded alley or the bathroom at the workshop.[10]

When a person with intellectual disabilities is evaluated and found capable of participating in a consensual sexual relationship, support staff must address several special concerns. Often, their greatest challenge is in reaching a consensus about what is appropriate sexual expression for the person receiving services. Another major concern is ensuring that the individual is capable of behaving with sexual responsibility. This requires counseling, education and training. These approaches must address:

- The importance of consent in a sexual relationship
- Reproduction and sexual hygiene
- Prevention of unwanted pregnancy
- Prevention of sexually transmitted diseases
- Appropriate times and places for engaging in sociosexual behavior (for example: public hand-holding and kissing versus private, direct sexual contact)
- Various forms of displaying sexual intimacy (including the right to decline any intimate practice at any time)
- General training in responsible adult relationships.[11]

Finally, provide individuals with disabilities with the opportunity for privacy in order to engage in consenting, responsible sexual relations.

Sexual Behavior Directed Toward An Inappropriate Person

An individual with disabilities may express sexual behavior toward an inappropriate person, such as support staff, a teacher, an acquaintance the person barely knows, and so on. Normally, we choose sexual partners from within our innermost circles, but it is not unusual to hear a support person complain, "My student is in love with me." Individuals who direct their sexual behavior inappropriately do so for a number of reasons related to the nature of their disability, the opportunities available to them, and the environments in which they live.[12]

INDIVIDUAL CHARACTERISTICS

■ The person usually does not have peer relationships with an adequate degree of intimacy and familiarity. Thus, she is choosing partners from the right circle of intimacy, but the wrong people are within that circle. It is comprised of people who serve and support her, not her peers.[13]

■ The person often lacks the social competency and ability to make accurate social judgments. This may take several forms:
    - Making inaccurate inferences about a relationship with another person
    - Having expectations that are unreal, irrational or fantasized
    - Misunderstanding the meaning of friendliness and familiarity
    - Misunderstanding the nature of sexual relationships
    - Difficulty discriminating sexual from nonsexual behavior.[14]

■ The person's peers are often unable to provide the guidance and direction she requires. If she is substantially cue-dependent but otherwise mentally competent, normal urges will draw her toward teachers or support persons who have provided guidance.[15]

• One man was severely language impaired and unable to learn without close, direct instruction. With this intensive instruction, he was able to learn and soon showed that his disability was mild. At the same time, he would fall in love with all of the teachers with whom he became "mentally intimate." When he attempted to dominate their time and was rejected, or when one of the teachers moved on, he would experience severe reactive depression.[16]

• One young woman was sexually aware and interested. She pleaded and demanded that a female support person come and sleep with her in her room. She would call any male support person who paid attention to her a boyfriend, and would attempt to give him neck massages.[17]

Interventions
Sexual Behavior Directed Toward an Inappropriate Person

PREVENTION

Every agency or individual providing support to a person with intellectual disabilities should have a pre-arranged plan for sexuality guidance and training. This ensures the rights as well as the safety of the individual receiving supports and/or services. The guiding philosophy should be:
    - Personal growth and self-determination
    - The best interest of the individual receiving support
    - Freedom from harm
    - Informed consent.[18]

GUIDANCE

■ The person needs immediate feedback–prompts and encouragement–and very clear guidance about social distance, levels of intimacy and appropriateness of partner selection. She should be led into relevant training programs as described below.

■ The person needs to expand her circle of intimates and, at the same time, gain the social skills required to sustain an intimate relationship.

■ Griffiths, Quinsey and Hingsburger (1989) suggest that "Any agency that advocates sexual rights and freedoms for individuals with handicaps must also stress that these freedoms be expressed in ways that are safe for the individuals involved."[19]

TRAINING

■ The person should be evaluated for a number of specific social skills. Where these are lacking, the Six Techniques for Developing Social Skills should be used to help her develop proficiency.

Six Techniques for Developing Social Skills

1. Direct instruction
2. Feedback
3. Reinforcement
4. Modeling
5. Practice
6. Role-play.

■ A number of specific social skills should be included in training.

Discrimination skills
- Affection versus intimacy
- Nonsexual versus sexual behavior
- Friend versus intimate
- Age-appropriate and peer-appropriate partners.

Basic friendship skills
- How to make and sustain friendly relationships with peers
- Verbal and nonverbal behaviors that can effectively elicit the desired response in a social interaction
- How to read a social situation: smiles, eye contact, proximity, facial expressions, friendly comments, and so on
- How to respond to social cues without losing social reinforcement from others.

Concrete aspects of a real relationship with a mutually consenting partner
- How to develop a relationship
- How to show and receive affection
- How to sustain a relationship
- How to resolve conflicts within the relationship
- The value of being in a relationship

- Understanding and caring about the effects of the relationship on a partner
- Coping with the complexity of sharing oneself with someone else, more than just sexually.

■ *Levels of intimacy.* Have the person describe the individuals in her life. Put each one within a concentric circle surrounding a picture of the person. The primary, inner-most circle contains closest and dearest friends to whom she can tell anything. These are the people she can allow to touch her. For a person with an intellectual disability, this inner circle is usually composed of staff or family members.

In the second circle are people she can touch with her mind, people she thinks about and who are important to her. Often, this is the social service blanket wrapped around the person.

In the third circle are the people at work. These are frequently other persons with no names. Finally, in the most outward circle are peers and community workers. These are often very close to the place held by complete strangers. (For more information, see *CIRCLES I: Intimacy & Relationships; CIRCLES II: Stop Abuse;* and *CIRCLES III: AIDS: Safer Ways* by Leslie Walker-Hirsch and Marklyn P. Champagne [James Stanfield Publishing, 1993, 1986, 1988].)

 These training techniques also provide critical skills for two other pur-poses: to assist in the protection of the sexually vulnerable individual, and to develop sociosexual skills in the individual displaying noxious and/or dan-gerous sexual behavior.

Protection of the Sexually Vulnerable Person

The incidence of documented and observable sexual harassment and sexual abuse of indi-viduals with intellectual disabilities is higher than the general population. Therefore, they have a greater need for training in self-protection. This is true for a number of reasons.

INDIVIDUAL CHARACTERISTICS

■ *Confusion about authority.* The person may have been thoroughly trained to com-ply with the direction and instruction of any number of non-disabled people. She may give no resistance to showing and receiving affection if the person touching her sexually appears to be in authority.[20]

■ *Confusion about physical contact.* The person may have spent years relying on a sup-port person or persons for physical care, which caused misunderstanding of social dis-tance, personal space and physical intimacy.[21]

■ *Lack of sexuality education.* The person may have a normal sex drive combined with impulsiveness and lack of judgment. Furthermore, she may have a normal need for emotional support and assurance of her self-worth, but little to no information about varieties of sexual experience. [22]

■ *Lack of discrimination in relationships.* Typically, the person has difficulty judging the character and motives of others. This leads to a limited ability to discriminate appropriate from inappropriate social behavior. An abstract idea like the importance of consent in a sexual relationship may be far beyond her comprehension. She may not know that she has the right to choose not to be sexually intimate.[23]

■ *Lack of self-protection skills.* The person may lack both the assertiveness to say no to a sexual advance and the physical skill to defend herself. Her communication difficulties may prevent her from reporting sexual abuse.[24]

■ *A history of abuse.* The person may have been sexually exploited by a relative, support person or authority figure who also provided pleasant, appropriate experiences. The person then becomes confused about what is "right" and "wrong" touching. She may have been threatened with harm or a withdrawal of support if she discussed the inappropriate sexual activity. Or, she was taught to refrain from discussing any sexual issue.[25]

Interventions
Protection of the Sexually Vulnerable Person

PREVENTION

■ Provide the person with opportunities for open communication and accurate knowledge about the varieties of sexual expression displayed in our society.[26]

There is no dumb question, and there is no issue too embarrassing to discuss. The person with a disability needs to know that she can comfortably go to a support person with any issue that bothers or confuses her, or sparks her curiosity.[27]

■ While statistics indicate that a large number of people with disabilities are sexually abused as they are growing up, they can avoid this by being taught to protect themselves. Parents, guardians and/or support staff begin by being open and responsive to any questions about sexuality; telling the truth; and using correct terminology and explicit details. Protective education should also include learning several critical facts.

Key to Training

Use positive intervention with the person. Employ motivation and skill development programs, and teach alternative coping skills over time.

   - Private and public places are different.
   - Sexual behavior occurs appropriately in private.
   - No one, not even someone you know, should touch your private parts.
   - You have the right to say NO.
   - Abuse is not the victim's fault should it occur.
   - You should respect the privacy of others, too.[28]

GUIDANCE

■ Attempt to provide the person with unambiguous experience about the meaning of touching during physical care. With sexually aware individuals who require assistance in toileting or in menstrual hygiene, care by a same-sex support person is advised. Where feasible, the support person should coach the person with disabilities to do her own care, while instructing her about the private and personal nature of physical self-care.

TRAINING

■ Try to ensure that the person can make a responsible decision about sex based on accurate, honest and well-informed teaching. Specific self-assertion skills should be taught directly and explicitly:
   - How to recognize, say NO to, and remove oneself from sexual interaction that is inappropriate to time, place or partner
   - How to recognize, say NO to, and remove oneself from sexual victimization in the form of force or manipulation
   - How to physically defend and protect oneself from unwanted sexual advances
   - How to request assistance–and from whom–following an unwanted sexual advance. (See the training techniques in "Sexual Behavior Directed Toward Inappropriate Persons.")

CRISIS MANAGEMENT

The person may be sexually responsive but unable to benefit from the suggested training approaches. In this case, it may be necessary to alter the person's environment to prevent any opportunity for sexual exploitation. Another option is to provide protective supervision in situations where she may be vulnerable.

Noxious and/or Dangerous Sexual Behavior

Definition: Noxious sexual behavior includes voyeurism, fetishes for non-dangerous objects, and talking about and threatening others with one's sexual fantasies. Dangerous sexual behavior includes exploitation (of a vulnerable person, such as a child or a less functional adult with disabilities); sexual coercion or violence; and rape.

The challenge of working with individuals who express their sexuality in a noxious and/or dangerous manner can be extremely difficult for the support person. These individuals actively seek opportunities to practice the deviant behaviors because they find them self-reinforcing. Typically, the person has an idiosyncratic learning history that has led to socially maladaptive ways of seeking sexual satisfaction.

■ As with any undesired behavior, the support person's goal is four-fold:
   - Determine acceptable replacement behaviors.
   - Teach the knowledge and skills the person needs to be able to exercise self-control.
   - Motivate the person to practice responsible self-control.
   - Provide the necessary supervision and support to prevent the person from harming himself or others.

BEHAVIOR CHARACTERISTICS

■ Typically, the person knows few or no ways whatsoever of expressing sexuality in an appropriate manner.

■ The behaviors are often responses by individuals who are unable to express anger in an appropriate way. This anger often stems from transient distress. The intensity of the distress typically matches the person's level of inner conflict and lack of adequate coping skills, not the actual threat posed by the stressor.

Key to Crisis Management

Use direct intervention with the problem behavior. Remain calm and always use guidance techniques first. Accommodate the person's special needs and disabilities. Respond to chaotic behavior with a prearranged plan for surviving the crisis while bringing challenging behavior to a stop! Interact positively with the person as soon as she exercises a degree of self-control. Have a plan for how to re-enter normal life.

- The person may lack an understanding of the seriousness of his deviant sexual behavior, especially if he sees himself as separate from society and, therefore, exempt from responsibility and blame.

- Often, the person has experienced a major life, vocational or interpersonal change, or conflict just prior to an occurrence of inappropriate sexual behavior.

- In new life situations, self-control becomes more challenging, leaving the person vulnerable to relapse. Symptoms of distress, such as insomnia or intense emotional reactions (anger, loneliness, depression or anxiety), can lead her to distort or misinterpret situations.

- For this person, distress is also generated by self-hate, guilt and shame. Alcohol or drug abuse, or another addiction, may also play a part. These feelings and habits increase the likelihood of the person finding herself in high-risk situations.[29]

GUIDANCE AND TRAINING

One effective approach was developed by Behavior Management Services of York Central Hospital in Richmond Hill, Ontario. This approach begins with a comprehensive assessment by experienced professionals, including:

- A preliminary survey
- An environmental assessment
- Assessment of the person's sexual knowledge
- Assessment of the person's social skills competency
- Assessment of the person's sexual preferences.[30]

Following this, a multidimensional treatment approach is developed for the person, which includes:

- Covert sensitization (methods for decreasing deviant arousal)
- Masturbatory conditioning (behavioral techniques for increasing arousal to non-deviant stimuli)
- Social skills training
- Sexuality education.[31]

The person's treatment also includes training in new coping strategies, and ongoing support to prevent relapse. However, these issues are extremely complex, requiring a skilled, comprehensive treatment plan that is beyond the scope of this book.

Readers wishing to learn more about York Central Hospital's approach to noxious and/or dangerous sexual behavior can find a detailed discussion of assessment and treatment protocol in *Changing Inappropriate Sexual Behavior: A Community-Based Approach for*

Persons with Developmental Disabilities by Dorothy M. Griffiths, Vernon L. Quinsey and Dave Hingsburger [Paul H. Brookes Publishing, 1989].

Appendices

Appendix A

Fundamental Training Approaches
For a Person with Severe Intellectual Disability

Training a person with severe to profound intellectual impairment is governed by two main principles:

Principle 1 (What Won't Work): It is not likely that the person will learn well from negative feedback. "No" or "try again" does not give any explicit cue about what the person should do next.

Principle 2 (What Will Work): With repetition, most individuals with severe to profound intellectual impairment are able to form expectations about the sequence of events. Remember the adage: Assist, insist and persist.

Keeping these principles in mind, use the initial training strategy of positive modeling, physical guidance, and rehearsal of error-free, prompted action.

1. Ask the question.

2. Prompt and model to give her the correct answer. (Use sounds or words that form a partial word or sentence for the person to recognize and complete. This is called the cloze technique.)

3. Prompt by supplying the person with the correct answer.

4. Praise every effort the person makes, no matter how small.

Training Essentials

- Before giving any prompts to task, the person's attention must first be focused by verbally and physically prompting both orientation and eye gaze.

- For most individuals with severe impairment, it is important to accompany any verbal cues with visual modeling, using concrete props, gestures, and signing.

- The "backwards chaining" and "error-free" learning techniques help the person know exactly what to do, and feel positive about their slightest effort.

- Until the person achieves a high degree of proficiency with any task, he will require graduated prompting. Practice sessions must be repeated daily, ideally several times a day, until the stimulus cues consistently evoke a correct response.

- If the person does not initiate a positive response within a few seconds, repeat the request, once again modeling the correct response.

■ If, for any reason, the person is not consistently making a correct response, immediately repeat the initial training strategy.

This is simply a brief overview. A number of publications, including the following books, offer comprehensive training approaches:

Hingsburger, Dave. *Do? Be? Do? What to Teach and How to Teach People with Developmental Disabilities.* Richmond Hill, ON, Canada: Diverse City Press, 1998.

McClannahan, Lynn E., and Patricia J. Krantz. *Activity Schedules for Children with Autism: Teaching Independent Behavior.* Bethesda, MD: Woodbine House, 1999.

Pryor, Karen. *Don't Shoot the Dog: The New Art of Teaching and Training.* New York: Bantam Books, 1999.

Appendix B

The 6-Step Training Ladder:
How to Support a Setback in Training

It is the nature of learning that anyone who is making progress in a learning task will have periods of "setbacks." For most people, this is not an issue. When our learning is built on a solid foundation, we just review and rehearse again the immediately previous steps. We consolidate our previous learning and carry on.

Some individuals with developmental disability can be making great progress, then run into a "setback" from which they do not recover. The 6-Step Training Ladder helps demonstrate some of the reasons why a person might be unable to recover from what seems to be one small slip.

The 6-Step Training Ladder

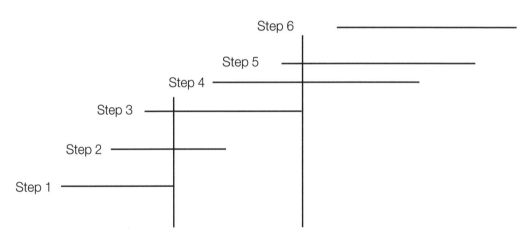

Step 1. We start teaching her at whatever level her natural ability dictates. At this spontaneous level, she may be secure but unfocused toward any progressive goal. She may function at this level as a dependent learner.

Step 2. We train her to enhance her natural level of ability by helping her acquire a few additional skills. These skills are steps towards a progressive goal that we believe will be within her reach eventually. Step 2 significantly overlaps and repeats what was learned at Step 1.

Step 3. Having helped her become secure and relatively independent at the second stage of learning, we raise the bar. We increase expectations for performance without support (or with less support) as she becomes practiced and familiar at performing at a higher level. By looking at the graphic, you can see that at Step 3 there is still some overlap between Step 1 and Step 2.

Step 4. By now she has made so much progress that anyone who was not observing from the beginning will be unaware of just how far she has come. Her original level of dependent functioning seems to be a matter of "ancient history." She is now doing things that many who knew her at the beginning could never have imagined.

The critical points occur at Step 4 and Step 6. At Step 4, her learning no longer overlaps Step 1 and just barely overlaps parts of Step 2. Her independent progress exceeds her starting point so much that she "loses touch" with her original, spontaneous level of ability. Her initial skills are no longer being rehearsed since they are now "assumed" to be permanent. She begins to lose her ground.

She can see the goals she wishes to achieve, but she is simply "getting ahead" of herself. She is smarter than she can independently be, so to speak. It is too much too soon for her to continue with confidence. She is able but inconsistent, and needs more support to consolidate her earlier learning.

Step 5. She has now progressed so far that she does not even remember how dependent she used to be. She seems ready for much more challenge and eager to do as much as she can. This is the point at which a person will typically run into some obstacle that she cannot independently overcome. Step 5 no longer overlaps Step 2 and just barely overlaps parts of Step 3. Her ground has slipped further and further away from her.

By this point, she expects to be able to overcome problems on her own. So, she tries to cope. Unfortunately, the coping skills that she requires were never among her original coping repertoire. Suddenly, she regresses and finds she is unable to sustain what she was able to do perfectly well just a short while ago.

Sometimes, support persons push the person with disabilities too fast. The person may also push herself. She may try to accomplish, without assistance, what she may only be able to accomplish with continuous assistance or structure.

Step 6. Her performance drops back a level or two. At this point, support staff will typically approach her with encouragement and support. "You knew what to do yesterday. You just have to try harder, and you can do it again."

This misses the point. Once a person who was initially dependent becomes insecure, she may be unable to make the connection between what she was doing at Step 4, and what she was supposed to do at Step 5, much less at Step 6. So, approaching her "from above" to reach back to where she has been experiencing failure and distress is likely to overwhelm her.

When you see regression, support from below. That is, just go back to the beginning. Do this as a means of giving her a chance to rehearse familiar territory and success without assistance. We always rebuild our efforts with a person who has had a setback from a place where she is naturally confident and certain of her ability to meet expectations.

To do this, it may be necessary to go back to Step 1, with very intense, dependent levels of support. From Step 1 she may be able to rapidly re-attain a level of ability where, with support, she can once again grow in a more independent fashion.

Appendix C

Working with Perfectionist Anxiety

Many individuals with autism and other developmental disabilities will not attempt to do things unless they are certain they know exactly what is expected, and that they can actually accomplish exactly that. They "lock in" on their concrete and literal interpretation of the "rules," as they understand them. Once they know how to do something they want to do it perfectly.

 One youngster could only do his schoolwork in pencil or on the computer. With an ink pen he could not turn in "perfect" work. This caused a major conflict with the school and a behavioral "meltdown" whenever he was required to use a pen. This boy had to be able to correct his "errors." His parent insisted that the school accept pencil or provide him with access to a computer to allow him to correct his work before turning it in. He was also given extra time to complete work to his own standard.

Perfectionism may affect the person with autism in another manner. It is so difficult for some to understand how the "rules of the world" work, that once they recognize what to do, they may feel that they have to do everything they know how to do. They try to do it all.

 One youngster was an excellent baseball player in many ways. He could catch, pitch and hit the ball hard. But when he was on the field he wanted to catch and field the ball and get the player out every time. When he could not accomplish this he would "melt down." He believed he was failing at the game of baseball. This was the end of his competitive ball playing, but he can still enjoy one-on-one catch and batting practice.

A person with this perfectionist tendency can become very depressed when he is unable to "win" in social situations.

 One boy always felt that he was playing life as a game and that the game was rigged. He needed to feel that those who were supporting him were in the game, on his side. And, the game itself always had to be "rigged" in this boy's favor.

Giving the "Answer Key to Life"

Try to remember your ninth grade algebra, or eleventh grade physics class. Remember the answer key at the back of the textbook? It gave students the correct answers in advance. Without that key, we might not have attempted to solve the difficult problems. With it, we felt confident that we would be able to correct our work if we made any simple mistakes. This prevented anxiety about appearing stupid, and reassured us that we would get credit for our effort.

These are powerful motivating circumstances; they allow a person to gear up and put out the effort needed to perform a difficult, new task. Having the answers available did not make us too dependent, not even if we looked at the answer first to get an idea about how we might do the problem. We still had to show our work. So, the answer key simply clarified the end goal, and allowed us to organize our effort. In short, it made us more efficient.

The Main Principle and Two Applications

When working with perfectionist anxiety, remember the main principle at work, and two of the most common situations in which you can offer help.

Main principle: Many individuals with autism and other developmental disabilities will not attempt to do things unless they are certain that they know exactly what is expected. They want to "lock in" on a concrete and literal interpretation of "the rules" as they understand them, and do things perfectly in line with those rules. It is our job to provide the person with the "answer key" to life in as many situations as possible.

Application 1: Solving social problems that are too full of conflict and ambiguous meaning.

- Write out every rule and every interaction, and have the person study them.
- Pre-rehearse this "life script" for successful interaction before each interaction. Make sure the person can "pass the test" because he has memorized, rehearsed, and externally generalized his role to the immediate situation.

Application 2: Helping a person get "unstuck" when perfectionist thinking "freezes" him, leaving him unable to apply himself.

Offer the person a suggestion to do something from his own ritualistic and sensory repertoire. Many individuals are so comfortable with ritual that this familiar "way out" is all they need to escape from their momentary anxiety.

What about Gray Areas?

The person's concrete or "black and white" thinking does not allow him to easily comprehend "maybe," "if-then" and "either-or." The phrase "sometimes this and sometimes that" can make him quite frustrated while "I don't know" can cause a near meltdown. It sometimes helps to explain the difference "black and white" versus "gray" areas, as follows.

Black and white means:
- There is just one rule.
- There is just one way to do things.

- Events and expectations are predictable because things stay the same.
- Rules seem fair and clear.

Black and white happens when:
- A schedule with an exact time is always the same. For example, the store always opens at 8 a.m. and closes at 10 p.m.
- All the rules apply to everybody with no exceptions. A driver must have a license to drive a car.

Gray areas mean:
- The rule is sometimes one thing and sometimes another.
- Events and expectations are unpredictable.
- Rules seem confusing and unfair.

Gray areas happen when:
- Different rules apply to different people. For example, everyone at a party enjoys pop, cake and ice cream except a person who is diabetic, because he cannot.
- Different rules apply at different times of the day or week. For instance, people pay parking at meters until 6 p.m. but not at all on Sunday.
- Different rules apply at different times of the year. For example, students go to school five days a week, except during spring break, holidays and summer vacation.
- Something is done one way some of the time, and another way at other times. For instance, some days your parents or friends drive you to the ball game. Other days, you take the bus because no one is available to take you.

Once you have explained the exact meaning of "black and white" or "gray" to the person, you can assist him by pointing out specific instances where "this is black and white" or "this is gray." Making this distinction helps the person handle confused emotions and understand why some things are not always the same for all people at all times.

Appendix D

Supporting Adults with Fetal Alcohol Syndrome and Similar Brain Dysfunction

Some adults who have Fetal Alcohol Syndrome (FAS) or Fetal Alcohol Spectrum Disorder (FASD), or another similarly disabling brain dysfunction, are likely to be unsafe when they are expected to function independently in the community. There are several reasons for their functional problems. Adults with FASD:

- Tend to be unorganized
- Tend to take on the role of influential persons in their environment who are accepting and friendly
- Have limited judgment about the consequences of their actions
- Have limited ability to apply what knowledge they have to making choices
- Do not generally learn from their own negative experiences.

These individuals are functionally dependent on an external "brain" to remind them what needs to be done and when. Therefore, the correct approach is to provide them with almost constant external organization.

The Psychosocial Goal Versus Functional Dependence

Adults with FASD who express a desire for more independence often find philosophical support from the professional mental health community. These professionals believe that the person with FASD can be rehabilitated through psychosocial methods. They define psychosocial rehabilitation as:

> The process of facilitating an individual's restoration to an optimal level of independent functioning in the community.... [P]sychosocial rehabilitation encourages people to participate actively with others in the attainment of mental health and social competence goals. (Cnaan et al. Psychosocial rehabilitation: towards a definition. *Psychosocial Rehabilitation Journal,* 11:4 [April 1988], p. 61.)

Applying psychosocial rehabilitation to all persons with FASD assumes that "restoration" of all brain dysfunctions is physically possible. It also assumes that all individuals with brain dysfunctions are capable of "participating actively with others" to attain social competence. Cnaan et al state that "people are motivated by a need for mastery and competence. This applies equally to those with brain dysfunctions such as FASD...."

However, in some individuals with disabling brain dysfunctions, it is not always correct that "new behavior can be learned and people are capable of adapting their behavior to meet their basic needs." (VICSERV.org.au–What Is Psychosocial Rehabilitation, http://www.vicserv.org.au/library/papers/whatispsr.htm.)

Becoming Independent and Responsible Versus Functional Dependence

In a mental health, forensic or other behavioral rehabilitation setting, increasing privileges are often contingent on increasing evidence of self-control. Programs are tailored to the needs of people who can learn over time to become independent based on their experiences. For individuals who are not independently capable of that, this contingent structure often leads to endless failure. The person with FASD does not benefit from this type of support system, and may feel unfairly treated or unable to establish trust. As a result, both support staff and the person receiving support sometimes experience mutual animosity and feelings of helplessness and futility. The behavioral model of tying privileges to an increasing display of responsible action is not a good fit.

Often, rehabilitation programs miss the fact that an adult with FASD may be able to take on responsibilities and follow programs if she first becomes dependent on functional support that allows her to feel accepted, fairly treated and positively focused.

With this type of success, the outside observer may conclude that the person's ability to act responsibly is 'inside," but the sad fact is that the individual with FASD would still be unable to sustain responsible behavior in a support vacuum. She is as trustworthy as the structure that supports her. While she may eventually learn from repeated experiences, it may also take enormous external support to help her remember and apply the concepts she learned. Therefore, instead of "eventual independence," the more appropriate goal is to protect an adult with FASD from being in situations where she cannot independently sustain herself in a responsible manner.

Disruptive behavior in a person with FASD may include:

- Impulsive actions (due to an absence of external structure);
- Repetitive or perseverative actions (when she becomes overfocused on random external stimuli);
- Extreme anxiety or disorientation behaviors (when she becomes overfocused on her internal fears).

Adapting Responses to the Individual

Support personnel may have reservations about treating a person with FASD differently from others in a program because of the message that might be communicated. Using the analogy of diabetics may allay some of those fears.

Diabetics are often served a different diet. At times when they are having an insulin reaction, they may be given ice cream or fruit not available to others who live in the same residence. Staff simply explain to residents that a person with diabetes has different biological and metabolic requirements.

Similarly, many individuals with disabling brain dysfunctions require a different level of external organization and support to achieve personal potential. Some require supports twenty-four hours a day to protect them from their own impulsive actions. Others may require twenty-four-hour-a-day supports to keep occupied so they do not become over-involved in their own overwhelming sensory states or emotional arousal.

Long-Term Goals

Eventually, the adult with both a disabling brain dysfunction (such as FASD) and mental health issues may be able to learn life-long routines for self-management. Even so, she will likely always need to live in some form of highly supportive environment to keep her focused and protect her from becoming overwhelmed.

For optimal results for adults with FASD, the general goal is to focus not so much on developing more independence as on achieving small, in-the-moment objectives. Increasing opportunities for positive interactions can enhance an individual's chances of accomplishing those objectives. For instance, support staff can provide more structure to the day in the form of positive guidance through modeling. Furthermore, they can use visual schedules and verbal reminders to create as many opportunities as possible to display the person's positive attributes.

Issues Related to Supporting Persons with FASD and Similar Brain Dysfunctions

Night staffing. Some persons with FASD may have difficulty getting to sleep, and conversely, difficulty waking up, because of a specific brain dysfunction. Therefore, support staff cannot assume that a fire alarm, for example, would necessarily arouse them. This naturally presents a safety issue for those individuals who are extremely unresponsive when asleep, and would require night staff to be available in case of an emergency.

Reducing sensory overload. Many individuals with FASD may become over-stimulated by too much visual clutter. In general, every environment should be assessed for and cleared of extraneous stimuli that can distract or trigger impulsive reactivity. Asking a person with FASD what can be done to fix a room is often the best guide to creating a comfortable environment.

Diminished taste sensation. Often, an underlying brain dysfunction will affect the sense of taste. Many individuals with FASD will eat only food that is very spicy or very sour since their sense of taste is so compromised. They may, for example, eat lemons rather than apples or oranges. Support staff should be made aware of the condition so they can respond with understanding.

Rituals to enhance coping. Working with people with FASD often requires adjusting to their functional competencies by fitting necessary changes into the rituals they have established to help themselves manage their lives. For instance, two parents with FASD prepared identical breakfasts, lunches and dinners day after day. This allowed them to budget finances, shop for themselves, and prepare familiar foods. The dietician working with the parents realized that expanding the family's diet was beyond their capacity, so she suggested a multivitamin as a nutritional enhancement.

Immediate behavior management suggestions. Situations occur repeatedly in which persons with FASD get stuck in the moment, demand immediate gratification and cannot move on with "regular" explanations. For example, a support person might set up a series of activities with a reward promised in two days. However, the individual wants the reward immediately. Her frustration begins to escalate out of control because she cannot understand "wait" or "coming soon." In such a case, a support person must take a different approach when positive motivations fail to work as expected. He should

- Avoid situations that require delayed gratification.

- Set up plans so that any reinforcement is delivered before the end of the day.
- Not assume that the individual can make the connection between the experiences of today and tomorrow.

Another example is the person who gets stuck in an argument and cannot drop the issue. In this case, the support person should
- Find a way to back off and distract the person.
- Have the targeted person "disappear," and replace him with a new face.
- Give up his side of the "argument."
- Ask for a break to go have a cup of tea or take a walk, then address the situation again once the emotion is diffused.

Appendix E

How to Create a Safe Relationship Habit and Serene Posture To Interrupt Extreme Behavior Episodes

It is very difficult to support a person who has a long history of dangerous and self-injurious behavior. Often, the most difficult person is the one who is aware and "testing" to find out how different people will respond. It is necessary to remain vigilant about the person's potential for violent reaction, as well as extremely calm and nonreactive when the person does become agitated. The goal of any intervention is to prevent and interrupt the chain of arousal.

Also very difficult to support is the person who goes out of control far too frequently and who requires rapid, external control. This person's variable functioning is often being driven by many, co-occurring biological, medical, psychological, environmental and social issues.

Regardless of the reason, some very simple responses are required for any extreme behavior. Initially, "ignoring" works for some. However, when ignoring has led to escalation and the person is already out of control, how can you tell that you needed to step in sooner? You cannot. Similarly, when a person is biologically over-stimulated, or has lost his focus due to some internal seizure event, how can you tell that you needed to step in sooner? You cannot.

The Safe Relationship Habit
There is an alternative to remaining eternally vigilant about the disruptive person's moments of threat, harm to others, or self-harm.

- Try to develop a continual, relationship-based connection to the person. This keeps him feeling safe and keeps those around him safe.

- Structure the person's life so that every moment is based on a support person's supportive, emotional connection with him.

- Try to develop as the person's strongest behavioral-social habit a continually practiced "safe relationship habit." This could be either a "serene posture" or a ritualistic activity that indicates that the person is ready to interact.

- Habituate the person to being continually calmed down. Create a habitual interaction that is so safe for the person that his natural condition will be a serene posture. In this posture, he calmly waits for someone to approach him with a choice to participate in his familiar routine.

- Practice self-calming behavior during times of quiet and appropriate behavior. Practice is accomplished best when it is not required! Practicing in advance ensures that the safe, habitual interaction is available when it is needed.

Shaping and Training a Serene Posture

Alternative behaviors. For the person with self-injurious behavior, always try to think about an alternative behavior that you can model, shape and prompt to assist him to express his frustration or inner turmoil. This alternative behavior must be something to which you can always say, "yes," "do this" and "start." For example, what behavior that uses the hands and arms can replace head butting, biting or pinching oneself or others?

Opposite behaviors. Try to think of a ritualistic, hand-arm action that can be modeled, coached and physically rehearsed to function as a momentary interruption in the chain of arousal. These "opposite" behaviors might include:

- Put both of his hands under his armpits and squeeze down with his arms.
- Take both of his hands and press them together.
- Model the sign for "finished."
- Place his hands onto his lap (for behaviors such as biting or pinching one's hands, or slapping one's face).
- Press his hands onto the table directly in front of him.

In choosing an opposite behavior, support staff should try whatever seems most natural for the person. For example, if the person spontaneously claps his hands, shaping clapping behavior might work best. If the person spontaneously hugs his own body, shaping hands under his armpits might work best. This alternative movement could become the person's serene posture.

Now imagine frequently doing this sequence without any requirement to assume control over the person's disruptive behaviors. Repeat this with him dozens of times a day. Each time, have him pause and wait for a moment. Then, give him a visual and/or verbal choice to engage in some aspect of his familiar, daily structure or schedule of activity. Move on as soon as the person becomes ready.

 Prompt "gentle hands" or "still hands" when giving physical guidance. Then pause. With repetition, the chosen, serene posture of passive-hand action could eventually become the person's visual signal that he is ready to be peacefully responsive to whatever is coming next.

Coach the person's "serene posture" between any and every event, action or transition—always the same. This ensures that life slows down and always comes back to the still, serene place.

 It may help to use the analogy of a short story when thinking about the reactive person's day. His activities are the "paragraphs" in the story. And, the support person's prompts to assume a serene posture are the "punctuation marks" between every paragraph. They keep things flowing in a sensible, predictable manner.

Ritualistic activities. An alternative to using opposite behaviors is to use ritualistic activities that also serve to interrupt an escalating chain of arousal systematically. Try to choose something that is portable and has the potential to generalize to multiple environments.

For example, one individual may benefit from looking at a picture album of a favorite camping trip. Another person may respond favorably to a quick game of cards.

Appendix F

A Brief Overview of Down Syndrome Dementia
By Bernice Seyfort, Ph.D., Registered Psychologist/Consultant,
Island Mental Health Support Team
Used by permission.

Unique Features of Down Syndrome and Dementia

- Early onset; usually by early 50s

- Early onset of age-related medical conditions

- High incidence of depression and hypothyroidism, which may overlap symptoms of dementia

- Sensory deficits, which may contribute to social withdrawal and therefore mimic symptoms of dementia; hearing and sight involvement (especially cataracts).

Other At-Risk Groups
Other populations who are also at risk for (relatively) early dementia include:

- Those with long-standing seizure disorders

- Those who have suffered brain damage through concussion or stroke.

Measuring Onset and Progression
How do we measure onset and progression in a person with developmental disabilities? A number of behavioral observation scales are available, but all of them have some flaws. Some neuropsychological memory tests that are typically used with the general population are not suited to a person with developmental disabilities. Measures of social adaptive behavior are useful only if there is a baseline.

- The best method starts by using as respondents support staff who have known the person for a long time. Then, use reliable scales. The key is to measure change.

- Also useful is a comparison with past testing done when the person was functioning optimally. These might include past psychological reports and social histories. (Again, this is baseline information.)

Drug Therapy for Dementia and Its Usefulness

- Cholinesterase inhibitors. The latest results from studies using drugs like Aricept are not too promising. They may slow progression if dementia is caught in the early stages, but they do not reverse the condition, nor do they halt the progress. These drugs are very expensive and are not covered by Pharmacare. New avenues of research are underway.

- Vitamin E as a preventative strategy. (Be aware of side effects that may accompany doses above 400 units, according to recent research.)

Behavioral Signs of Dementia

- Retention of long-term memories but increasing difficulty laying down and retrieving new information. Also, difficulty learning new tasks.

- Loss of specific, well-learned skills such as knitting, puzzles or workshop-related tasks. Plus, increased reliance on prompts and assistance in carrying out these tasks.

- Skipping of steps (or stalling) in routine hygiene tasks, such as dressing or bathing. Greater reliance on assistance. Also, confusion about dressing, such as putting clothes on the right way.

- Failure to keep even simple instruction in mind, especially when the task involves going to another room to carry it out. Increased reliance on visual and motor prompts.

- Most people with DS experience language as an area of weakness. During early years and mid-life, this can be compensated for by other strengths, such as visual learning. As these skills weaken during aging and dementia onset, language weaknesses become more noticeable. And, hearing problems may accelerate the process.

- Less spontaneous speaking.

- Spatial confusion in formerly familiar settings or routines.

- Greater susceptibility to choking. Pocketing of food in the mouth.

- Slowing of movements and greater caution. Possibly related in some cases to depth perception problems due to cataracts (especially with DS).

- Fatigue and loss of energy. A wish to engage in quiet pursuits. Often bothered by complex environments such as too many people, too much noise and not enough structure or predictability. Resistance to formerly enjoyable socialization opportunities.

- Incontinence, with decreasing awareness of accidents.

- Night wakefulness with day/night confusion. Similar disorientation following daytime naps.

- Misplacement or hiding of valued items with no recall of whereabouts.

- General disintegration of executive skills, such as the ability to get started on an action, or plan an action, or suppress an action (stop when finished).

- Emotional outbursts for little reason (also known as catastrophic action).

- Day-to-day fluctuation in mood and functioning (some good and some bad days).

- Increased signs of perseveration (repeating an action or a phrase over and over).

Four Types of Dementia

Alzheimer's dementia. Most common form of dementia and generally age related, characterized by gradual forgetfulness.

Vascular dementia. Usually associated with numerous small strokes or transient ischemic attacks (TIAs), but may also be caused by major strokes, which often affect one side of the body. Sudden onset.

Lewy body dementia. Parkinson's-like symptoms (rigidity and tremors). Falls and hallucinations in the later stages.

Fronto temporal dementia. Affects mainly the anterior of the brain and is associated with loss of social awareness and emotional disinhibition. May also be associated with major loss of language, especially the ability to express.

Tips for Support Staff

 When a person is showing signs of aging or dementia, be aware that changes are neurological in nature.

- Reduce expectations. A person with DS who is fifty years old may have the needs of a seventy-year-old. In brief, reduce work routines and allow more leisure time.

- Maintain familiarity of place, support staff and routine. This avoids confusion, fearfulness and emotional meltdowns.

- Make use of comfort objects such as a favorite purse, tote bag or blanket. Create a quiet space at home with favorite items nearby.

- Senses are diminished, especially taste and smell. Test out foods that are tolerable and enjoyable, both in taste and texture.

- Encourage tasks that are repetitive and can be performed in a quiet environment. Examples are coloring, sorting items by color and size, folding towels, or simple food preparation (such as putting out crackers). These activities can also serve to divert and defuse cycling anger.

- Be alert to space and time deficits. Avoid getting too close or approaching too quickly, and give hugs only when you are sure the person is ready. Allow more time to get things done. Obsessive slowness is particularly characteristic of a person with DS.

- Give prompts and assistance when needed. When giving directions, try to pair brief verbal messages with nonverbal prompts (show and tell).

- Try to avoid nonverbal messages that may relay your frustration, such as facial expression, body language and tone of voice.

- Keep all communications in the here and now.

- Correct for visual and hearing deficits, if possible. Ensure that ears are kept clear of wax to cut down on conductive hearing loss. This is especially important for a person with DS who has narrow ear canals.

- Ensure that pain is addressed. Sometimes irritability or crying is a sign of pain the person is not able to express, especially joint and muscle pain.

- Persons suffering from dementia do not fare well when moved. Keep them in their homes with appropriate supports, if at all possible.

- Be sensitive to sensory changes that may accompany dementia, such as feeling too cold or too warm, or discomfort with certain clothing (too tight or too rough in texture).

■ Discuss end-of-life issues and prepare for them. For example, discuss palliative care and the degree to which certain extreme interventions will or will not be employed in cases of terminal illness. This is as important for support persons as it is for the family and the person with disabilities.

■ Caring for a person experiencing dementia is very taxing. Take care of your own health and emotional well being.

■ Using PRNs for catastrophic reactions is usually not recommended since PRN (pro re nata or "as needed") medications take a minimum of fifteen or twenty minutes to work. This comes too late. Instead, try diversionary tactics and calming environments. Allow time alone. If emotional meltdowns last for a lengthy period, PRNs are useful. A person with dementia is particularly sensitive to benzodiazepines and may experience increased disorientation.

■ Do not worry about the behavior modification rule of possibly rewarding "undesirable" behavior. Memory and learning are impaired with dementia. The person's thinking is "in the moment."

Appendix G

**Suggestions for Creating
a "Prader-Willi Syndrome-Friendly" Place**
By Rita Di Gangi, M.Ed., Behavioral Consultant
Used by permission.

A Prader-Willi Syndrome-friendly place is a safe setting that provides a person with Prader-Willi Syndrome (PWS) with a sense of security. The person is surrounded by people who understand him and are sensitive to his struggles. Punitive measures are a thing of the past.

In order to avoid serious health concerns, people with PWS need to be on a life-long diet. No matter how much a person with PWS eats, he continues to live with a constant need to satisfy an insatiable appetite. Although this need is never extinguished, a person is more likely to seek food, and even think about food, when there are both opportunity and cues present in the immediate setting.

Each time a person with PWS is successful in obtaining food that is not on his diet (an "unapproved" food), it seems to tell him that his support person cannot provide him with the security he needs. This impression can create worry and may increase his anxiety. This, in turn, sometimes contributes to the presence of such negative behavior as stealing, aggression and power struggles. So, consistently controlling access to food and avoiding food-related cues not only aids in weight control, but also recognizes and addresses this worry.

Often, people with PWS appear able to cope with food. When they cannot, it becomes extremely difficult to get back on track within the same setting. The support person's challenge, then, is to prevent the person from reaching a point from which it is difficult to return. One of the goals is to provide a sanctuary, a PWS-friendly place, where someone with PWS can live and work without the anxiety of potentially acquiring "unapproved" food. It is also a place where he can exist in a state of calm, in which visual, auditory, olfactory and social food-related cues are absent. In this setting, the person is not bombarded with temptation and reminders that seem to invite him to think about what he cannot have. Gone is the sense of unfairness he feels each time he witnesses someone eating what he cannot have.

This article notes and expands on Dr. B. Linder's (2002) writing on suggestions on how to control access to food and on ways to remove or avoid food-related cues. Consistent application of these suggestions is as vital as the suggestions themselves.

Control Over Access to "Unapproved" Food

- Make all food and drink consistently inaccessible by either locking it up or by not having it in the setting at all. This includes such uninviting foods as raw or frozen meats, onions, spices and condiments. Some people have been known to eat pet food or other nonedibles, such as soaps that smell like fruit. This too may need to be restricted.

- Locking up food and drink may include restricting access to the kitchen by keeping the door (and windows) under lock and key or by securing all the individual cupboards, drawers, refrigerator/freezer, storage units and other places food may be kept. Some people have eaten contaminated food or have become water toxic from drinking too much water. Therefore, access to garbage bins and water may also need to be restricted.

- Some support staff have tried not keeping any food in their setting. This involves shopping for all food on a daily basis or having it all brought in per meal and snack. This may be more expensive and time consuming to implement, but it does avoid the need for locks.

- Indirect access to food must also be considered and consistently controlled. This includes restricting access to spending money, a bank account, and a bank card.

- This also involves recognizing potential ways of "sneaking" in food or breaking into food storage units. Examples: Getting a friend to stow a chocolate bar in his knapsack, phoning in a pizza order while the support staff are outside, getting hold of the keys to unlock a door, using a library card to slip open a latch, or finding a bobby pin to pick open a lock.

- When such innovative attempts are tried, methods of addressing these include protocols involving the use of more secured locks (such as dead bolts), regular preventative checks and searches, and direct supervision when access to food is possible. Example: When a friend visits. When implementing these methods, the concern is always one of safety for the individual and not one of punishment. The message is always: "I'm on your side."

Sensitivity to Bombardment of Food-Related Cues
Avoid visual cues by:

- Requesting support staff to not chew gum while working.

- Paying attention to not opening the doors to locked food units while the person with PWS is present.

- Delivering groceries when the person with PWS is not present and watching.

- Not displaying any artwork that is food-related. This may include molds of vegetables and fruit (ceramic, soaps, candles), paintings and prints, calendars, magazines and cookbooks.

- Blocking the food network and generally decreasing television time where shows are filled with persuasive food commercials.

Avoid and remove food smell (olfactory) cues by:

- Preparing meals when the person with PWS is not home or organizing a day program activity such as baking when the person is out of the building for a couple of hours. Follow this up with airing out the building.

- Remembering to use the stove vent when cooking or mask minor food smells with pine air fresheners.

- Not purchasing or using products with a food type scent including:
    - Air fresheners, such as country apple or cinnamon
    - Cleaners, strippers and waxes such as orange or lemon
    - Soaps, candles, shampoo and conditioners, sunscreen, perfumes, talc, such as watermelon, papaya, apple, coconut and vanilla.
- Requesting support staff not to arrive to work smelling like food (on their clothes or breath).

Avoid social type cues by requesting support staff to:
- Not encourage or discuss food related topics. Instead, redirect the conversation to another topic of interest.
- Not eat or drink "unapproved" food or sneak around with "unapproved" food, such as eating something in the office. Therefore, do not bring any to work.
- Not set up the person with PWS by asking for his permission for you to pick up or eat food in front of him. He will likely say yes.
- Encourage (or insist) guests bring gifts other than food.

Pay attention to possible auditory cues and reduce or eliminate them:
- Food-related sounds can include the clattering of dishes, the blender or coffeemaker, as well as wrapping off a chocolate bar in the office or jingling pop cans in a purse.
- Establish a routine in which all "approved" meals and snacks are punctually served at set times. Provide a schedule so meals are known ahead of time. Be precise about measurements (Forester & Gourash, 2005).

How can someone with PWS participate in his community with less worry?
With sensitivity and careful planning, opportunities to access food and food-related cues can be greatly decreased while still enjoying community involvement. Some suggestions:

- Make choices that are PWS-friendly whenever possible. For example: If there are two parks to go for a walk, one with an ice cream vendor and one without, go to the park without the ice cream vendor.
- Weigh the anxiety of going to a place where there is food present. Investigate other places that are just as much fun that do not have any food around.
- Recognize that food is not available everywhere and at all times. Therefore, take advantage of periods in which a community outing is PWS-friendly. For example: Schedule going to the gym when the cafeteria is closed.
- Continue to avoid and remove food-related cues when possible. Examples:
    - Take travel routes that are free of visual, olfactory and auditory reminders, such as restaurants, ice-cream trucks, and bulletin boards.
    - Call organizers of events and find out when food will be served and how they will dispose of garbage. Decide to show up after the food is cleaned up.
    - Before the person with PWS enters an area, check for any garbage and food or packages left out.

- Choose to sit away from places where food or drink is kept. Example: Do not sit near the pop machine. Be aware of people who may keep food in their purses or pockets and decide to sit away from them.
- Visit restaurants at times when there are few patrons. Service is faster.
- Also during these times, there is less food on tables and you can choose a table away from them.
- Stay a shorter period of time.

- Educate and encourage other support services to promote PWS-friendly places by:
  - Suggesting to the organizers of a dance or social group that they sell low-calorie foods and drinks or, at least, offer food in smaller portions. For example: small bags of hot-air popcorn instead of larger bags of chips, and diet pop and bottled water instead of sugared drinks.
  - Suggesting that they sell or offer food for a shorter period of time or not at all.
  - Helping out and clearing the garbage bins and tables of leftover food frequently.
  - Providing constant supervision of areas that contain food or suggest locking these areas up.
  - Offering the suggestions you find helpful in your own setting.

Sometimes, when support persons have less control over the environment, direct supervision may be important to provide a sense of safety and security. For some individuals, "eyes on" supervision is needed.

References

Forester, J.L., and L.M. Gourash. *Food Security for PWS*. Pittsburgh Partnership, 2005.

Linder, B.A. *Managing Difficult Behaviors with Persons with Prader-Willi Syndrome*. Ontario Prader-Willi Syndrome Association, 2002.

Some helpful websites to visit:
- http://members.allstream.net/~opwsa/index.htm
- http://www.cafamily.org.uk/Direct/p33.html
- http://www.praderwilli.org.za/news4.htm
- http://www.pwsa.co.uk/

August 17, 2006
Rita Di Gangi Behavioural Consulting
6620 Razor Point Rd.
Pender Island, BC, V0N 2M1
Rita.DiGangi@cablelan.net

Notes

Chapter 2

1. Thanks to Ken Martin, MD, for his assistance with this discussion of the pain reflex.

2. Thanks to Janet Groves-Fullerton, OT, for her assistance with this discussion of the startle reflex.

3. Thanks to Janet Groves-Fullerton, OT, for her assistance with this discussion of defensive reflexes.

Chapter 8

1. R. S. Sprick, M. Garrison and L. Howard, *CHAMPs: A Proactive and Positive Approach to Classroom Management* (Eugene, OR: Pacific Northwest Publishing, 1998).

2. See the following references for more information on developing and maintaining relationships: William Glasser, *Reality Therapy: A New Approach to Psychiatry* (New York: Harper & Row, 1991); Haim G. Ginott, Alice Ginott and H. Wallace Goddard, *Between Parent and Child: The Bestselling Classic That Revolutionized Parent-Child Communication* (Emeryville, CA: Three Rivers Press, 2003); and Gordon Neufeld and Gaber Mate, *Hold On to Your Kids: Why Parents Need to Matter More Than Peers* (New York: Ballantine Books, 2006).

Chapter 9

1. See the following works by William Glasser for further discussion of self-sabotage and failure identity, and how to address the issues: *Reality Therapy: A New Approach to Psychiatry* (New York: Harper & Row, 1991); *Choice Theory: A New Psychology of Personal Freedom* (New York: Harper Paperbacks, 1999); *Counseling with Choice Theory: The New Reality Therapy* (New York: Harper Paperbacks, 2001); *Unhappy Teenagers: A Way for Parents and Teachers to Reach Them* (New York: HarperCollins, 2002).

2. For more information, see Christopher Petersen, Steven F. Maier and Martin E. P. Seligman, *Learned Helplessness: A Theory for the Age of Personal Control* (New York: Oxford University Press, 1995).

3. For more information, see *The Habilitative Mental Healthcare Newsletter*, a bimonthly publication covering issues of mental health and intellectual disabilities. Write to Psych-Media of NC, Inc., P.O. Box 57, Bear Creek, NC 27207, or call (336) 581-3700.

Chapter 10

1. Dave Hingsburger, Focus 1989 and Focus 1990 (Presentations at conference in Victoria, British Columbia, Canada, 1989, 1990).

2. Hingsburger, Focus 1989 and Focus 1990.

3. Hingsburger, Focus 1989 and Focus 1990.

4. Hingsburger, Focus 1989 and Focus 1990.

5. Hingsburger, Focus 1989 and Focus 1990.

6. Hingsburger, Focus 1989 and Focus 1990.

7. Hingsburger, Focus 1989 and Focus 1990.

8. Hingsburger, Focus 1989 and Focus 1990.

9. Hingsburger, Focus 1989 and Focus 1990.

10. Hingsburger, Focus 1989 and Focus 1990.

11. Hingsburger, Focus 1989 and Focus 1990.

12. Hingsburger, Focus 1989 and Focus 1990.

13. Hingsburger, Focus 1989 and Focus 1990.

14. Hingsburger, Focus 1989 and Focus 1990.

15. Hingsburger, Focus 1989 and Focus 1990.

16. Hingsburger, Focus 1989 and Focus 1990.

17. Hingsburger, Focus 1989 and Focus 1990.

18. Steve Baker and Amy Tabor, *Human Rights Committees: Staying on Course with Services and Supports for People with Intellectual Disabilities* (Homewood, IL: High Tide Press, 2006): 17-22.

19. Dorothy M. Griffiths, Vernon L. Quinsey and Dave Hingsburger, *Changing Inappropriate Sexual Behavior: A Community-Based Approach for Persons with Developmental Disabilities* (Baltimore: Paul H. Brookes, 1989): 73.

20. Hingsburger, Focus 1989 and Focus 1990.

21. Hingsburger, Focus 1989 and Focus 1990.

22. Hingsburger, Focus 1989 and Focus 1990.

23. Hingsburger, Focus 1989 and Focus 1990.

24. Hingsburger, Focus 1989 and Focus 1990.

25. Hingsburger, Focus 1989 and Focus 1990. (For additional information, see Hingsburger, *Just Say Know: Understanding and Reducing the Risk of Sexual Victimization of People with Developmental Disabilities* [Eastman, QC, Canada, 1995].)

26. Hingsburger, Focus 1989 and Focus 1990.

27. For additional information, see the following publications: Sol Gordon, *Sexual Rights for the People Who Happen to Be Handicapped* (Syracuse, NY: Center on Human Policy, Syracuse University Division of Special Education and Rehabilitation, 1974); Sol Gordon, *A Better Safe Than Sorry Book: A Family Guide for Sexual Assault Prevention* (Fayetteville, NY: Ed-U Press, 1984); Orieda Horn Anderson and Shirley Paceley, *Safe Beginnings: Protecting Our Children from Sexual Abuse* (Decatur, IL: Blue Tower Training Center, 2003); and Dave Hingsburger, *Just Say Know: Understanding and Reducing the Risk of Social Victimization of People with Developmental Disabilities* (Baltimore: Paul H. Brookes, 1995).

28. Irving Dickinson and Sol Gordon, *One Miracle at a Time: How to Get Help for Your Disabled Child—From the Experience of Other Parents* (New York: Simon and Schuster, 1985).

29. Griffiths, Quinsey and Hingsburger, *Changing Inappropriate Sexual Behavior: A Community-Based Approach for Persons with Developmental Disabilities* (Baltimore: Paul H. Brookes, 1989): 56-88. (This provides a more detailed analysis of the characteristics associated with extremely inappropriate sexual behavior.)

30. Griffiths, Quinsey and Hingsburger, *Changing Inappropriate Sexual Behavior: A Community-Based Approach for Persons with Developmental Disabilities*, 34-51.

31. Griffiths, Quinsey and Hingsburger, *Changing Inappropriate Sexual Behavior: A Community-Based Approach for Persons with Developmental Disabilities*, 53-86.

About the Author

Nathan Ory has been a registered psychologist for nearly 30 years. He has worked in Victoria, British Columbia, since 1978 with children and adults with intellectual and developmental disabilities. Mr. Ory specializes in autism spectrum disorders, fetal alcohol syndrome, extremely challenging behavior, and persons who are dually diagnosed with one of these conditions and a mental health disorder. In addition to his work with the Island Mental Health Support Team in Victoria, he speaks throughout the United States and Canada about these issues. Mr. Ory holds a master's degree in psychology from The Ohio State University, and a bachelor's degree in psychology from Georgia State University.